ROME
AND THE VATICAN

COMPLETE GUIDE
FOR VISITING THE CITY

D1015252

EB
BONECHI

HISTORICAL OVERVIEW

Rome got its start when groups of shepherds and farmers settled on the hill now known as the Palatine. Etymologically, the name *Roma* may mean the city of the river, or more probably "the city of the Ruma" (an old Etruscan family).

After the semi-legendary period of the monarchy, the first authentic references date to the moment of transition from the monarchy to the republic (509 BC), when the Etruscan civilization, which had dominated in Rome with the last kings, began its slow decline. During the long period of the republic, there arose a sort of democracy governed by the consuls and the tribunes (the representatives of the plebeians) which progressed to the point of instituting equal rights for patricians and plebs.

By the 4th century BC, Rome already held sway over all of Latium. The city later extended its rule to many other regions in Italy, subjugating numerous Italic peoples and the great Etruscan civilization; even the Gauls, and the Greeks in southern Italy, laid down their arms to Rome. By 270 BC, the entire Italian peninsula was under Roman domination. In the 3rd century BC, the Romans began to extend their sphere of influence beyond the borders of the peninsula: with the Punic Wars (264 - 201 BC), the entire Mediterranean came under Roman rule; in the east, Rome extended its frontiers into the kingdom of Alexander the Great and in the west subjugated the Gauls and the peoples of Spain. At this point, with Augustus, the republic became an empire, and auspices of power and greatness accompanied its foundation.

As it was first conceived, the empire was intended to provide a balanced form of government administered by the various republican magistratures in accordance with the will of the people and under the direct control of the senate. This was what it was meant to be, but in reality the administration grew increasingly dictatorial and militaristic as time went on. Eventually, with its far-flung frontiers, the empire became divided and ungovernable; central authority inevitably began to weaken and a slow but inexorable decline set in. The city of Rome was no longer the absolute center of imperial power; the emperors moved their courts elsewhere and the senate gradually lost its political identity. The decline of Rome reached its nadir following the first barbarian invasions. Nonetheless, the city never lost its moral force, that awareness which for centuries had made Rome *caput mundi*, and its survival was abetted by the advent of Christianity, which consecrated it the seat of its Church.

By the mid-6th century AD, Rome had become just one more of the cities of the new Byzantine empire, which had its capital in Ravenna. Even so, two centuries later, thanks to the growing importance of the papacy, Rome had returned to occupying a central position in this new empire and its history began to intertwine with that of the Frankish Carolingian dynasty. Charlemagne chose to be crowned emperor in Rome, as did all the Holy Roman emperors who followed him.

The city proclaimed itself an independent commune in 1144, and in this period it was governed by local factions, the papacy, and the feudal nobility. The communal forces were often in open contrast with the pope; the life of the new commune was for a long period marked by conflicts and harsh struggles. At the beginning of the 14th century, when the papacy moved to Avignon, the popular forces were freer to govern.

But in the late 14th and the early 15th century the situation was reversed: the pope returned to Rome and managed to gain control of city government, returning to the Church most of the power the popular government had gained in the preceding century. The city flourished in this

3

period as capital of the Papal State; it was returned to its ancient splendor and became one of the most important crossroads for culture and art. In the centuries that followed, Rome tended toward increasing political isolation. The Papal State remained aloof from the various international contrasts; while on the one hand this policy limited its importance on the international political scene, on the other it laid the bases for development of trade and above all of the arts and culture.

This situation continued until the end of the 18th century, when due to the revolutionary climate that swept through Europe in those years the power of the Church entered an unexpected state of crisis and the papal rule of the city passed to the Republic (Pius VI was exiled to France). The temporal power of the Church was restored for a brief period under Pius VII, but only a few years later Napoleon once more reversed the situation when he proclaimed Rome the second city of his empire. After a series of alternating events, and another period of papal rule (1814), came the period of the Risorgimento when, during the papacy of Pius IX, Rome was a hotbed of patriotic and anticlerical ideals. A true parliament was formed in 1848; the following year the Roman Republic was proclaimed and the government passed into the hands of a triumvirate headed by Giuseppe Mazzini until the intervention of the French army restored the temporal power of the Church. In 1860, with the formation of the Kingdom of Italy, the pope saw his sphere of influence contract to Latium - the area around Rome - alone. Ten years later, with the famous episode of the breach of Porta Pia, the French troops protecting the pope were driven out of the city. Rome was thus annexed to the Kingdom of Italy and became its capital. The dissension that arose between the Papal State and the new Italian government was eventually resolved with the Lateran Treaty of 11 February 1929 conciliated the Italian state and the Church and set up an independent Vatican city-state. After World War II, when Italy repudiated the monarchy and became a republic, Rome became the seat of the Italian Parliament.

ARCHITECTURAL DEVELOPMENT

The city of Rome developed from a nucleus on the Palatine hill and gradually increased in size to embrace the surrounding hills as well. The *Servian walls* date to the 4th century BC.; the *Aurelian walls* are of later date. The urban fabric changed radically during the felicitous period of the Republic, when the city underwent rapid expansion; the *Cloaca Maxima* and the *Basilica Aemilia* in the Roman Forum date to this period. With the advent of the empire, the city expanded still further; examples of imperial construction are the grandiose *Imperial Forums*, the *Basilica Julia*, the reliefs of the *Arch of Titus* and of that of *Septimius Severus*, the *Pantheon*, the *Colosseum*, Nero's *Domus Aurea*, Trajan's

Markets, the *Baths of Caracalla* and *Diocletian's Baths*. After the fires of 64 and 80 AD, Rome was almost completely rebuilt on more modern and rational bases. By the 2nd century AD, the population of the city had increased to about one million, an exceptional number for the times. The city began to decline in the 3rd century and the new Aurelian walls went up. The haunting catacombs (brought to light in the 20th century) date to the 3rd and 4th centuries AD, the magnificent mosaics of *Santa Pudenziana* and of *Santi Cosma e Damiano* to only a little later. The arrival of the Goths, and then of the Lombards, reduced Rome to a mere 50,000 inhabitants; the development of the arts came to a standstill. Many churches, including those of *Santa Maria Maggiore*, *Santa Sabina*, and *San Clemente*, were built in the early Christian period. Rome was overrun by the Saracens in the 9th century and again by the Normans in 1084.

The cultural awakening of the city began in the 10th, 11th, and 12th centuries and saw the building of the Romanesque churches of *San Clemente*, *Santa Maria in Trastevere*, and *San Crisogono*. The Romanesque style was replaced by the Gothic, of which few signs have survived (the Church of *Santa Maria sopra Minerva*, the altar canopies by Arnolfo di Cambio for the Churches of *San Paolo fuori le Mura* and *Santa Cecilia*). But only when the papacy returned to Rome from exile in Avignon did Rome began its rapid comeback as an exceedingly important crossroads for culture and trade. During the 15th century, under the impulse of the Church, the city again flourished. Many of the most illustrious artists of the times worked for the Vatican, creating such masterpieces as the *bronze doors of St. Peter's* (Filarete), the decoration of the *Vatican Chapel* by (Beato Angelico), the *bronze funeral monuments of Sixtus V and Innocent IV* (Antonio del Pollaiolo); *Palazzo Venezia* and the *Palazzo della Cancelleria* were built. With the arrival of the 16th century, Rome was once more its old self, the *caput mundi*. One after the other, the greatest artists of the time - Raphael, Michelangelo, Bramante, Giulio Romano, Baldassarre Peruzzi, the Sangallos, Vignola, and many others - regaled the city with unique masterpieces, and churches, squares, fountains, palaces and streets, all of unequaled beauty, came into being. This felicitous period continued throughout the 17th and 18th centuries. The Carraccis (*Galleria Farnese*), Guido Reni, and Guercino worked in Rome, as did Gian Lorenzo Bernini, who laid out *St. Peter's Square* and also revealed himself to be a peerless sculptor (works in the *Museo Borghese*). The city grew at a prodigious rate in the 19th and 20th centuries, when new districts, new roads and new social realities intertwined with the old urban fabric.

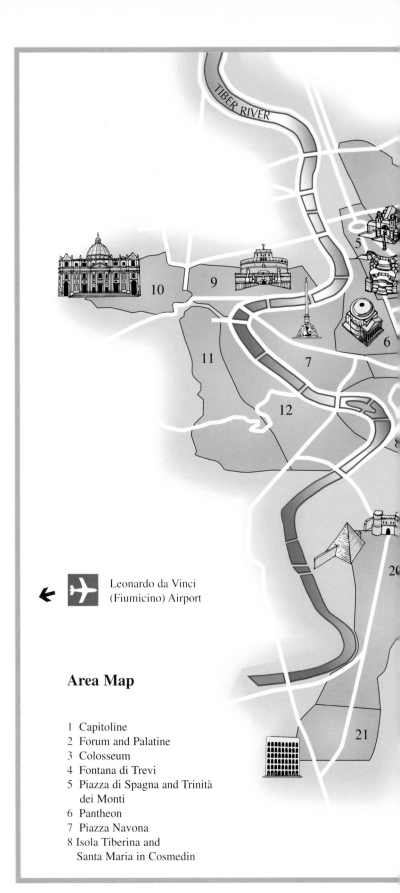

Leonardo da Vinci
(Fiumicino) Airport

Area Map

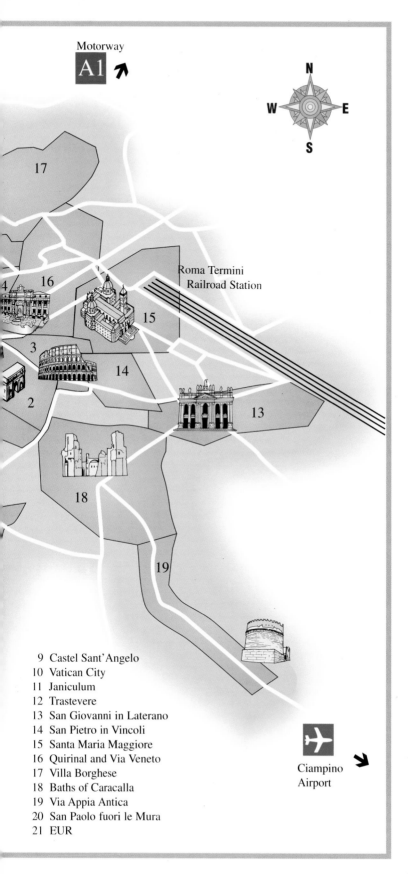

Motorway
A1 ↗

N
W E
S

17

Roma Termini
Railroad Station

4 16

15

3

14

2

13

18

19

Ciampino
Airport

CAPITOLINE

**Capitoline Hill - Palazzo Senatorio - Capitoline Museums -
Palazzo Nuovo - Palazzo dei Conservatori -
Pinacoteca Capitolina - Church of Santa Maria in Aracoeli -**
San Marco - Palazzo Venezia -
Monument to Vittorio Emmanuele II - **Mamertine Prison**

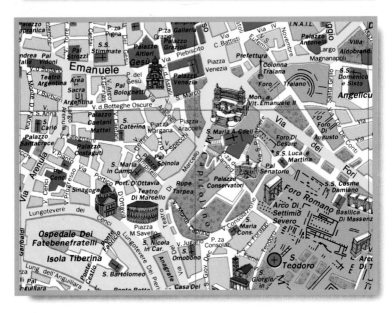

The statue of Minerva near the staircase of Palazzo Senatorio in Piazza del Campidoglio.

Capitoline Hill - From the earliest times, the Capitoline hill (or Campidoglio) was the center of the political, social, and religious life of Rome. This was the site of the ancient *asylum* (sanctuary), but also that of the great Italic temple dedicated to the Capitoline Jupiter: the name of *Capitolium* was used almost exclusively to designate the temple rather than the entire hilltop. Also on the north summit of the two knolls which comprise the site was the *arx* (sacred enclosure) with the Temple of Juno Moneta (the Admonisher) and the temple of the Vetus. The *Clivus Capitolinus* was the carriage road which led to the hill of the forum; there was once also a flight of stairs leading to the *arx* alone; the famous *Scalae Gemoniae* branched of from it near the Mamertine Prison. The most sacred (even though the smallest) of the hills of Rome has continued to be the seat of power throughout the centuries. Its summit is now crowned by Michelangelo's **Piazza del Campidoglio**, defined by illustrious palaces and magnificently decorated with the statue of *Marcus Aurelius* set at the center of the intriguing interplay of ellipses and volutes designed by Michelangelo for the grey pavement of the square. Formerly in Piazza di San Giovanni in Laterano, Marcus Aurelius was moved to the Campidoglio in 1538: apparently, Michelangelo had not previously tak-

...en the statue into consideration as decoration for the square. The statue we see today is a copy of the original that now stands in the adjacent Palazzo Nuovo.

Palazzo Senatorio - This building stands on a site on which functions linked to the political life of the city have always been carried on. It was originally that of the *Tabularium*, an impressive building housing the state archives, ordered built by Quintus Lutazio Catulus in 78 BC. In the eighth century, the senate of Rome met in the Curia, but when this old building was damaged and isolated by the marshes that were invading the forum, it was decided to reorganize administrative activity in another location. The first site chosen was the cloister, today no longer in existence,

1 - Piazza del Campidoglio. 2 - Palazzo Nuovo.
3 - Palazzo Senatorio. 4 - Palazzo dei Conservatori.
5 - Monument to Vittorio Emanuele II.
6 - Santa Maria in Aracoeli. 7 - Tarpeian Rock.

of Santa Maria in Aracoeli, but later, as city independence grew and with it the prestige of the senators, a more fitting meeting-place was sought. Thus, in 1143, work began for construction of a new building on the ruins of the *Tabularium*, then used as a storehouse for salt. In 1160 the col-

Above, the statue of Tiber decorating the staircase of Palazzo Senatorio; below, a view of Piazza del Campidoglio with the copy of the statue of Marcus Aurelius at the center.

lege of senators was already meeting in the halls of the new building. It was remodeled in 1299, when a loggia and two corner towers were also added. The building was severely damaged by the assault of the troops of Henry VII but was restored in the early 15th century under Pope Boniface IX, who donated it to the city of Rome. Halfway through the same century, Pope Nicholas V had the central tower added, but the building took on its modern-day look only a century later, under Pope Paul III, who charged Michelangelo with redesigning it. Michelangelo directed the work of building the staircase personally; it was later decorated by order of Sixtus V with the statue of the goddess *Roma Capitolina*, originally Minerva, in the center niche, and those of the *Nile* and the *Tiber* (originally the *Tigris*), brought to the Capitoline from the Baths of Constantine on the Quirinal hill, in those on each side. The work planned by Michelangelo was completed, with some liberties taken, between 1582 and 1605 by Giacomo della Porta, Girolamo Rainaldi, and Martino Longhi the Elder. The latter architect is the author of the brick bell tower that replaced the medieval turret.

The statues of the Dioscuri *at the summit of Michelangelo's staircase to Piazza del Campidoglio; below, the facade of Palazzo Senatorio.*

CAPITOLINE MUSEUMS

*T*he Capitoline Museum complex hosts one of the world's oldest and most prestigious public collections of art. It contains above all statues of the Classical era, some of which are of considerable historical-artistic importance and worldwide fame. The collections are housed in the **Palazzo Nuovo** and the facing **Palazzo dei Conservatori**, which includes the **Pinacoteca Capitolina**.
The history of the collections of the Capitoline Museums dates far back in time and greatly predates the construction of the buildings that today house them and in which they were arranged beginning in 1753 under Pope Clement XII. The original nucleus of all these precious collections was the Lateran collection of Roman bronzes donated to the city of Rome by Pope Sixtus V in 1471. Other donations soon followed: popes Leo X and Pius V contributed in the sixteenth century to enlarging the collections with some of the most important examples of Classical statuary; two centuries later, the statues in the private collection of Cardinal Albani were added. Later, during the pontificate of Benedict XIV, the museums were enriched by an influx of works from Hadrian's Villa at Tivoli. The last large donation was the Castellani collection including; many works unearthed during the excavation work carried on when Rome was made capital of Italy.

PALAZZO NUOVO

The exterior of Palazzo Nuovo and, below, a view of the Room of the Emperors.

In 1734, Palazzo Nuovo became the first home of the Capitoline Museums. The building houses some of the most interesting examples of Roman statuary, and boasts one of the most complete collections of Imperial portraiture. The so-called **Room of the Emperors** in fact contains 65 *busts of Roman emperors* arranged in chronological order around an evocative statue of the *Seated Helena* in which the head of Constantine's mother is set on the body of a 5th-century BC Greek original. The masterful *Marcus Aurelius* may be considered as being a latecomer to this museum. His gilded bronze equestrian statue, for centuries at the center of the Campidoglio square, found a permanent home here following a decade of

restoration concluded in 1990. Thought in the Middle Ages to be the effigy of Constantine (and for this reason not destroyed), the statue served as a model for the equestrian statues of the Renaissance. Other works on display on the halls of Palazzo Nuovo include the famous *Capitoline Venus*, a Roman copy of a Hellenistic original, the *Wounded Amazon* and the *Dying Galatian*, unearthed in the Horti Sallustian together with the *Galatian Killing his Wife* which is today in the Palazzo Altemps Museum.

PALAZZO DEI CONSERVATORI AND THE PINACOTECA CAPITOLINA

Since the Middle Ages the seat of one of the most important city magistratures, the **Palazzo dei Conservatori** was completely restructured to Michelangelo's plans beginning in 1563. Guidetto Guidetti and Giacomo Della Porta, pupils of the great Tuscan artist, collaborated on realization of the harmonious facade

with its colossal pilaster strips and crowning balustrade adorned with statues. The original destination of the palace is evident in the splendid Sale dei Conservatori, which are now used as exhibit space for some of the most celebrated of the works in the Capitoline collec-

tions: for example, the *Spinario* and the *She-Wolf (Lupa Capitolina)*, a marvelous bronze from the 5th century BC. The twins, quite probably the work of Antonio del Pollaiolo, were added in the 15th century when the statue was raised to the status of symbol of the city. A few Gothic arches of the original fifteenth-century building still remain in the courtyard, which also contains evocative fragments, among which the head and one hand, of the *colossal Constantine*, the mag-

From top to bottom: the busts of emperors Augustus and Marcus Aurelius, a view of Palazzo dei Conservatori, and the bronze equestrian statue of Marcus Aurelius, in Palazzo Nuovo following restoration.

niloquent statue that once stood in the apse of the Basilica of Maxentius. The museum as such is housed in the rooms and galleries of one of the wings of the palace, and contains such masterpieces as the bust of the *Emperor Commodus*, the *Esquiline Venus*, the *Warrior Hercules* and the *Punishment of Marsyas*, found together with other statues in the Lamiani Gardens and the gardens of Maecenas' villa on the Esquiline. The Castellani collection, which includes many black- and red-figured Greek vases, is a very interesting section of this museum, which continues on into the **Braccio Nuovo** and the **Museo Nuovo**. During reorganization of the latter exhibit space, much attention was paid to the reconstruction of those sculptural groups that once adorned public and sacred buildings in ancient Rome. The museum itinerary is brought to a close with the **Pinacoteca Capitolina**, established in 1748 in the other wing of the palace by Benedict XIV. His primary intention was to provide a home for the numerous paintings belonging to the Sacchetti collection and to that of Pio di Savoia. Among the many important works on exhibit here are paintings by Titian, Tintoretto, and Guido Reni, as well as the celebrated *Saint John the Baptist* by Caravaggio.

From top to bottom: the bronze She-Wolf *and two fragments (a hand and the head) of the colossal statue of the emperor Constantine.*

Church of Santa Maria in Aracoeli -
Mention of the church is made as early as the 7th century; in the 10th century it became a Benedictine abbey and then passed to the Friars Minor, who saw to its reconstruction around 1320. A place for associative life as well as a place of worship, the church continued in this unique calling into the 16th century: for example, the civic victory ceremony celebrating Marcantonio Colonna's victory at Lepanto (1571) was held here in 1571.

The **exterior** has a gabled roof and a facade with three doorways under three windows. A sort of vestibule is set against the central portal. Renaissance elements of some importance in the austere 14th-century **facade** are the reliefs with *Saints Matthew and John* over the two smaller portals.

In the **interior**, with its typical basilica plan, the nave is separated from the two side aisles by 22 reused antique columns. The Bufalini Chapel, in the right aisle, contains the *frescoes* by Pinturicchio that are considered his masterpieces.

Above, the exterior of Santa Maria in Aracoeli. Below, the tomb of Luca Savelli and two details of the monument to the Cardinal of Acquasparta: the Madonna Enthroned with the Child and Two Saints *is by Cavallini.*

Church of San Marco - The church, opening onto Piazza San Marco, has to all intents and purposes been incorporated into Palazzo Venezia, but its origins date to the 4th century, when it was founded by Pope Mark, himself later sanctified, in honor of Saint Mark the Evangelist. Major rebuilding was ordered by Pope Paul II Barbo when he had Palazzo Venezia built, and around the middle of the 18th century the church was made over in the Baroque style that is especially apparent in the interior.

The *facade* stands out for its tasteful travertine arcade and the graceful loggia that bears the mark of Giuliano da Maiano.

The basilica-plan *interior*, with a nave and two aisles, is richly decorated and frescoed, in line with the 18th-century plan by Filippo Barigioni. Of particular note are the *mosaics* in the conch of the apse, which date to the time of Pope Gregory IV (early 9th century).

Palazzetto Venezia - Built between 1455 and 1468 for Cardinal Pietro Barbo, later Pope Paul II, the edifice was razed and rebuilt in the early 20th century when demolition work was undertaken for the monument to Vittorio Emmanuele II. The three-story *facade* features fine arched windows and an elegant portal. In the *interior* is a porticoed courtyard, with an Ionic-columned loggia.

1 - Palazzo Venezia.
2 - Church of San Marco.
3 - Palazzetto Venezia.

Palazzo Venezia - In about the mid-15th century, Cardinal Paolo Barbo began work for the construction of his residence incorporating the medieval Torre della Biscia, which he had raised, and adding mighty battlements like a crown along the whole top of the side of the building facing on what is today Piazza Venezia. The work continued even after the election of the cardinal to the papal throne with the name of Paul II, and the palace, suitably enlarged in a style that in many respects presaged that of the Renaissance, became the papal palace. During the pontificate of Paul II, the building, which had incorporated in its architectural fabric the adjoining **Saint Mark's Basilica**, the facade of which was redesigned by Alberti, underwent considerable modification: the wing which was to become the **Palazzetto Venezia** was added along Via del Plebiscito, and in the interior there was created the famous **Sala del Mappamondo**, probably decorated by Mantegna, which hosted Mussolini's cabinet during the Fascist era. In the early 16th century,

The exterior of Palazzo Venezia.

Cardinal Lorenzo Cybo enlarged the Pauline layout and made further modifications to it with the creation of the so-called Cybo Apartment, which between 1564 and 1797 was home to the cardinals of San Marco. During the same period the palace was the property of the Republic of Venice, which used it as the residence of its ambassadors and further modified the original fifteenth-century structure. Still further remodeling was carried out during the two centuries that followed, until in 1924, following lengthy restoration of questionable value, the building became a museum and, from 1929 onward, the seat of the Gran Consiglio of the Fascist government. Today's **Museo di Palazzo Venezia** overflows into the rooms of the adjoining Palazzetto Venezia, which communicates with the main building through the so-called "Passetto" or Corridor of the Cardinals, an ancient guard-walk modified in the eighteenth century, and houses rich collections of art including some pieces from the collection of Athanasius Kircher. Terra-cotta and pottery, porcelain, bronze and silver objects, church ornaments and vestments, wooden sculptures, paintings, weapons, ivory, crystal, tapestries and *objets d'arte* of the most disparate types, both Italian and foreign, fill the numerous rooms of the museum to offer the visitor an exhaustive panorama of the evolution of the arts from the Middle Ages through the eighteenth century.

Monument to Vittorio Emmanuele II - Following an extenuating competition, the commission for the monument to the first king of united Italy was entrusted to Giuseppe Sacconi. It was begun in 1885, and finished and inaugurated in 1911. The theme of the competition was celebration of the splendor of the nation after the Unification of Italy, and with this in mind Sacconi envisioned a medley of classicistic forms leading into the emotional and patriotic "heart" of the monument, the **Altar of the Nation**, which was in turn envisioned as architecture within architecture with the solemn statue of Rome standing watch over the **Tomb of the Unknown Soldier**. Note should also be taken of the decidedly classicistic *equestrian statue of Vittorio Emmanuele II*, an integral part of the monument, as are the fateful words from the Bulletin of Victory of 4 November 1918 carved in the stone of the last level. The entrance to the **Museo Sacrario delle Bandiere della Marina Militare** is on the left side.

Mamertine Prison - Under the church of San Giuseppe dei Falegnami, on the slopes of the Capitoline hill north of the Temple of Concord, is the "prison" given the name "Mamertine" in the Middle Ages. The travertine *facade* of the building can by dated from the inscription referring to the consuls Gaius Vibius Rufinus and Marcus Cocceius Nerva, who served between 39 and 42 BC. A modern entrance leads into a trapezoidal

chamber built in blocks of tufa stone and dating to the mid-2nd century BC. A door, now walled up, led into the other rooms of the prison, called *latomie* because they were adapted from the tufa quarries. A circular opening in the pavement of this room was originally the only entrance to an underground chamber where those condemned to death and enemies of the State were tortured and killed, generally by strangulation. According to later Christian legend, it was here Saint Peter was held a prisoner.

The Monument to Vittorio Emmanuele II and, below, a view of the interior of the Mamertine Prisons.

FORUM AND PALATINE

Roman Forum - Via Sacra - **Basilica Aemilia - Curia -
Arch of Septimius Severus - Basilica Julia** - Temple of Castor and
Pollux - Temple of the Divus Julius - **House of the Vestals -**
Regia - Temple of Antoninus and Faustina - **Basilica of Maxentius -
Santa Francesca Romana - Arch of Titus - Palatine Hill -**
Domus Augustana - Domus Tiberiana

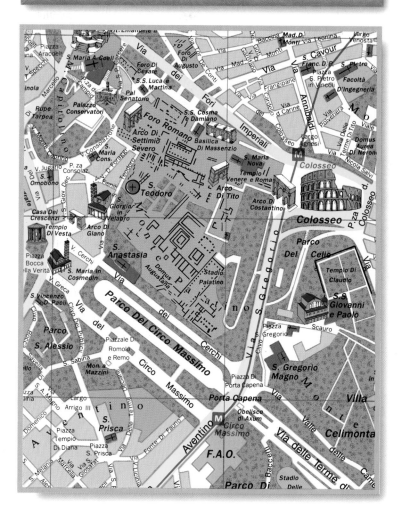

Roman Forum - Situated in the depression surrounded by the Palatine, the
Capitoline and the Esquiline hills, the area was originally most inhos-
pitable, swampy and unhealthy, until the surprisingly modern reclamation work carried out by king Tarquinius Priscus provided the area with a
highly-developed drainage system (*Cloaca Maxima*). Once this complex
reclamation work was finished, the Roman Forum became a place for
trade and barter. Numerous shops and a large market square were built.
An area was also set apart for public ceremonies: it was here that the
magistrates were elected, the traditional religious holidays were kept, and
those charged with various crimes were judged by a court with all the
forensic appurtenances. The urban fabric of the forum took on a new look
after the Punic wars, thanks to the extraordinary development of the city.

17

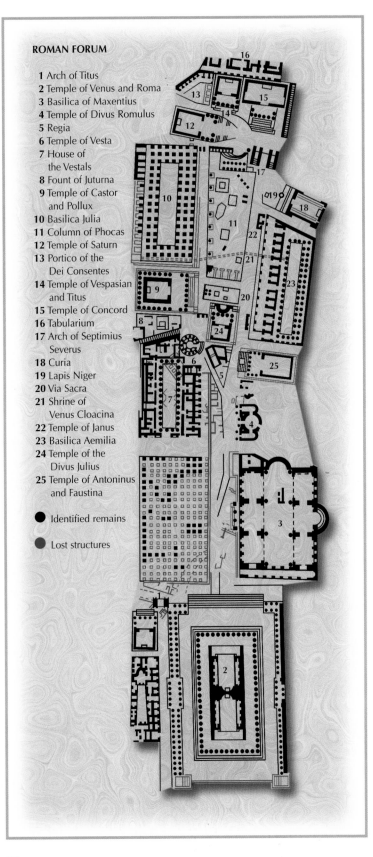

ROMAN FORUM

1 Arch of Titus
2 Temple of Venus and Roma
3 Basilica of Maxentius
4 Temple of Divus Romulus
5 Regia
6 Temple of Vesta
7 House of the Vestals
8 Fount of Juturna
9 Temple of Castor and Pollux
10 Basilica Julia
11 Column of Phocas
12 Temple of Saturn
13 Portico of the Dei Consentes
14 Temple of Vespasian and Titus
15 Temple of Concord
16 Tabularium
17 Arch of Septimius Severus
18 Curia
19 Lapis Niger
20 Via Sacra
21 Shrine of Venus Cloacina
22 Temple of Janus
23 Basilica Aemilia
24 Temple of the Divus Julius
25 Temple of Antoninus and Faustina

● Identified remains

● Lost structures

By the early 2nd century BC, various basilicas (Porcia, Sempronia, and Aemilia) had been built, the Temple of Castor and Pollux and the Temple of Concord had been rebuilt, and the network of roads connecting the forum to the other districts of the city had expanded considerably. After various transformations, the Roman Forum became so large as to be considered the secular, religious and commercial center of the city in Augustus' time.

There followed a period in which secular and political interests centered on other parts of the city, but the Roman Forum reacquired its original prestige under Maxentius and Constantine, who ordered construction of the Temple of Romulus and the great Basilica of Constantine. With the decline of the Roman Empire, the splendid but venerable structures of the forum were severely damaged during the barbarian invasions, especially those of the Goths (410 AD) and of the Vandals (455 AD). The Roman Forum meanwhile became a place of worship for the early Christians, who built the churches of Santi Sergius e Bacco (on the Via Sacra), of Sant' Adriano (near the Curia), and of Santi Cosma e Damiano (Temple of Peace).

As time passed, the forum area was completely abandoned; the ruins of the ancient monuments were used by the population and in large part demolished. During the Middle Ages, it became a pasture for sheep and cattle (hence its name of "Campo Vaccino"). For many centuries the prestige of the Roman Forum was a thing of the past; not until the early 20th century was the area systematically rehabilitated with excavation campaigns that lasted for decades on end. Thanks to these efforts, much splendid evidence of the Rome of the kings as well as that of the republic and the empire has again been brought to light.

A view of the Roman Forum with Phocas' Column, the Temple of Saturn, and, on the right, a portion of the Arch of Septimius Severus.

Via Sacra - Regarding the Via Sacra we have much detailed evidence from various ancient sources, but the entire course of this route, which changed along with the history of the city of Rome, has not yet been completely identified. Various hypotheses regarding the use of the term "*sacra*" have also been advanced. Varro tells us it was called thus because it was the route taken by the sacred processions, and Festus adds the mythical episode of the sacred pact between Romulus and Titus Tatius, which by tradition occurred here. In any case, it seems likely that a decisive element in the acquisition of the name is the fact that the oldest and most important places of worship were situated along this route. As far as the route itself is concerned, we know from historical sources that the sacerdotal terms stipulated that the Via Sacra was to run from the *arx* on the Capitoline to the shrine of Strenia near the Colosseum, crossing the Roman Forum by way of the Regia and the house of the *rex sacrorum*. This last brief stretch was the one the people knew best. The route then passed in front of the Basilica Aemilia, the Regia and the Temple of the Divus Romulus, at which point it probably veered left between this temple and the Basilica of Maxentius in the direction of the *Carinae*. The road that led from the Temple of the Divus Romulus toward the Arch of Titus may also at a later point in time have been called Via Sacra.

The route was considerably modified after Nero's fire of 64 AD. The street level was raised and the road was straightened out toward the site of the bronze colossus of the emperor. Stretches of two lower layers of the cobble paving dating to the republican period have also come to light. The Via Sacra was further modified by Hadrian after the construction of the Temple of Venus and Roma.

Basilica Aemilia - The basilica runs along the entire long side of the square of the Roman Forum and its west side is delimited by the *Argiletum* road.

This is the only basilica of the republican period still in existence; the others were the Sempronia, the Opimia and the Porcia. The Basilica Aemilia was founded in 179 BC by the censors M. Fulvius Nobiliores and M. Emilius Lepidus, after whom it was originally called (*Basilica Aemilia et Fulvia*). The *gens* Aemilia made numerous modifications to the building down through the centuries.

In 55 BC, the curule aedile L. Emilius Paulus (brother of the triumvirate Lepidus) began a thorough restructuring action, which was completed, not without a contribution from Caesar, by his son L. Emilius Lepidus Paulus in 34 BC, the year of his consulate. It was at this time that the basilica acquired its basic ground plan and was superimposed on the *tabernae*

A stretch of the Via Sacra in the Roman Forum.

novae which lay in front of the site, just as the Basilica Julia had been superimposed on the *tabernae veteres*. Together, these two structures constituted the long sides of the forum square, in line with Caesar's project. In 14 BC the basilica was destroyed by fire; it was rebuilt by L. Emilius Lepidus Paolus and Augustus. The decoration of the portico and the cella date to this time. The basilica was rebuilt one last time after the fire of 410 AD during the invasion of Rome by Alaric's Goths, an event of which the early 5th-century coins found fused on the pavement of this period provide striking evidence.

Detail of the paving of the Via Sacra.

The basilica as a type is probably of eastern Hellenistic origin; in Rome, these buildings provided a place for carrying on the political, economic and judiciary functions of the forum when the weather made it impossible to proceed in the open air.

The Basilica Aemilia consisted of a large hall (70 x 29 meters) divided into aisles by rows of columns. The nave, about twelve meters wide, was flanked by one aisle on the south and two aisles on the north. Part of the colored marble paving still survives. The side of the building toward the forum square was adorned with a two-story portico with sixteen arches on pilasters; the three columns we see standing belong to the reconstruction after the 410 AD fire. Behind the portico is a series of tabernae (shops) for bankers, built to take the place of the *tabernae novae* that were demolished during the construction work for the basilica. The three entrances to the hall open between one shop and the next.

Shrine of Venus Cloacina - The round marble base in front of the Basilica Aemilia was part of a shrine, consisting of an open-air enclosure, to the goddess Cloacina, who was charged with purifying the waters of the Cloaca Maxima that entered the area of the Roman Forum at this spot. This goddess was later identified with Venus, who inherited her name as one of her epithets as well as her attributes. Historical sources tell us that the shrine contained the cult statues of Venus and Cloacina. As tradition has it, it was here that one of the mythical episodes of the history of Rome occurred: the killing of Virginia by her father in his attempt to preserve her honor from the lustful advances of the tyrannical decemvir Appius Claudius.

Curia - The building touches on the southwest side of Caesar's Forum, of which it is in a sense an adjunct, between the *Argiletum* road and the Comitium.

It is also representative of the seat of the Roman Senate. Tradition attributes the founding of the first permanent curia to king Tullus Hostilius, hence the name *Curia Hostilia*. The Curia was rebuilt and enlarged in 80 BC by Silla, but in 52 BC it was destroyed in a fire provoked by incidents connected with the funeral of the tribune Clodius. It was then moved from its original site by Caesar, who built his forum there. Caesar began to rebuild the Curia on its present site, but his death in 44 BC interrupted work; the new Curia, renamed *Curia Julia* by decree of the Senate, was not finished until 29 BC by

1 - Curia. 2 - Church of Santi Luca e Martina.
3 - Arch of Septimius Severus.

Augustus, who also erected the portico known as the *Chalcidicum*. The damage suffered by the Curia in the fire of 64 AD was set right by Domitian in 94 AD, but the building again required restoration following the fire under Carinus in 283 AD.

The ground plan we see today dates to this period, even though Honorius I transformed the building, in 630 AD, into the church of Sant'Adriano, which was in turn rebuilt more than once and finally torn down between 1930 and 1936 during excavation work in the archaeological site. The building is on a rectangular plan, with four large buttress piers at the external corners in line with the facades. The main facade has an entrance portal and three large windows that illuminate the hall, which is 21 meters high, 27 meters long and 18 meters wide: proportions these that fully respect the Vitruvian canon for such buildings. It originally had a flat timber roof: the present one is blatantly modern. The fragments of marble pavement date to Diocletian's time, as does the decoration of the walls in the interior, where niches framed by small columns on projecting supports are topped by pediments typical of the taste of the 4th century AD.

A sector of the hall along each long side presents tiers on which the chairs of the senators were set. The podium for the president is at the back of the hall, between two doors; near it is the base of the statue of Victory which Octavianus had brought from Taranto.

Two bas-reliefs found in the central area of the forum in 1872 are on exhibit in the Curia. These, the so-called **Plutei of Trajan**, are sculpted on both sides and must have once been part

Trajan's Plutei inside the Curia and, below, the exterior of the building. Facing page: the cippus of the Lapis Niger.

of some lost monument, perhaps the enclosure of the *Ficus Ruminalis*, or decoration for the Rostra. On one side of each of the panels are represented a pig, a sheep, and a bull prepared for the *souvetaurilia*, as the sacrifice of these animals was called. On the other sides are two historical friezes that depict events that occurred during Trajan's reign. One panel commemorates the institution of the *Alimenta*: loans granted to smallholders, the interest from which was used by the state

for the education of orphaned children. The scheme provided assistance both to agriculture and to education.

The scene on the other panel illustrates the nullification of the outstanding debts of the citizens in regard of the state (back taxes): archive officials bring the registers and burn them in the presence of the emperor, in the forum.

Lapis Niger - This is the only surviving monument of the ancient Comitium, in what became the northwest corner of the Roman Forum, near the Curia, after Caesar and Augustus reorganized the area. It was discovered in 1899 by Giacomo Boni during the course of the excavations of the Roman Forum. It consists of a nearly square area paved in black marble and separated from the travertine pavement of Augustus' time by a balustrade of marble slabs. Under it was found a religious complex dating to the archaic period, in the form of a U-shaped altar of two superposed cushions (only the lower one has been preserved), a base in the form of a truncated cone, probably for a statue, and a pyramidal cippus or stele with a boustrophedon inscription (that is, one which may be read either from top to bottom and from bottom to top) in archaic Latin. It is unfortunately partially destroyed and not completely comprehensible even today.

Evidently what we have here is the *lex sacra* of the sanctuary. It contains a curse directed against those who dare defile the holy place, and the king (*Recei*) and the calator (*Kalatorem*) are mentioned. This is the oldest known monumental inscription in Latin; it dates to the second quarter of the 6th century BC. The votive pottery, some of which is Greek, and the bronze statuettes found here support the theory that the entire cult complex dates to that same century, and lead us to infer that the *"rex"* really refers to the kings of the period of the monarchy and not to the republican *rex sacrorum*, a priest who inherited the king's religious functions. In this respect the mention of the *calator*, or herald, also makes sense: it was in the Comitium, where the sanctuary is situated, that the king convoked the archaic assemblies of the Roman people and made the ritual sacrifices demanded on such occasions.

This cult site is mentioned in Roman literary sources (by Festus, in particular) as being ill-omened, since it was connected with the death of Romulus, and as the site of the tomb of Faustulus or of Hostus Hostilius, grandfather of king Tullus Hostilius. The area is now thought to have been the *Volcanal*, the ancient sanctuary of Vulcan, where according to a tradition which is echoed in Plutarch's *Life of Romulus*, Romulus found his death at the hands of the senators.

Arch of Septimius Severus - The arch is situated between the Rostra and the Curia and closes off the Roman Forum to the northeast. It was built in 203 AD to celebrate the two Parthian campaigns conducted by Septimius Severus in 195 and 197 AD.

The arch is about 20 meters high, 25 meters wide and more than 11 meters deep, with three passageways, a large one in the center and two smaller

ones at the sides; short flights of steps lead up to each. On top is a tall attic with a monumental inscription dedicating the arch to Septimius Severus and his son Caracalla. Septimius' other son Geta was also originally mentioned (we can still see the holes for the bronze letters, which in one point do not coincide with those there now, that spelled out his name and title), but when Caracalla killed his brother in the struggle for power after the death of their father, he also removed his name from the monuments of Rome. Representations of the monument on antique coins show that on the summit there was also once a bronze quadriga with the emperors.

The arch is built of travertine and brick and is faced with marble. On the front are four columns standing on tall plinths, decorated with reliefs of Roman soldiers and Parthian prisoners. The decoration includes two Victories above the Genii of the Seasons that frame the central opening, and personifications of the major rivers on the side openings; above, a small frieze commemorates the triumphal procession of the emperors. The keystones represent various gods: Mars appears twice in the main arch, while two female and two male

The Arch of Septimius Severus and, on the facing page, a detail of the base of the Decennalia column in the Roman Forum.

figures, one of whom is Hercules, adorn the lesser arches.

But the most interesting part of the decoration is the series of four panels (each 3.92 x 4.72 meters) set above the side openings, in which the most significant episodes of the two Parthian campaigns are narrated.

Temple of Concord - The temple, which faces on the square of the Roman Forum, is back to back with the *Tabularium* and north of the Temple of Vespasian and Titus. One of the first Roman temples built in honor of the personification of an abstract concept, the Temple of Concord occupies a particularly important place in the city's civil history. Tradition relates that it was founded in 367 BC by Marcus Furius Camillus, leader of the aristocratic party, in celebration of the pacification between patricians and plebeians following the promulgation of the Licinio-Sextian rogations establishing the concept of equal political rights for both portions of the population. The temple was drastically restored and rebuilt in 121 BC, when it was again dedicated to Concord by the patrician consul Lucius Opimius after the assassination of Gaius Gracchus and his followers. At this time, Opimius also founded a basilica, which stood near the temple and took his name.

Between 7 BC and 10 AD, Tiberius completely rebuilt the temple and had it newly inaugurated. The remains of the building date to this phase. There is a cella, curiously wider than it is deep (45 x 25 meters), set on a podium to which a central staircase gives access; it is preceded by six Corinthian columns that formed a jutting pronaos, a sort of avant-corps. The only parts still *in situ* are the podium and the doorstep of the cella, in red-veined grey marble (a type called "portasanta"), on which a caduceus is represented. Fragments of the entablature and a capital decorated with a pair of rams have also been found.

Tabularium - The Tabularium is at the westernmost end of the Roman Forum, behind the Temple of Concord, the Temple of Vespasian and Titus, and the Portico of the Dei Consentes. It was built in 78 BC by the consul Q. Lutatius Catulus as part of the reconstruction of the Capitoline after the fire of 83 BC to house the state archives, hence its name (the documents of the time were stone tablets called *tabulae*).

The building stands on the slopes of the Capitoline hill on a massive substructure that compensates the difference in height between the level of the forum and that of the valley of the *asylum*. It is trapezoidal in plan and has a recess on the southwest side to accommodate the preexisting Temple of Veiove. The facade facing on the forum is 73.60 meters long and formed of a row of ten arches framed by Doric semicolumns behind which runs a gallery divided into rooms roofed with cloister vaults. The Tabularium originally had a second story with a porticoed facade of Corinthian columns. Six windows in the long corridor in the interior of the substructure face on the forum.

The Tabularium, by the architect Lucius Cornelius, is an example of the late republican current of monumental architecture that made extensive use of substructures (see the sanctuaries of Tivoli, Terracina and Palestrina). It also introduced a number of features that met with great success in later times, such as facades with arches and semicolumns, and the cloister vault.

Temple of Vespasian and Titus - Set against the east side of the *Tabularium*, the temple is just south of the adjacent Temple of Concord and faces the west side of the Temple of Saturn.

A mutilated inscription discovered on the architrave of the temple corresponds to the inscription reported in its entirety by the Einsiedeln traveler of the 8th century. We thus know that the building is the one the

25

Senate dedicated to the deified Vespasian after his death in 79 AD, and thereafter to his son Titus who died two years later.

The temple was built by the emperor Domitian, son of Vespasian and brother of Titus.

The layout is strongly influenced by the lack of available space in the forum: the temple develops in width rather than depth (23 x 33 meters) and its builders adopted the unique solution of embedding the staircase in the pronaos between the columns.

The temple consists of a cella on a podium, with columns along the long walls of the interior. At the back is the plinth on which the cult statues of the two emperors stood. The pronaos consisted of six Corinthian columns on the front and two on the sides (a prostyle temple).

Three of the 15.70 meter-high columns still stand to delimit a corner. Alongside the inscription on the architrave were *bucrania* and representations of other sacrificial objects. The podium and the staircase were consolidated by Valadier in 1811.

Two images of the remains of the Temple of Vespasian.

Portico of the Dei Consentes - In 1834, a unique structure was brought to light in a raised area near the *Tabularium*, south of the Temple of Vespasian and Titus, consisting of a portico divided into two wings which meet in an obtuse angle, with eight rooms behind. The cipolin marble columns of the portico were restored to a standing position as part of the restoration work conducted during the 1858 excavation campaign.Six of the rooms contained paired gilded bronze statues of the twelve *Dei Consentes* ("counselors," or the highest gods in the Roman *pantheon*), mentioned by Varro. On the lower floor there are seven rooms fitted as shops. The building as we see it now is the result of reconstruction under the Flavian dynasty and later enlargement (367 AD) carried out, as an inscription on the architrave informs us, by the then-prefect of the city Vettius Agorius Pretextatus.

Temple of Saturn - This is one of the oldest temples in Rome, erected in 497 BC. Festus and Servius tell us that it was preceded by an altar, dedicated to the god Saturn, for which a special area was later set apart as we see in the *Forma Urbis* (the monumental marble plan of the city from the time of Septimius Severus). Some authors argue that the foundation of the temple ought to be attributed to the last kings, even if the actual building did not take place till the beginning of the republican period. The temple was dedicated on the day of the *Saturnalia*, the Roman "New Year" celebration held on 17 December. It was completely rebuilt in 42 BC by the curule aedile L. Munatius Plancus. The large podium from this phase in the life of the temple still exists; it is entirely faced in travertine and is 40 meters long, 22.50 meters wide and 9 meters high.

The inscription on the architrave tells us that the temple was once again restored in 283 AD, following a fire. The six grey granite columns on the front, the two in red granite on the sides, and the pediment, made mostly of reused blocks, date to this period. A great deal of building material used in the 42 BC reconstruction was in fact again turned to use: even the columns, which do not always pair up stylistically with the bases or with the Ionic capitals.

This temple was built at a particularly critical time in Rome's history, one marked by extensive famine, epidemics, and the severe economic and commercial crisis which characterized the years subsequent to the fall of the monarchy. The great number of temples built at the time is eloquent testimony to the sense of distress which took hold of the Roman people at this turning: the Temple of Saturn in 497 BC, that of Mercury, protector of commerce, in 495 BC, that dedicated to Ceres, goddess of the earth and fertility, in 493 BC. This analysis explains the building of a temple to the god Saturn, who before being identified with the Greek Kronos was venerated for his special power known as *Lua Saturni* (the verb *luo* means to loosen, to liberate; *lustrum* means purification); in other words, the power to free the city from its afflictions.

Above, a relief from the base of the Decennalia column and, below, the colonnade of the Temple of Saturn.

Basilica Julia - The basilica runs along the entire long south side of the forum and is bordered on the west by the *Vicus Jugarius* and on the east by the *Vicus Tuscus*, which separate it from the Temple of Saturn and the Temple of Castor and Pollux, respectively. Work on the building was begun in 54 BC by Julius Caesar, from whom it took its name, and it was dedicated in 46 BC. The area was previously occupied by the *tabernae veteres* (market shops) and the Basilica Sempronia, built in 169 BC by Tiberius Sempronius Gracchus, the father of the plebeian tribunes Tiberius and Gaius. The house of Scipio Africanus and various shops were torn down to permit its construction.

The Basilica Julia was finished by Augustus, who also had to reconstruct it after its destruction in the fire of 14 BC. In 12 AD he dedicated the Basilica to his adopted sons Gaius and Lucius. The fire under Carinus (283 AD) caused considerable damage and Diocletian later saw to restoration of the basilica. It was once more partially destroyed when Alaric sacked Rome in 410 AD and was reconstructed six years later (416) by the then-prefect of the city Gabinius Vettius Probianus.

The court of the centumvirs met in the Basilica, which also served as a meeting place for those who frequented the forum. The impressively-sized building (96 x 48 meters), was composed of a large central space (82 x 18 meters) delimited by four aisles that served as corridors. They were vaulted and set on two stories, with arches framed by semicolumns.

The only part of the original building still standing is the stepped podium; the brick piers are a modern addition.

Various pedestals for statues, with inscriptions, three of which name Polycleitus, Praxiteles, and Timarchus as sculptors, are still in place. The "gaming boards" (*tabulae lusoriae*) scratched into the pavement and steps and the graffiti sketches of some of the statues we suppose to have stood nearby are probably the work of ancient Roman idlers.

Column of Phocas - This marble Corinthian column, which stands in front of the Rostra on a stepped brick base, was the last erected in the Roman Forum. It is 13.60 meters high and was undoubtedly taken from an older monument. The dedicatory inscription informs us that in 608 AD Smaragdo, then the exarch of Italy, set a gilded bronze statue of the Byzantine emperor Phocas atop the column. Although the inscription sings the praises of the emperor, Phocas was instead famous for his cruelty. To begin with, he acquired the throne by assassinating his predecessor Mauricius and his children. But he redeemed himself to some extent, at least in Rome, by making a gift of the Pantheon to Pope Boniface IV in 608 AD. The temple was converted into a church the following year.

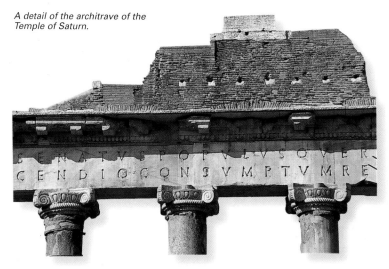

A detail of the architrave of the Temple of Saturn.

On the right, Phocas' Column, located near the Rostra; below, the columns of the Temple of Castor and Pollux.

29

A view of the remains of the Basilica Julia, begun by Julius Caesar and completed by Augustus.

Temple of Castor and Pollux - The temple faces on the square of the Roman Forum to the west of the Arch of Augustus, and is separated by the *Vicus Tuscus* from the east side of the Basilica of Gaius and Lucius (Basilica Julia).

Tradition links the founding of the temple to a popular legend of ancient Rome. During the battle of Lake Regillus between Romans and Latins in 496 BC, two unknown young horsemen appeared, seemingly from nowhere, to lead the Romans to victory. Immediately thereafter the two were seen in the forum watering their horses at the fountain of Juturna; after announcing the rout of the enemy, they disappeared into thin air. They were identified as the Dioscuri, and in thanks for their aid the dictator Aulus Postumius Albinus vowed to build them a temple. The building was dedicated by his son, *duumvir* in 484 BC, and in 117 BC it was completely rebuilt with a larger podium by L. Caecilius Metellus Dalmaticus after his victory over the Dalmatians.

The temple was restored again by Verres (governor of Sicily, attacked by Cicero in his *Verrine Orations*) in 73 BC. The last, definitive reconstruction was by Tiberius after the fire of 14 BC; the temple was rededicated in 6 AD. What remains dates back to this time. The temple was peripteral with eight Corinthian columns on its short sides and eleven on its long sides. The cella stood on a on a concrete base, an *opus caementicium* (50 x 30 x 7 meters) that was originally faced with blocks of tufa stone, removed in modern times and reused as construction material.

The podium we now see dates to the restoration by Metellus in 117 BC, as do the stretches of black and white mosaic on the floor of the cella.

During the republican period, the senate met in the temple; in the mid-2nd century BC the podium became a tribune for magistrates and orators in the legislative *comitia* that were held in this part of the forum square: it was here, for example, that Caesar proposed his agrarian reforms. The building became the headquarters for the office of weights and measures as well, and in imperial times a part of the treasury of the tax office was kept in rooms in the long sides. Some of these were also bankers' offices.

The cult of the Dioscuri was originally Greek and was imported to Rome via the cities of Magna Graecia. The twins, sons of Zeus and Leda, were skillful horsemen both in war and in competitions and were therefore patrons of the Olympic Games in Greece and later, in Rome, of the Circus games.

Fount of Juturna - A spring that probably supplied the archaic settlement on the Palatine rises between the Temple of Castor and Pollux and that of Vesta; in ancient times it was identified with Juturna, sister of Turnus, king of the Rutulii (a figure connected with the legend of the origins of Rome). Juturna was loved by Jupiter, who transformed her into a nymph.

A square basin in *quasi reticolatum* masonry and faced with marble was built in the republican period to collect the water of the spring. At the center was a base supporting the marble statues of the Dioscuri, placed there to celebrate the mythical episode relating how they were seen watering their horses after having announced the Roman victory over the Latins in the battle of Lake Regillus (496 BC). The statues were found in fragments at the bottom of the basin, while on its border is the cast of a stele dating to Trajan's time, with a relief of the Dioscuri, Juturna, Jupiter and Leda. The aedicula near the basin, with a dedicatory inscription to Juturna, dates to the same period. The basin was probably built in the late 2nd century BC by Metellus and later restored by Tiberius at the same time that the neighboring Temple of Castor and Pollux was being restored.

Church of Santa Maria Antiqua - Raised over the remains of structures of the imperial period that were probably part of the Palatine complex, this church was rebuilt a number of times during its long history, in the first millennium as well as later, and although its present form is a mix of styles, the original nucleus is unquestionably anterior to the 10th century and therefore one of the most interesting examples of early Christian architecture in Rome.
The vast **atrium** was originally part of a building dating to the time of Domitian; on its walls are remains of what are probably seventh-century paintings. The atrium leads to the old hall, divided into a nave and two aisles. At the center of the nave are the remains of an enclosure, the old *schola cantorum*. The wall paintings and decorations in the splendid left aisle depict *Scenes from the Old Testament*; in the right aisle are coeval paintings of the *Virgin and Child with Saints*. Other fine and well-preserved frescoes are found in the left chapel of the apse and in the apse itself.

Temple of the Divus Julius - This temple is at the eastern end of the forum square between the Basilica Aemilia to the north, the Temple of Castor and Pollux to the south and the Regia to the east.
It was built in 29 BC by Augustus, as part of his project for the restructuring of the area of the Roman Forum. Augustus' aim was to modernize, and with this building he closed off the square on its short east side to exclude once and for all the archaic monuments, such as the Regia and the Temple of Vesta.
The temple, dedicated to the deified Julius Caesar (the first example of such deification in Rome), stands on the site where Caesar's body was cremated before his ashes were taken to the Regia, his official residence as pontifex maximus. A marble column was erected here in memory of the "father of the country," as we read in the inscription. The column was later replaced by a semicircular exedra with an altar, which opens at the center of the temple podium on the facade. The Temple of the Divus Julius, of which only the base remains, consisted of a cella on a podium with a flight of stairs on either side, with a pronaos with six Corinthian columns on the front and two on each side, and was enclosed by a colonnade, identifiable as the *Porticus Julia*, on all sides except the facade. The rosters taken from the ships used by Antony and Cleopatra in the battle of Actium in 31 BC would seem not, as formerly believed, to have decorated the podium, but instead to have been exhibited on the front of an orator's tribune that stood before the

The Temple of Caesar in the Roman Forum, with in the background the Curia building.

temple. The building is connected to the Basilica Aemilia by the portico dedicated to Gaius and Lucius, Augustus' grandsons, and to the Temple of Castor and Pollux (rededicated to the brothers Tiberius and Drusus) by an arch of the Augustan age. The arch originally celebrated the victory at Actium, but was replaced in 19 BC by one celebrating the Parthian victory, and therefore may be said to reflect a true propagandistic effort by the emperor, whose aim was to have the whole forum echo with the name of the *gens* Julia.

Temple of Vesta - Located to the south of the Via Sacra in front of the Regia, this is one of the oldest temples in Rome, although its present appearance dates to 191 AD when it was restored by Julia Domna, wife of Septimius Severus. The fire sacred to Vesta, the goddess of the household hearth, had to be kept perennially burning in this temple, for disaster threatened if the flame were to go out. But this fact obviously meant that the building was frequently in danger of fire, hence the many restorations. It would seem, however, that the various reconstructions all retained both the original orientation, with the entrance to the east as dictated by ritual, and the original circular plan, which, as Ovid informs us in his *Fasti*, takes as prototype the duellingo of the early Iron Age. The original temple may very well have been no more than a round hut with walls in interlaced wood and reeds plastered with clay, and with a straw roof.

The remains of the Temple of Vesta with its characteristic circular form.
On the facing page: above, the House of the Vestals with the statues of the senior members of the religious order; below, a statue of a vestal in the interior of the priestess' house.

As we have said, the building is circular; it consists of a cella surrounded by twenty Corinthian columns set on a podium 15 meters in diameter, faced with marble, to which a staircase leads up on the east. The roof was conical with an opening for the smoke. The cella, on the outside wall of which semicolumns rose at intervals, contained no cult statue but only the hearth that was sacred to the goddess. A trapezoidal cavity in the podium, accessible only from the cella, may be the *penus Vestae*; that is, the *sancta sanctorum* of the temple, a sort of storeroom that only the vestal virgins could enter that contained the objects Aeneas was said to have brought back after the destruction of Troy as proof of the universal glory of Rome. These treasures included the Palladium, an ancient wooden image of Minerva, and the images of the Penates. The temple was closed by Theodosius in 394 AD.

House of the Vestals - The *Atrium Vestae*, on the south side of the Via Sacra, was a complex consisting of the Temple of Vesta and the House of the Vestals. As priestesses of the cult of Vesta, the vestals were the custodians of the sacred hearth and were charged with performing the various cult rites. The six vestal virgins of the only body of female priests in Rome were chosen, between the ages of six and ten, from among the daughters of the patrician families. They were required to remain in the order for thirty years and to keep a vow of chastity. Vestal virgins who broke this vow were buried alive in a subterranean chamber outside Porta Collina, in a place suitably called the "field of iniquity," while their accomplice in the transgression was condemned to death by flogging in the Comitium. But in exchange for their chastity, they enjoyed important privileges: they were subtracted from parental authority and the *patria potestas* passed to the pontifex maximus, they could travel in the city in a wagon (which was forbidden to ordinary women), they had reserved seats at the spectacles and ceremonies, and they were permitted to do as they best saw fit with a sort of stipend they received from the State.

The order of the vestal virgins is extremely ancient and traditionally dates to the time of king Numa Pompilius.

About a meter below the level of the present building, we can still see the remains of the *Atrium*

Vestae of the republican era. It was a much smaller structure and, unlike the later one, oriented north-south. It was joined to the Temple of Vesta by a courtyard, to the south of which was a complex of six rooms (remember that there were six vestal virgins). Part of the mosaic pavement with irregular inserts of marble tile (*lithostroton*) is still intact.

After the fire of Rome in 64 AD, the House of the Vestals was rebuilt by Nero in the form that was destined to endure as least as far as size and orientation (shifted to northwest-southeast, following that of the forum) were concerned. Trajan completely remodeled it and afterwards Septimius Severus restored the entire complex, including the temple. The vestals abandoned the building in 394 AD when the pagan cults were abolished; from that time onward the buildings were used for other purposes.

The **entrance** to the House of the Vestals is to the west, adjacent to an aedicula which probably served as a lararium. The door leads into a large rectangular central courtyard surrounded by a double colonnade with eighteen columns on the long sides and six on the short sides.

The porticoes originally housed the statues of the Virgines Vestales Maximae (the senior members of the order), many of which have been found in the courtyard together with bases naming them. The earliest inscriptions date to the time of Septimius Severus. Some of the statues have been left in the courtyard, set arbitrarily on pedestals which do not necessarily belong to them.

At the center of the east side of the complex is the so-called tablinum, a spacious hall that was originally vaulted and from which six rooms open off. The rooms were also vaulted and all about the same size (4.15 x 3.50 meters); this fact leads us to believe that they were the rooms of the six vestal virgins.

On the ground floor, opening off a corridor on the south side, is a series of what must have been service rooms: a bakery, a mill, a kitchen, etc. Upstairs are the rooms of the vestals, with baths. There must also have been a third floor. The western part of this sector contains an apsed hall, which may be the republican-era reconstruction of the shrine to Aius Locutius. This was the name given to a voice heard in the sacred grove of Vesta (*Lucus Vestae*) in 390 BC warning the Romans of the attack of the Gauls.

A large room, which may have been a triclinium, opens in the west side. Not enough remains of the north side to tell what was there; underneath are visible remains dating to the archaic and republican periods, including the houses of the *rex sacrorum* and of the pontifex maximus, where Caesar too lived when he was pontifex. An apsed hall used as *thermae* must also have been connected to this portion of the complex.

Regia - The building stands on an old tract of the Via Sacra, with the Temple of the Divus Julius on the west, the Temple of Vesta and the House of the Vestals on the south, and the Temple of Antoninus and Faustina on the north. Ancient sources (Festus, Servius, Plutarch) tell us that the Regia was built during the monarchy as the dwelling of Numa Pompilius, traditionally the second king of Rome. Recent archaeological studies, which have revealed a complicated alternation of building phases going back to the monarchic phase of Roman history, support the sources.

In the 8th century BC, the site was occupied by huts. In the late 7th century BC, the first "permanent" building, in sun-dried brick on a foundation of tufa blocks, with rooms arranged around an unroofed enclosure, was erected. It was rebuilt three times during the 6th century BC and the arrangement of the rooms around the courtyard was modified. Confirmation of the importance ascribed to the building, and perhaps even that it was the palace of the kings, has been provided by the discovery of architectural terracotta blocks and facing slabs from the third and fourth buildings (dating, respectively, to 570 and 530 BC) and the stand of a bucchero-ware bowl from the last quarter of the 6th century BC, bearing the inscription "*rex.*" The radical modification of the ground plan of the Regia at that time remained unaltered throughout the republican period and has survived to our time. The building was remodeled in the second half of the 3rd century BC after a fire, in 148 BC, and again in 36 BC by the pontifex Gneus Domitius Calvinus, who is also responsible for having added the marble facing, but all these actions respected the irregular republican ground plan.

The Regia was the site of extremely ancient cults and rites, with a sanctuary to Mars in which the twelve *ancilia*, the sacred shields used by the ancient college of the *Salii* for the processions in honor of the god, and the *hastae*, the spears said to vibrate as a portent of impending ruin, were jealously preserved. There was also a sanctuary to Ops Consiva, an ancient goddess of the harvest.

For a better understanding of the relationship between these two gods, it helps to recall that Mars was originally connected with the agrestic world, as god of vegetation and the fields and protector of the townsfolk. In his honor, in a ceremony known as *Equos October* held at the ides of October, a horse was sacrificed and the tail and genitals were taken to the Regia.

How basically important the Regia was for the religious and civil life of the city is proved by the fact that up to the time of Augustus this was where the archives of the pontifices were kept and where the annals and calendar drawn up by the pontifex maximus were exhibited. The final ground plan of the building, that which has come down to us from the 6th century BC, has three rooms on the south: the central one serves as an entrance from the Via Sacra to the other two and to the courtyard, which lay to the north. The room to the west is the sanctuary of Mars, paved in tufa and with a circular base which may have been an altar, while the room to the east is thought to have been the sanctuary of Ops Consiva. The trapezoidal courtyard is paved with slabs of tufa and provided with drainage channels; it had a portico of wooden columns on the north, an entrance on the east and an altar near the west side.

Temple of Antoninus and Faustina -
The temple faces on the Via Sacra, in front of the north side of the Regia to the east of the Basilica Aemilia.

The monumental inscription on the architrave identifies this building as the temple of the emperor Antoninus Pius and his wife Faustina. It was originally erected in honor of Faustina alone, by her husband, after her death in 141 AD. When Antoninus Pius also died, in 161 AD, the temple was dedicated to the deified imperial couple by senate decree.

There are two reasons why the building has reached us in good condition; first, because the Church of San Lorenzo in Miranda was built inside it in the early Middle

Above, a detail of the remains of the Regia, the residence of Numa Pompilio. At the center, the Temple of Antoninus and Faustina over which the church of San Lorenzo in Miranda was built. Below, the Temple of the Divus Romulus, with its original bronze portal.

35

Ages, and secondly because it was unusually solidly built. Attempts to tear down the pronaos so as to reuse the marble were to no avail, as is shown by the oblique grooves cut in the upper part of the columns, into which ropes could have been fitted to topple the columns by pulling from below. The temple, of grandiose dimensions, consists of a cella, built in blocks of peperino and originally faced with cipolin marble, placed on a podium with a brick altar at its center. Access to the podium is afforded by a modern-day staircase. The pronaos has six Corinthian columns in cipolin marble on the front and two on each side. Each is seventeen meters high; some are engraved with images of gods. The frieze is decorated with facing griffins and plant motifs. Interesting fragments of sculpture, which belonged to the cult statues of the imperial couple, have been found near the temple.

Temple of the Divus Romulus - The building faces on the Via Sacra between the area occupied by the archaic burial grounds and the Basilica of Maxentius. It would by now seem certain that this was not a temple dedicated to Romulus, the deified son of Maxentius, but was instead built under Constantine. It was thus probably that Temple of the Penates we know to have originally stood in the area occupied at the beginning of the 4th century AD by the Basilica of Maxentius and to have been later transferred to an adjacent site. The building is circular in plan and built in brick; the entrance with its original bronze portal that opens at the center of the curved facade is framed by two porphyry columns, with bases in travertine and marble capitals, supporting a marble architrave. To the sides of the entrance are four niches for statues. Two elongated apsed rooms, preceded by two columns in cipolin marble, flank the temple; they probably housed the statues of the Penates. In the 6th century AD, the temple became the atrium of the Church of Santi Cosma e Damiano, originally built in a large space in the Forum of Peace that lay behind the temple. One hypothesis identifies this temple with that of Jupiter Stator, which has never been localized but which is mentioned together with other buildings on the left of the Via Sacra in literary sources of Constantine's time, whereas no mention is made of the Temple of the Divus Romulus.

1 - Basilica of Maxentius.
2 - Temple of Antoninus and Faustina.
3 - Temple of Romulus and Church of Santi Cosma e Damiano.

A view of the remains of the Basilica Aemilia with the Temple of Antoninus and Faustina on the left.

Basilica of Maxentius - Access to the Basilica of Maxentius, which stands outside the current archaeological area of the Roman Forum, is from the Via dei Fori Imperiali. The building was begun in 308 AD by Maxentius and completed by Constantine, who modified the internal layout by shifting the entrance from the east to the south side on the Via Sacra.

The building occupies an area of 100 by 65 meters and stands on a platform which is in part a superstructure over storerooms of considerable size. The original **entrance**, which Constantine also retained, opened into a narrow elongated atrium from which three openings led into the large central area. This is oriented east-west; it is 80 meters long, 25 meters, wide and 35 meters high, and was covered by three cross vaults supported by eight columns in proconnesian marble, each 4.50 meters high and set against piers (none of which are still *in situ*). At the back, facing Maxentius' entrance, there was a semicircular apse which contained an enormous acrolithic statue of Constantine (with the uncovered parts of the body in marble and the rest probably in gilded bronze). The head, 2.60 meters high, and a foot, two meters long, were found in 1487.

The aisles on either side of the nave were divided into three communicating bays with transversal coffered and stuccoed barrel vaults. Constantine's new plan maintained the three-part division, but shifted the axis of the basilica from east-west to north-south and moved the entrance, with four tall porphyry columns, to the south. Here, a flight of steps led from the Via Sacra to the floor of the building, which was partly cut into the Velian hill. Across from this entrance a new semicircular apse was set into the wall at the center of the north aisle; it was preceded by two columns and had niches for statues framed by small columns on projecting supports.

The nave was illuminated by a series of large windows in the clerestory, while the side aisles had two tiers of arched windows.

The ground plan and dimensions of the building were inspired by the majestic halls of the imperial baths, which were also called "basilicas."

Church of Santa Francesca Romana - The church was originally built in the second half of the 10th century, but has been remodeled more than once over the course of time. The profiled white facade in travertine dates to the early 17th century; it is the work of Carlo Lombardi, who was extremely active in Rome at the time. The gabled *facade* is crowned by statues and has two orders of paired

Santa Francesca Romana.

The ruins of the Temple of Venus and Rome.

pilasters set on high stylobates; above, there are a large balcony and a porch with three arches.

The single-nave **interior** has a beautiful coffered *ceiling* and a very old square of Cosmatesque mosaic in the pavement. At the back of the nave is an arch known as the *Holy Arch*, with a *Confession* in polychrome marble by Bernini and a four-columned shrine containing the marble group of *Santa Francesca Romana with an Angel* by Giosuè Meli (1886). On the back wall of the right transept, protected by a grating, are two blocks of basalt said to bear the print of Saint Peter's knees, made when he knelt to pray here. On the left wall is the lovely *Funeral Monument of Gregory XI* by Olivieri. The apsidal mosaic portrays the *Madonna and Child with Saints*, dating to about 1160; on the high altar is the reputedly miraculous image of the *Virgin with Child* (also from the 12th century). The altar in the **Crypt** conserves the mortal remains of the saint; facing it is a lovely relief medallion of *Saint Francesca and an Angel* by the school of Bernini. The **Sacristy** houses some excellent paintings, including the panel of *Santa Maria Nova* (or the *Madonna del Conforto*) dating to the 5th century, a *Virgin Enthroned* by Sinibaldo Ibi from Perugia (1524), an imposing altarpiece depicting the *Miracle of Saint Benedict*, by Subleyras, and various paintings by the school of Caravaggio. The adjacent **Convent** is the seat of the *Antiquarium Forense*.

Temple of Venus and Roma - The temple, set between the Basilica of Maxentius and the Colosseum, stands on a huge artificial platform on substructures built to extend the area offered by the Velian hill over what remained of the monumental atrium of the Domus Aurea, Nero's regal residence. To increase the available space, the gigantic bronze statue (36 meters high) of Nero as Helios was moved to a new site nearer the Colosseum.

Begun in 121 AD and inaugurated in 135, the Temple of Venus and Roma was personally designed by Hadrian, who was known as a "cultured" emperor with a passionate love for art and architecture. The building was set within a double colonnade that left the two principal facades free and featured an entrance propylaeum at the center of each of the long sides. The proportions of the complex as a whole (145 x 100 meters) are quite impressive.

The temple itself was a large Corinthian decastyle structure (with ten columns on the front and nineteen on the sides). It lacked the traditional podium of Roman temples, and stood instead on a stylobate with four steps. The temple had two cellae set back to back; entrance to the cellae was through two porches with four columns between the antae. Originally, neither cella was apsed, having instead flat timber roofs. Their present aspect is the result of the restoration ordered by Maxentius in 307 AD, following a fire: on this occasion, the *cellae* were given rear apses to contain the cult statues of Venus (in the cella facing the Colosseum) and of the goddess Roma (facing the forum), coffered and stuccoed barrel vaults replaced the original flat ceiling, porphyry columns were installed on the long sides in the interior, and niches meant for statues, framed by small porphyry columns resting on corbels, were cut; finally, the floor was repaved in polychrome marble.

The cella of the goddess Roma is the better preserved of the two. It is now part of the former convent of Santa Francesca Romana, and the peristasis has been replaced by a hedge. Only a few of the grey granite columns of the portico are still standing.

Arch of Titus - The arch rises in the eastern part of the forums area, south of the Temple of Venus and Roma.

As part of the medieval fortifications of the Frangipane fami-

Facing page, the monumental Arch of Titus, erected by Domitian in 81 AD. On this page, a detail of the arch and its inscription.

ly, it survived into the 19th century and in 1822 was restored by Valadier, as recorded in the inscription on the attic on the side facing the forum. The inscription on the side toward the Colosseum is instead coeval with the arch; it tells us that the arch was dedicated to the emperor Titus by his brother and successor Domitian to commemorate the victory of the former in the Judaic campaign of 70 AD, probably after Titus' death in 81 AD.

The arch, with a single passageway, is 5.40 meters high, 13.50 meters wide and 4.75 meters deep. It is faced with pentelic marble (with piers in travertine restored by Valadier) and on the front and back has four semicolumns with composite capitals. The decorative sculpture on the outside includes two figures of Victories on globes, with banners, on the archivolt, the *Goddess Roma* and the *Genius of the Roman People* on the keystones, and a high-relief frieze of the triumph of Vespasian and Titus over the Jews on the architrave. Inside the arch, the panel at the center of the coffered vault contains a relief of the apotheosis of Titus as he is carried to heaven by an eagle, while two large panels with scenes from the Judaic triumph adorn the sides. The panel on the north depicts a procession in which the bearers of the lictor's fasces precede the Emperor, riding on a quadriga, being crowned by a figure of Victory; the horses are led by the goddess Roma (or perhaps Virtus) and the chariot is followed by personifications of the Roman People (a youth with a bare torso) and the Senate (a man wearing a toga), in a *summa* of the traditional motifs of imperial propaganda.

The panel on the south side presents the procession as it passes through the Porta Triumphalis, which is represented in a perspective view; the spoils from the Temple of Jerusalem, including the seven-branched candelabrum, the silver horns, and the golden tablet, are carried on litters (fercula); various other figures bear tablets with handles on which the names of the conquered cities were probably inscribed.

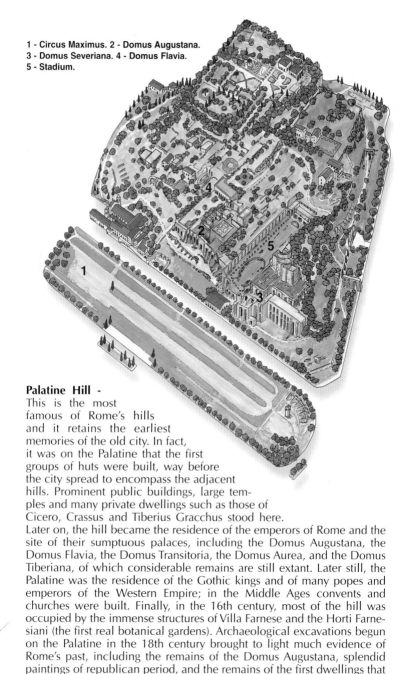

1 - Circus Maximus. 2 - Domus Augustana.
3 - Domus Severiana. 4 - Domus Flavia.
5 - Stadium.

Palatine Hill -

This is the most
famous of Rome's hills
and it retains the earliest
memories of the old city. In fact,
it was on the Palatine that the first
groups of huts were built, way before
the city spread to encompass the adjacent
hills. Prominent public buildings, large temples and many private dwellings such as those of
Cicero, Crassus and Tiberius Gracchus stood here.
Later on, the hill became the residence of the emperors of Rome and the
site of their sumptuous palaces, including the Domus Augustana, the
Domus Flavia, the Domus Transitoria, the Domus Aurea, and the Domus
Tiberiana, of which considerable remains are still extant. Later still, the
Palatine was the residence of the Gothic kings and of many popes and
emperors of the Western Empire; in the Middle Ages convents and
churches were built. Finally, in the 16th century, most of the hill was
occupied by the immense structures of Villa Farnese and the Horti Farnesiani (the first real botanical gardens). Archaeological excavations begun
on the Palatine in the 18th century brought to light much evidence of
Rome's past, including the remains of the Domus Augustana, splendid
paintings of republican period, and the remains of the first dwellings that
stood on the hill, not to mention the magnificent 16th-century entrance
portal to the Horti Farnesiani.

The Domus Augustana on the Palatine.

Domus Augustana - The building
of Domitian's grandiose palace on
the Palatine gave the hill its definitive topographical disposition and
firmly established its role as the
site of the imperial residences. The
building was begun in the early
years of Domitian's reign and in
the main completed by 92 AD,
although some parts, such as the
stadium, were finished later. It was
used as the emperor's palace until

the end of the Empire. The complex is divided into three parts: the **Domus Flavia**, which was used for state functions, the Domus Augustana proper, a private wing, and finally the Stadium, or large garden in the shape of a circus.

The core of the Domus Flavia was a large peristyle with an octagonal fountain at the center; all that is left of the portico today are the bases of the columns. A series of large rooms surrounded the courtyard. On the north side was the so-called *Aula Regia*, with two entrances framing an apse. The walls of this stately hall were decorated with niches containing statues flanked by tall columns. From the apse at the center back of the room, on its main axis, Domitian granted official audiences and received the homage of his subjects, in a setting that was perfectly in keeping with his self-asserted divinity (he was the first emperor to have himself called "god").

Two large rooms, the *Basilica* and the so-called *Lararium*, communicated with the Aula Regia on its two sides. The Basilica is a rectangular hall terminating in an apse and divided into three aisles by two rows of columns. Its form would seem to indicate that it was used for some kind of public ceremony which required the presence of the emperor, for whom the apse was reserved.

The function of the Lararium is more problematical. The name seems to be purely conventional and not actually indicative of the sanctuary of the Lares.

The *Triclinium*, with its colonnaded front, opens on the south side of the peristyle. This grand space, which terminates in an apse at the back and has columns along

Above, the Domus Augustana. Below, the oval fountain of the Domus Flavia.

the walls, was the emperor's luxurious dining room. At the sides, clearly visible through large windows, are two large nymphaea with oval fountains, of which only one is still extant.

Two earlier dwellings have been brought to light under the Domus Flavia, called the *House of the Griffins* (late 2nd century BC) and the *Aula Isiaca* (ca. 20 BC) from the decoration on the walls.

The Domus Augustana, the term originally used to indicate the entire complex, now refers only to the emperor's private apartments. The complex spreads out over two levels, following the lay of the artificial leveling of the hill. The curvilinear facade of the southern part, at ground level, opens onto the Circus Maximus. A vestibule, with two semicircular rooms at the sides, leads to a large peristyle with a monumental fountain with ornamental pelta motifs in the center. This courtyard is surrounded by rooms on two stories; flights of stairs lead to the upper level (the same on which the Domus Flavia is built) and to the interconnecting rooms that lead into a second peristyle with a small temple on a small island at the center of a large basin. There may have been a third peristyle to the north, in an area that is very poorly preserved; on the east, a large elliptical room with a double internal colonnade runs parallel to the stadium.

The eastern sector of the complex was composed of the so-called **Stadium**, a large garden in the form of a circus, measuring 160 x 50 meters, with the back set against the curve of the Circus Maximus. A portico on two levels ran all around it, and at its center was a *spina*, of which only the semicircular extremities remain. The east side has an exedra-shaped tribune at the center.

The Domus Aurea represents an important moment in Roman architecture. Here, Domitian's architect Rabirius created what was to become the canonic formula for the dynastic residence: a synthesis of structural functionality - with the division into official and private sectors - and extravagant decoration, in which the blend of curved and straight lines in the ground plan and the illusionistic and perspective effects, already present in Nero's Domus Aurea and here reproposed, were made a near science.

Palatine Antiquarium - Built over a small part of the earlier Domus Augustana, the Antiquarium houses exhibits of archaeological finds and sculpture unearthed on the Palatine from the late 19th century on. Of particular note are two heads of *Attis*, two *ideal heads* (copies of 5th-century BC Greek originals), a torso of *Mercury* and a torso of *Artemis* (also copies of Greek originals), and above all the famous *Graffito of the Crucifixion*, dating to early Christian times.

Domus Flavia - This construction consisted of three aisles separated by columns and terminating in an apse. At the center of the structure are the remains of the Aula Regia, or throne room, in which the emperor held audience. Significant parts of another room, the **Lararium**, or the emperor's private chapel, are also still extant. Excavations begun in the 18th century have brought to light interesting architectural elements predating the Domus Flavia and below the present ground level. These are only partially visible, but include an apsed room dedicated to the cult of Isis and completely decorated with fine paintings, and an entire apartment, the **House of the Griffins**, hidden under the *lararium* and dating to the 2nd century BC.

The area in which the octagonal fountain of the Domus Flavia once stood.

House of Livia - The house of Augustus' wife Livia, in which the Emperor himself probably also lived, is one of the most precious examples of early imperial Roman architecture. The house consisted of various rooms, including the *triclinium* (dining room) and the *tablinum* (a reception suite), the *central room* of which, with its Pompeiian style wall painting of *Mercury Rescuing Io*, is particularly beautiful. An adjacent room (the hall on the right) is decorated with equally excellent paintings of scenes of Egyptian life.

House of Romulus - Traces of ancient structures have come to light across from the remains of the Temple of the *Magna Mater*. They include a cistern and remains of prehistoric structures, with three huts datable to the early Iron Age (9th - 8th centuries BC). They are the earliest examples of architecture found in Rome; tradition identifies these vestiges with the House of Romulus, the legendary first king of the city.

Temple of the Magna Mater - This temple, dating to 204 BC, was erected in honor of Cybele and contained a black stone, the symbol of the goddess. It was often rebuilt, the last time during the reign of Augustus. Excavations have brought to light a splendid winged statue of the goddess, which is now on display in the nearby Domus Tiberiana.

Domus Tiberiana - The house of Tiberius was the first of the imperial palaces to be conceived organically as such, and the first to be built on the Palatine. It rose behind the Temple of the Magna Mater on the western slope of the hill, overlooking the Roman Forum. Only a small part of the building complex has been excavated, since the area it occupied became the Horti Farnesiani in the 16th century.
Still visible on the south side of the complex is a series of rectangular rooms, built of brick and with barrel vaults, which may date to Nero's time. The vaults preserve traces of pictorial decoration in the form of scenes and figures set in panels, datable to the third century AD. In the south corner of this side of the building is an oval basin with steps, which seems to have been a fish pond. The eastern side consists of a long cryptoporticus, again with painted walls and mosaic pavements. At the north end is a section branching off to the west that was built later to link the complex with the Domus Augustana.
The north side of the Domus Tiberiana overlooks the Roman Forum

and is the best preserved part of the complex. It consists of two differently-oriented nuclei of rooms that both flank an old road, the Clivus Victoriae. The easternmost sector, in which the rooms follow the orientation of the rest of the building, is a reconstruction dating to Domitian's time, after the palace had been gutted by the fires of 64 and 80 AD. The obliquely-oriented rooms that flank this sector date from Hadrian's time, and extend even beyond the *Clivus Victoriae*, passing over it on wide arches.
A portion of the central part of the building was excavated in the second half of the 19th century and then filled in again. The excavations revealed a vast peristyle, off which various rooms open, that is connected to the cryptoporticus on the east side via two corridors.

Drove By

COLOSSEUM

Colosseum - Arch of Constantine - Imperial Forums -
Forum Transitorium - Forum of Augustus -
Caesar's Forum - Trajan's Forum - Basilica Ulpia -
Trajan's Markets - Trajan's Column -
Santa Maria di Loreto and the Santissimo Nome di Maria

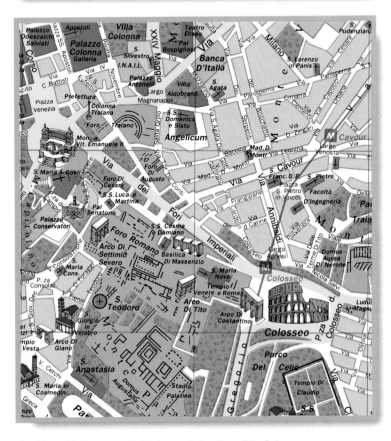

On this and facing page: Aerial view and elevation of the Colosseum.

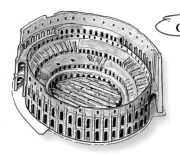

Colosseum.

Colosseum - The largest amphitheater ever built in Rome and the symbol par excellence of Romanism was the work of the Flavian emperors and was for this reason called the *Amphiteatrum Flavium*. The name "Colosseum" was first used in the Middle Ages and derives from the colossal bronze statue of Nero as sun god which stood on the site of the vestibule of the Domus Aurea, near the amphitheater.

Emperor Vespasian began construction of the Colosseum in the valley between the Caelian, Palatine, and Esquiline hills, on the site of the artificial lake around which Nero's royal residence was centered and which he had drained for the purpose. Vespasian's intentions were to restore to the Roman people what Nero's tyranny had subtracted from them, and to provide Rome with a large permanent amphitheater in place of the Amphitheater of Taurus in the Campus Martius, a temporary wooden structure, erected by Nero after the fire of 64 AD, that had become insufficient to meet the needs of the populace.

Work began in the early years of Vespasian's reign; the building was dedicated in 79 AD, when only the first two exterior orders with the first three tiers of steps inside were completed. After Titus had completed the fourth and fifth tiers, the amphitheater was inaugurated in 80 AD, with magnificent spectacles and games which lasted a hundred days. It assumed its present aspect and size only under Domitian. According to the sources, he added the *ad clipea*; in other words, he set in place the bronze shields which decorated the attic level; he also added the *maenianum summum*, the third internal order made of wooden tiers, and had the substructures of the arena built. This meant that the *naumachie* (naval battles, for which the arena had to be flooded) could no longer be held in the Colosseum as the literary sources tell us they had previously been.

Additional work was carried out by Nerva, Trajan and Antoninus Pius. Alexander Severus restored the building after it had been damaged by a fire caused by lightning in 217 AD. Further restoration was carried out by Gordian III and later by Decius, after the Colosseum had once more been struck by lightning in 250 AD. Other works of renovation were made necessary by the earthquakes of 429 and 443 AD. The German usurper Odoacer had the lower tiers rebuilt, as we read on the inscriptions of the names of senators that date from between 476 and 483 AD. The last attempt at restoration was made by Theodoric king of the Ostragoths; after his time, the building was totally abandoned.

It thus became the fortress of the Frangipane family in the Middle Ages, until with the advent of further earthquakes the fallen material began to be removed for use in new constructions. From the 15th through the mid-18th century, the once-great amphitheater was transformed into a simple quarry for blocks of travertine until it was consecrated by Pope Benedict XV.

The building is elliptical in form and measures 188 x 156 meters at the perimeter and 86 x 54 meters inside; it is almost 49 meters in height. The four-story facade is built entirely of travertine. The three lower stories have 80 arches each, supported by piers and framed by encased three-quarter columns that are Doric on the first level, Ionic on the second, and Corinthian on the third. The three lower levels are crowned by a fourth-

story attic, on the exterior of which, in the walls between one Corinthian parastade and the next, there alternate square windows and blank spaces where the gilded shields once hung. The beams that supported the large canopy (velarium) that protected the spectators from the sun were fitted into a row of holes in the upper cornice. The canopy was unfurled by a crew of sailors of Misenus' fleet.

The arches of the ground floor level were numbered to indicate the entrance to the various tiers of seats in the cavea. The four entrances of honor, reserved for upper class persons of rank such as magistrates, members of the religious colleges, and the Vestal Virgins, were situated at the ends of the principal axes of the building and were unnumbered. The entrance on the north side was preceded by a small two-columned portico opening on a corridor, decorated with stuccowork, that led to the imperial tribune.

The external arcades led to a twin set of circular corridors from which stairs led to the aisles (*vomitoria*) of the cavea; the second floor had a similar double ambulacrum, and so did the third, but with a lower ceiling than the other two, while at the attic level two single corridors ran one over the other.

Inside, the cavea was separated from the arena by a podium almost four meters high, behind which the seats of honor were arranged. The

Four images of the Colosseum today in all its remaining splendor: above, the exterior; below and facing page, the theatrical remains in the interior.

cavea was divided in the horizontal sense into three orders (*maeniana*) separated by walls in masonry (*baltei*). The first two maeniana (the second was subdivided once more into upper and lower sections) had marble seats and were cut through vertically by the entrance aisles (*vomitoria*) and stairs. The result was to create sectors called cunei; it was therefore possible to assign seat numbers by tier, cuneus and single seat. The third *maenianum*, or *maenianum summum*, had wooden tiers and was separated from the *maenianum secundum* below by a high wall. There was a colonnade with a gallery reserved for the women, above which a terrace provided standing room only for the lower classes.

Access to seats in the cavea was based on social class: the higher up the seat, the less influential its occupant. The inscriptions still readable on some of the extant tiers inform us that they were reserved for specific categories of citizens. The emperor's box was at the south end of the minor axis, where the consuls and Vestal Virgins also sat. The box at the north

extremity was for the prefect of the city (*praefectus Urbis*) and other magistrates. The tiers closest to the arena were reserved for senators.

The arena was originally covered with wooden floorboards which could be removed as required. In the case of hunts of ferocious animals, the spectators in the cavea were protected by a metal grating topped by elephant tusks and rotating cylinders placed horizontally in such a manner as to make it impossible for the wild animals to claw their way up.

The area below the arena floor contained all the structures necessary for the presentation of the spectacles: cages for the animals, settings and illusionistic devices, storerooms for the gladiators' weapons, machines, etc. These service areas were arranged along three concentric walkways with openings that made them all functionally interconnected. A series of thirty niches in the outer wall was apparently used for the elevators that were used to raise the gladiators and the beasts up to the level of the arena. The rational exploitation of the artificial basin previously created for the lake of Nero's Domus Aurea saved an enormous amount of excavation work during the building of the Colosseum. Once the lake had been drained, the foundations for the amphitheater were cast and travertine piers were set into the large elliptical concrete platform to form a framework reaching up to the third floor level; radial walls in blocks of tufa and brick were then raised between one pier and the next. It was thus possible to work on the lower and upper portions at the same time, and as a matter of fact the building was subdivided into four sectors, with four different construction sites operating simultaneously.

Various types of **spectacles** were held in the Colosseum: the *munera*, or contests between gladiators, the *venationes*, or hunts of wild beasts, and the previously cited *naumachie*. Christians may or may not have been sent to their death as martyrs in the Colosseum. A final point to consider is the number of spectators the Colosseum was capable of containing: opinions vary, but the figure must have been around 50,000.

Below, a view of the interior of the Colosseum. On the facing page, details of the friezes decorating the monumental Arch of Constantine.

Arch of Constantine - The largest of the arches erected in Rome, on the route followed by triumphal processions of antiquity between the Caelian and the Palatine hills, is 21 meters high, almost 26 meters wide and more than 7 meters deep; of the three passageways, the central one is largest. The arch was built in 315 AD by decree of the Senate and the Roman people to celebrate the 10th anniversary of Constantine's ascent to the throne and his victory over Maxentius in the Battle of the Milvian Bridge in 312. For decoration of the arch, a number of reliefs and sculptures from other monuments were employed. The four detached marble columns on each of the principal sides, surmounted by eight statues of Dacians, are in pavonazzetto marble (white with purple veining, from Asia Minor) and date to Trajan's time. Eight tondi from Hadrian's time, each about two meters in diameter, are set, paired, in porphyry slabs over the side passageways. The presence in some of these medallions of Antinous, Hadrian's favorite, verifies their attribution to this emperor's reign. Four scenes of the hunt (bear, boar, lion and departure for the hunt) and four sacrificial scenes (to Apollo, Diana, Hercules and Silvanus) are represented. The figure of Hadrian appears in each, although his head was replaced by that of Constantine in the hunting scenes and by that of Licinius in the sacrificial scenes. In some of them the *nimbus* (a sort of halo), used in Constantine's time to confer an air of sacrality to the figure of the emperor, was added. On either side of the inscription, which is repeated both on the front and the back of the monument, are eight paired-up reliefs from the period of Marcus Aurelius that were probably taken from a now-lost honorary arch. Taken together, the reliefs of a series of exemplary episodes, the same scenes presented in the Aurelian column, form a cycle celebrating the return of the emperor in 173 AD after his campaigns against the Marcomanni and the Quadi.

A large marble frieze from Trajan's time was also reused in the arch. It was cut into four parts, two of which are on the short sides of the attic and two on the interior of the central passage. The frieze, of which we have other fragments, was originally three meters high and more than eighteen meters long, but its provenance is not known. The scenes represented have to do with Trajan's two Dacian campaigns (101-102 and 105-106 AD).

But there are also many decorative elements that date to the building of the arch. On the principal facades of the monument, these are the reliefs at the bases of the columns with Victories, Roman soldiers and Barbarian prisoners, those on the keystones of the arches with divinities and allegorical personifications, the winged victories with trophies and personifications of the seasons at the sides of the central passageway, and the river gods flanking the minor openings. On the short sides, in correspondence to the eight Hadrianic roundels on the main facades, are two medallions, one of the Sun God and another of the Goddess of the Moon, on chariots. The most significant part of Constantine's decoration is, however, the large historical frieze above the lesser openings and on the short sides of the arch. The story begins on the western side, with the departure of Constantine from Milan on a chariot preceded by infantry and cavalry. It continues on the south side with the representations of the siege of Verona by Constantine's troops and of the emperor protected by two bodyguards while a Victory places a wreath on his head. On the same side is a representation of the Battle of the Milvian Bridge, with Constantine on the bridge accompanied by the personification of Virtus and a Victory, and the defeat of Maxentius and his troops. The short eastern side presents the emperor's triumphal entrance into Rome on a chariot preceded by Roman foot soldiers and horsemen. On the north side, Constantine is shown addressing the crowd near the Rostra: he is the only person presented frontally, in accordance with the hieratic concept of sovereignty which had by this time become well established. The emperor is represented in the same manner at the center of the last scene: he is seated on a high throne in a frontal position, surrounded by his court and personages in togas, while he oversees the work of his officials as they distribute gratuities to the people behind in a high arched portico. Conventionally, the sizes of the figures vary according to their positions in the hierarchy of power.

Via dei Fori Imperiali - This great thoroughfare, which connects various characteristic quarters of the city with the historical center, was opened only relatively recently (1932); it is about one kilometer long and lined with pines and gardens. The thoroughfare crosses much of the archaeological zone and ends at the Imperial Forums.

Two images of the Arch of Constantine. On the facing page, a detail of the remains of the portico of the Forum Transitorium (also known as Nerva's Forum).

Imperial Forums - Although the Imperial Forums were built near the earlier forum of republican times, the underlying concept was more rational and the scope more grandiose. Each of these enormous public squares (80-90,000 square meters) was enclosed by porticoes and closed off at the back by a massive temple, and quite probably had an equestrian statue of the emperor at the center.

The Imperial Forums were created with the scope of enhancing the prestige of the city and providing the citizens with a place for their markets and one where they could listen to the harangues and participate in religious ceremonies. The first of these forums was the Forum Julium (Caesar's Forum, 56-54 BC), built under the auspices of Julius Caesar. Next came the Forum of Augustus (32-31 BC), the Forum of Vespasian or of Peace (71-75 AD), the Forum Transitorium or Nerva's Forum (98 AD), and lastly Trajan's Forum (113 AD). From the 6th century AD onward, the forum area was completely neglected and gradual destruction began. During the Middle Ages, a minimal portion was recovered and a small residential district came into being among the Roman ruins. Most of the area, however, was invaded by water and became a mud-field, called at the time the Pantani ("bogs"): the splendid buildings of Imperial times were destroyed or gravely damaged. Forgotten for centuries, the area was partially urbanized in the Renaissance, but not until the 19th and above all the 20th centuries were the remains of this once magnificent architecture brought to light and the Via dei Fori Imperiali created.

Temple of Peace - The Temple of Peace closed off the Imperial Forums on the southeast. The old route of the *Argiletum* separated it from the Forum of Augustus, to which it was later joined when Nerva's Forum was built. The temple was built in about 74 AD by the emperor Vespasian on the site of the old *Macellum*, the covered public market, to celebrate the success of the Judaic campaign and the return of peace. It was destroyed by fire in 192 AD, under Commodus, and was restored by Septimius Severus.

The complex, later known as "Forum of Peace," consisted of a large square with gardens, enclosed on three sides by porticoes.

In addition to the Greek and Latin libraries, the Temple of Peace also housed a true museum of Greek art that included including statues by Polycleitus, Phidias, Leochares, and Myron, and paintings by Nicomachus and other artists. The works had been taken in part from Nero's Domus Aurea and installed in the Temple of Peace by Vespasian. The museum also contained the sacred objects from the Temple of Jerusalem brought to Rome by Titus in 70 AD. Besides two halls that were adjacent to the temple, the remains of the complex include nothing more than a column in African marble, a fragmentary entablature, and one of the exedrae of the portico now under the Torre dei Conti.

Forum Transitorium and Temple of Minerva - The Forum Transitorium takes its name from the fact that it lies between the republican Roman Forum, the Forum of Augustus, Caesar's Forum, and Vespasian's Temple (or Forum) of Peace.

It was built by Domitian and inaugurated by Nerva (which is why it is also called Nerva's Forum) and was meant to unify the various forum areas of Rome. It is superposed on a stretch of the old *Argiletum* road. Its long, narrow shape (120 x 45 meters) was dictated by the limited space available, and this also explains the absence of an internal portico and the illusionistic device of setting up a row of columns a short distance from the outer wall. Above the columns was an attic with reliefs illustrating myths connected with Minerva and a frieze with scenes of the womanly arts. On the south side there still stands a stretch of the outer wall, in blocks of peperino, and the two Corinthian columns called the "Colonnacce." The frieze illustrates

The remains of the Temple of Mars Ultor in the Forum of Augustus. Below and on the facing page, the statues of Augustus and Trajan.

the myth of Arachne and the attic is adorned with a figure of Minerva. The short entrance side of the Temple of Minerva, a Corinthian hexastyle on a podium with a tripartite apsed cella, was curved, while the pronaos projected from the back. In 1606, Pope Paul V had it torn down so he could use the building materials and the decorations in the monumental Acqua Paola fountain on the Janiculum. All that is visible today are the now formless foundations of the podium, under wich ran a stretch of the Cloaca Maxima.

Forum of Augustus and Temple of Mars Ultor - The Forum of Augustus

lies between the Caesar's Forum on the west and the *Subura* district to the east. It was later delimited to the north by Trajan's Forum and to the south by the Forum Transitorium.

The Forum of Augustus was constructed after costly expropriations on the part of the emperor so that he could free the area of the private dwellings that occupied it. Desirous of avenging the death of his adoptive father Julius Caesar, he had vowed a temple to Mars Ultor (the Avenger) before the battle of Philippi of 42 BC, in which he confronted and finally defeated Brutus and Cassius, but it was not until forty years later, in 2 BC, that the work was completed and the great square (125 x 118 meters) could be inaugurated. The forum has colonnades on its long sides and ends in the mass of the temple on the short southeast side.

Two large symmetrical semicircular exedrae were set into the wall behind the porticoes, at the height of the temple, and a bronze quadriga with the emperor was placed at the center of the square.

The southwest entrance side, adjacent to the eastern side of Caesar's Forum, is now underneath Via dei Fori Imperiali, as is the case with the front part of the square and the colonnades. There were also two secondary entrances at the back of the forum, near the large wall in peperino and *pietra sperone* (lithoid tufa) that with its thirty-three meters height effectively isolated the complex from the *Subura* district. The one to the north had three openings, while the so-called "Arco dei Pantani" to the south had one opening which led, via two flights of stairs, to the arches dedicated to Drusus Minor and Germanicus on either side of the Temple of Mars Ultor. The porticoes on the long sides have Corinthian columns in cipolin marble and were decorated at the top by caryatids and shields with the portraits of divinities. It is uncertain whether or not the porticoes had two floors or were topped by an attic.

The Temple of Mars Ultor consisted of a cella on a tall podium faced in marble, with an altar at the center and two fountains at its outer edges; a staircase gave access to the podium. The temple had eight seventeen-meter-plus Corinthian columns on the front and eight on the long sides, while the back was columnless (*peripteros sine postico*). The inside had seven columns in two rows along the walls and, at the back, an apse with the cult statues of Venus, Mars and the Divus Julius.

Caesar's Forum and Temple of Venus - This first of the great forums of the Imperial Age, lies northeast of the republican Roman Forum along the *Clivus Argentarius*. Caesar had to spend enormous sums of money (sixty million sestercians, according to Cicero, one hundred million according to Suetonius) simply to purchase the land and to remove the private buildings that occupied the area.

The complex was planned as an elongated esplanade (160 x 75 meters) with porticoes on three sides, and, in the back, the large Temple of Venus Genetrix which Caesar had vowed before the battle of Pharsalus against Pompey in 48 BC. The forum was designed in 54 BC and dedicated in 46 BC, but work was actually finished later by Octavianus. Trajan reconstructed the temple and the porticoes and also added the Basilica Arenaria. A new inaugura-

tion of the whole was held in 113 AD. Diocletian was the last to intervene here, with restoration works following the fire of 283 AD. Of the forum area, the Temple of Venus Genetrix and about half of the square in front and the portico on the west have been studied by the archaeologists. A series of shops from Caesar's time has been brought to light. They vary in size and are built in tufa or travertine on three floors, with vaulted roofs added in Trajan's time and with a double colonnade in front. There was a statue of Caesar on horseback at the center of the square.

The Temple of Venus Genetrix has a single cella on a high podium with a flight of stairs on each side. There were eight Corinthian columns on the front and nine at the sides, in line with the formula of the *peripteros sine postico*. Two square fountains were set in front of the podium. The temple decoration that has come down to us is from Trajan's time.

The Caesar's Forum is an outstanding example of personal propaganda. It was paid for by the dictator, who at the time was a consul, out of his own pocket; his intention was to enlarge the republican forum, which no longer sufficed to meet the city's needs.

The layout of the complex recalls the typically axial and frontal stylistic features of the oriental models; all this aligns perfectly with the absolutist tendencies the dictator was beginning to develop. Caesar's Forum provided the model for the later Imperial Forums.

A view of the colonnade of Trajan's Forum; in the background, Trajan's Markets with the Loggia of the Knights of Rhodes.

Trajan's Forum and Basilica Ulpia - Trajan's Forum extends northwards from Caesar's Forum and is oriented in the same direction, and is at right angles to the Forum of Augustus, with which it borders on the west. This last and most imposing of the Imperial Forums was the most important public work carried out by Trajan and his architect Apollodorus of Damascus, and involved elimination of the ridge between the Capitoline and the Quirinal hills. The impressive complex (300 meters in length by 185 in width) was built between 106 and 113 AD and was financed by the proceeds of the Dacian war that had just been concluded.

Practically none of the forum square is visible, since it lies under the Via dei Fori Imperiali. All that remains are the eastern exedra and the ground level of the portico on the same side, with the bases of the columns still *in situ*. The Basilica Ulpia, which closed off the back of the square, has also been excavated only partially. This is the largest basilica ever built in Rome. It is 170 meters long and almost 60 meters wide, and takes its name from the family name of the emperor.

Statues of Dacian prisoners and fragments of sculpture and a frieze with figures of Victories killing a bull and decorating a candelabrum with garlands were found in the area of the basilica.

Two openings on the northwest side of the basilica led to a courtyard in which Trajan's column still stands, flanked by the two libraries which according to the sources contained the emperor's private archives and a collection of praetorial departmental orders. The library to the southwest, lying under the Via dei Fori Imperiali, has been excavated. It is a rectangular room; the walls have two orders of niches raised on three steps and framed by columns, in which the closets which contained the volumes were set. On the back wall is a larger niche, with marble architectural decoration: it probably contained the statue of a god.

Trajan's Forum terminates to the northeast with the Temple of the Divus Trajanus and the Diva Plotina. It was built in 121 AD by Hadrian, after Trajan's death. Not much is known about this temple, which stood on what is today the site of the church of Santa Maria di Loreto; it must, however, have been colossal in size, with eight Corinthian columns more than 20 meters tall on the front and eight on each side.

Trajan's Markets - The construction of Trajan's Forum required the removal of part of the Quirinal hill; the architect, Apollodorus of Damascus (who also built Trajan's Forum), made brilliant use of the cutaway face to realize a unified structural complex which we call Trajan's Markets.

The front of the markets is a large brick hemicycle behind the eastern exedra of Trajan's Forum. It echoes the shape of the exedra and is separated from it by a road paved with large, irregularly-polygonal blocks of polished lava. A series of *tabernae*, with doorways with jambs and lintel in travertine, opens on the bottom floor; overhead are arches framed by brick pilasters, with travertine bases and capitals in travertine, that support small pediments. These arched windows provide light for the corridor on the upper floor, onto which another row of shops, set against the cut rock of the hill face, opens. At the sides of the *tabernae* on the ground floor are two large semicircular halls with windows, covered by half domes, that may have been used for schools.

The third level of the complex is a steeply-rising road that was called "Via Biberatica" in the Middle Ages. The name may refer to the types of shops found there (*biber* = drink, or *piper* = spice). Most of the tabernae on the side towards the forum have been destroyed, but those uphill of the road are still well preserved.

A staircase leads from the Via Biberatica to a great basilica-like hall covered with six cross vaults springing from travertine corbels. On the long sides are various rooms, on two levels: on the lower floor, six shops with doorways with travertine frames, open off on each side, while on the upper floor, reached via internal stairs, a series of *tabernae* opens onto a corridor that faces onto the central hall.

This fifth level leads, on the south side of the basilica hall, to another series of rooms on two floors (for an overall total, therefore, of six stories) that includes an apsed room that was probably the main management and supervision office for the complex as a whole.

Trajan's Markets probably functioned as a sort of wholesale outlet for staple foodstuffs such as grain, oil and wine, managed by the state through imperial personnel who supplied the *negotiatores* of the provinces. Retail sales were probably also conducted at "political" prices inferior to going market prices - and it was probably here that on occasion the emperor distributed foodstuffs to the people (the so-called *congiaria*).

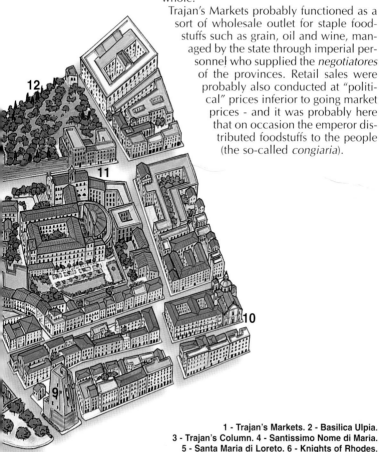

1 - Trajan's Markets. 2 - Basilica Ulpia.
3 - Trajan's Column. 4 - Santissimo Nome di Maria.
5 - Santa Maria di Loreto. 6 - Knights of Rhodes.
7 - Forum of Augustus and Temple of Mars Ultor.
8 - Nerva's Forum or Forum Transitorium. 9 - Torre dei Conti. 10 - Madonna dei Monti.
11 - Santi Domenico e Sisto. 12 - Villa Aldobrandini and Gardens. 13 - Torre delle Milizie.

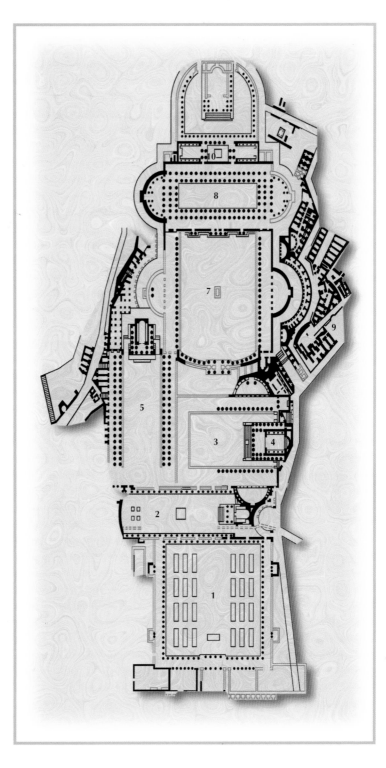

IMPERIAL FORUMS

1 Temple of Peace
2 Nerva's Forum (Forum Transitorium)
3 Forum of Augustus
4 Temple of Mars Ultor
5 Caesar's Forum

6 Temple of Venus Genetrix
7 Trajan's Forum
8 Basilica Ulpia
9 Trajan's Markets
10 Trajan's Column

Above, an aerial view of the area of Trajan's Markets. At the center, details of the ruins and the Loggia of the Knights of Rhodes. Below, Trajan's Column.

Trajan's Column - The column that stands in Trajan's Forum between the two libraries, behind the Basilica Ulpia and in front of the Temple of the Divus Trajanus, was dedicated in 113 AD. The Doric *centenaria* (that is, 100 Roman feet or 39.77 meters tall) column is composed of 18 drums of Luna marble. It stands on a high cubic base with four eagles holding garlands at the corners and low relief trophies of stacks of Dacian weapons on three sides. All together, it is almost 40 meters high; the statue of Trajan that once topped it was lost; in 1587 Pope Sixtus V set one of *Saint Peter* in its place.

The entrance door to the monument is on its main side facing the Basilica Ulpia. Set above it is a panel supported by two Victories, with an inscription celebrating the donation of the column to the emperor by the Senate and the Roman people as an indication of the height of the hill before it was leveled to make way for the new forum. Actually, the column was meant to serve as the tomb of the emperor: the entrance in the base leads, on the left, to an antechamber

Trajan's Column and a detail of the friezes that winds around it.

and then a large room where a golden urn containing Trajan's ashes was kept. From the same entrance, but to the right, is a spiral staircase of 185 steps, cut in the marble, that leads to the top of the column.

A continuous frieze, about 200 meters long and varying in height from 90 to 125 centimeters, moves around the shaft of the column like an unrolled *volumen* to represent Trajan's two victorious Dacian campaigns of 101-102 and 105-106 AD. The two narrations are separated by a figure of Victory writing on a shield. All the phases of the two wars are minutely described with precise geographical and topographical details. Battle scenes alternate with representations of troop movements, the construction of encampments, bridges, and roads, speeches made to the troops, sieges, the deportation of the conquered enemy, etc. The documentary and didactic purpose is evident from the inclusion of detailed items of information meant to help the spectator understand the events more clearly.

There are more than 2500 figures in the frieze and Trajan appears about 60 times. The relief was originally painted, but the chromatic decoration has survived only in few places. There may also have been painted inscriptions with the names of the places where the action took place. The work is attributed to the so-called "Master of the Feats of Trajan," who may perhaps be identified with Apollodorus of Damascus, the architect of Trajan's Forum.

A general view of the twin churches on the Largo del Foro di Traiano.
Below, separate images of the churches: Santa Maria di Loreto and Santissimo Nome di Maria.

Church of Santi Cosma e Damiano - Erected in 527 AD for Pope Felix IV on the remains of a hall in the Forum of Peace, the church was largely rebuilt in 1632 to designs by L. Arrigucci. The entrance is preceded by a **vestibule** adapted from the Temple of the Divus Romulus. **Inside**, chapels line both sides of the single nave. The first chapel on the right contains a 13th-century fresco of *Christ on the Cross*; the second chapel has an impressive altarpiece by Giovanni Baglioni, with the *Healing of the Lame Man.*
In the second chapel on the left are pleasing mid-17th century frescoes by F. Allegrini. The famous 6th-century mosaics in the apse represent the Mystic Lamb surrounded by seven candelabra, four angels, the symbols of the Evangelists Luke and John, and certain of the twenty-four elders offering crowns.

Churches of Santa Maria di Loreto and of the Santissimo Nome di Maria - These "twin" churches, both on the Largo del Foro Traiano, are both on central plans, although the former, dedicated to the Madonna of Loreto, was founded at the turn of the 16th century, in 1501, while the latter was built between 1736 and 1738 to plans by Antonio Derizet. Instead, the plans for the robust, square main body of Santa Maria di Loreto, the cupola, and the corresponding octagon in the **interior** have been tentatively attributed to artists as prestigious as Bramante and Antonio da Sangallo the Younger.
Despite the fact that the two churches resemble each other externally, the **interiors** are quite different, that of the Santissimo Nome di Maria being on an elliptical plan with seven sumptuous chapels opening off the perimeter.

FONTANA DI TREVI

Palazzo and Galleria Colonna - Church of the Santi Apostoli -
Fontana di Trevi - Galleria dell'Accademia di San Luca -
Sant'Andrea delle Fratte - **Column of Marcus Aurelius** -
Palazzo Chigi

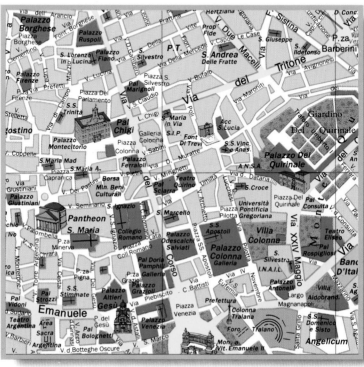

1 - Palazzo Colonna.
2 - Santi Apostoli. 3 - VillaColonna.
4 - San Silvestro al Quirinale.

PALAZZO AND GALLERIA COLONNA

As far back as the Middle Ages this was the residence of the noble Colonna family, descendants of the counts of Tusculum, whose violent disagreements with the papacy led to the demolition of the original buildings by Boniface VIII. The palace, rebuilt in the 15th century by Pope Martin V, a member of the Colonna family, was rebuilt again in 1730 by Niccolò Michetti and

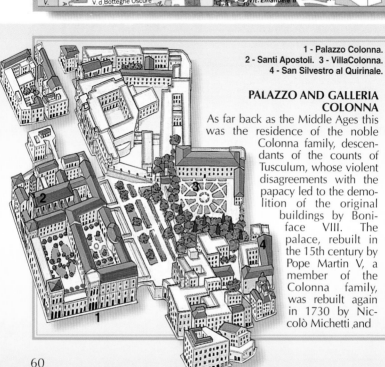

finely decorated by artists of the time. The paintings by Italian and foreign masters collected by various members of the family adorned the
rooms of the palace and formed the nucleus of the *Galleria Colonna*,
today open to the public. The gallery, formally established in the mid-
17th century by Cardinal Girolamo Colonna, is set out in a series of
sumptuously-decorated rooms with pictorial cycles and stuccowork
that celebrate the annals and the glory of the family. The **Sala della
Colonna Bellica** owes its name to the column of red marble, the emblem of the family, at the center of the room. The ceiling is decorated
with fresco of the *Apotheosis of Marcantonio II Colonna*. The room
hosts masterpieces by Tintoretto and a beautiful panel by Bronzino depicting *Venus, Cupid, and a Satyr*. Marcantonio II is also celebrated in
the ceilings of the **Sala Grande**, designed by Girolamo Fontana and
abounding in stuccowork and works of such great masters as Salvatore
Rosa and Rubens. The episode of Marcantonio's victory at the Battle of
Lepanto, painted by Sebastiano Ricci, adorns the room known as the
Sala dei Paesaggi in which many landscapes by Flemish masters are
displayed. To the *Apotheosis of Martin V*, painted on its ceiling by
Benedetto Luti, is instead dedicated the room in which alongside the
compelling portraits by artists of the caliber of Tintoretto and Veronese
are displayed works by Bronzino, Guercino and Annibale Carracci. The
many 14th- and 15th-century paintings acquired in the 1800s are apt-
ly arranged in the so-called **Sala dei Primitivi** adjacent to the **Sala del
Trono** in which, in accordance with the ancient tradition of the noble
Roman families, was intended for receiving the pope. Today it contains
many documents relating to the victory of Marcantonio II at Lepanto.

Church of the Santi Apostoli - First mention of this church was made in
the 6th century; it was almost completely rebuilt in the 18th century by
Francesco and Carlo Fontana.
The wide Neoclassical **facade**, designed by Giuseppe Valadier (1827), is
preceded by a spacious **portico**, the work of Baccio Pontelli (ca. 1495),
on nine arches in two tiers. In the porch, on the left, is a stele by Canova
(1807) dedicated to the engraver and sculptor Giovanni Volpato, and, on
the right, a compelling imperial eagle in a Roman relief of the 2nd century AD. To the left of the doorway is the tomb with the *Portrait of Giovanni Colonna* and, on the right, the tombstone of Girolamo Frescobaldi,
both by L. Capponi.
The vast interior, with a nave and two aisles, has three spacious chapels
on either side, and is closed by a dome. The striking fresco in the vault of
the *Triumph of the Order of Saint Francis* is an excellent work by Baciccia (1707). The first chapel on the right contains a charming altarpiece by
Lapiccola with the *Madonna and Child with Saint Bonaventure* and, below, a canvas known as the *Madonna of Bessarion*, attributed to Jacopo
Ripanda; of note in the second chapel is the *Immaculata* by Francesco
Coghetti; the chapel at the back is especially attractive, with its three
small aisles separated by 4th-century tortile columns. In the apse is the
enormous altarpiece (the largest in the city) by Domenico Muratori
(1704) depicting the *Martyrdom of Saints Philip and James*. The left aisle
leads to the **sacristy**, with its magnificent 17th-century wardrobes and the
splendid canvas, the finest in the church, set into the vault: the *Ascension*
by Sebastiano Ricci (1701). The walls are for the most part covered with
frescoes (*The Conversion of Constantine, Saint Bonaventure Proclaimed
Doctor of the Church*) by Domenico Bruschi.
Entrance to the old **cloister**, with its columns and Ionic capitals, is from
the sacristy.
Back in the church, we find Canova's superb *monument to Clement XIV*
at the beginning of the nave; in the third chapel on the left, a powerful altarpiece of *Saint Francis*, by Giuseppe Chiari, and the *monuments* to *Cardinal Carlo Colonna* and *Maria Lucrezia Rospigliosi Salviati*, both by
Bernardo Ludovisi; in the second chapel, the altarpiece of *Saint Joseph of
Copertino* by Giuseppe Cades (1777); and lastly, on the altar of the first
chapel, a lovely *Pietà* by Francesco Manno.

Fontana di Trevi.

Fontana di Trevi - This may not be the most beautiful fountain in Rome, but it is without doubt the most famous. The imaginative concept, the theatrical composition, the sober and dignified beauty of the sculptured marble figures make it a true masterpiece both of sculpture and of architecture. Both Pietro da Cortona and above all Bernini, who began the undertaking, had a hand in the project. The death of Pope Urban VIII brought work to a standstill and it was not until about a hundred years later that Clement XII entrusted the work to Nicola Salvi, who finished the fountain between 1732 and 1751.

The design of the fountain is highly symbolic, with various intellectual connotations. A tall and sober *Arch of Triumph* (the Palace of Neptune) dominates the scene from on high, with a row of four Corinthian columns surmounted by an attic with statues and a

Below and on the facing page: views of the Fontana di Trevi.

balustrade. A large niche at the center of the arch lends balance and symmetry to the whole ensemble. A smaller niche to the left contains the statue of *Abundance* by F. Valle, above which is a relief by Andrea Bergondi depicting *Agrippa Approving the Plans for the Aqueduct.* The niche on the right contains the figure of *Salubrity*, also by F. Valle, surmounted by a relief of the *Virgin Showing the Soldiers the Way*, by G. B. Grossi.

The central niche seems to impart movement to the commanding figure of Neptune, who with a firm hand guides a chariot drawn by two sea horses, known as the "spirited horse" and the "placid horse," names obviously derived from the way in which the two animals have been represented. As they gallop over the water, the horses are guided in their course by the figures of Tritons emerging from the water sculpted by P. Bracci in 1762. The setting all around consists of rocks.

GALLERIA DELL'ACCADEMIA DI SAN LUCA

The Accademia di San Luca, heir to the long tradition of the "Università dei Pittori" founded in the 1400s at the Church of Santi Luca e Martina (hence its name), moved to Palazzo Carpegna in 1932. This building was first built for the Carpegna family but was renovated in the mid-17th century by Borromini, who left his distinctive mark on the entrance portal and the staircase. Besides the Galleria, with its splendid collection of works of art housed on the third floor, Palazzo Carpegna also hosts the Accademia itself. In its rooms are found the portraits of its many honorary members and the award-winning works of art as well as a historical archives section

and a well-stocked library; the well-known *Saint Luke Painting a Portrait of the Virgin*, which through the centuries has been the subject of lively debate that has attributed its authorship now to Raphael, now to this or that of his followers, hangs in the Accademia portion of the *palazzo*. The Galleria proper, instead, is home to many masterpieces of Roman Mannerism which are exhibited alongside works of intense evocative value and great artistic worth by foreign masters. Thus, majestic paintings by Baciccia, the Cavalier d'Arpino and Federico Zuccari alternate with canvases by Rubens, Van Dyck, and Poussin, not to mention works of the Venetian school by artists of the caliber of Titian and Jacopo Bassano, author of the celebrated *Annunciation to the Shepherds.*

Via del Tritone - One of the most characteristic thoroughfares in Rome owes its name to a sculpture by Bernini of a Triton, situated in the final stretch. The street was widened considerably when Rome became capital of Italy; some of the large buildings, with their proudly massive silhouettes that lend the street its refined and monumental air, date to that period.

Church of Sant'Andrea delle Fratte - This church has stood on the site since the 12th century, but in 1612 the Marquis del Bufalo had it almost completely rebuilt by Gaspare Guerra. Work continued even later, and may have been terminated by Borromini, who is certainly responsible for the design of the *cupola* and the fanciful bell tower, a true masterpiece of Baroque architecture. The layout of the two-tier *facade* (late 16th-century) possesses a charming simplicity despite the elaborate 17th-century forms. The *bell tower* is, instead, a work of pure fantasy. It is square in plan, with complex superposed tiers with corner columns and windows; further up is an open colonnade with an entablature surmounted by a balustrade; the terminal part of the tower is on a composite plan, with eight piers crowned by a series of candelabra. The single-nave *interior* has three chapels on either side. Two *Angels* flank the apse: one with a crown of thorns, the other with a scroll, both by Bernini and originally meant for Ponte Sant'Angelo.

Piazza Colonna - One of most famous and lively squares in the city is to be found halfway up the Corso. It is surrounded by various superb buildings: on the north *Palazzo Chigi*, on the west *Palazzo Wedekind*, and on the south *Palazzo Ferraioli* and the small *Church of Santa Maria della Pietà*. The Column of Marcus Aurelius stands in the center of the square.

Column of Marcus Aurelius - Set at the center of Piazza Colonna, the column takes its name from the Roman emperor Marcus Aurelius, who had it erected between 189 and 196 AD in honor of his victories over the Marcomanni, the Quadi and the Sarmatians. The shaft, almost 30 meters high, is enveloped by a bas-relief scroll that unrolls like the one on Trajan's Column to narrate the events of the Germanic and Sarmatian campaigns. The statue of Marcus Aurelius that originally topped the column was replaced in 1599 by one of *Saint Paul* by Domenico Fontana.
The column originally stood between the ancient Temple of Marcus Aurelius and the Temple of Hadrian, in the heart of the imperial Rome of the Antonines.
It now rises in Piazza Colonna, on a base restored by Fontana who, as shown by the inscription, erroneously thought the column had been dedicated to Antoninus Pius. The interior of the column is hollow and a spiral staircase of 190 steps leads to the top.

Palazzo Chigi – Begun in 1580, it was completed in 1616. In 1659 the palace became the property of the Chigi family who kept it until 1917 when it was bought by the State. It has been the seat of the Presidency of the Council of Ministers since 1961.
Inside, particularly fine is the spacious courtyard, Baroque in feeling and decorated with stuccoes, the wide Staircase of Honor, the large Room of the Mappamondo and the magnificent Sala d'Oro which has a fine oval painting by Baciccia (1668) on the ceiling.

The Column of Marcus Aurelius with the reliefs narrating the events of the imperial wars. On the facing page, the figure of the god Neptune that dominates the Fontana di Trevi.

PIAZZA DI SPAGNA AND TRINITÀ DEI MONTI

**Piazza di Spagna - Trinità dei Monti -
Church of Trinita dei Monti - Piazza del Popolo -
Church of Santa Maria del Popolo**

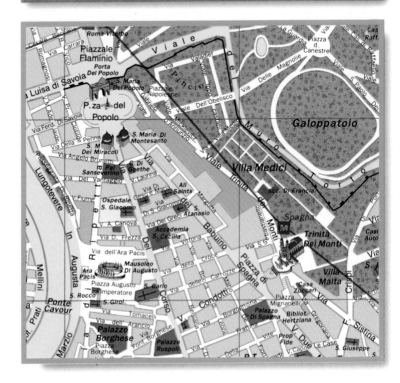

1 - Trinità dei Monti.
2 - Convent of the Sacro Cuore.
3 - Sallustian Obelisk.

Piazza di Spagna and Trinità dei Monti - One of the most characteristic of Roman squares, Piazza di Spagna runs for 270 meters and is divided into two triangular areas. The square takes its name from the **Palazzo di Spagna**, seat since the 17th century of the Spanish ambassador to the Holy See. It is famous for its magnificent buildings, elegant shops, and for the illustrious personages who sojourned here in the past: from the enigmatic Cagliostro, who held his masonic meetings tinged with magic in an inn, to Casanova, who mentioned the square in his famous *Memoirs*, to Keats, who lived and died at No. 26, now a small **museum** dedicated to the great poet. Other notable buildings, such as the **Palazzo di Propaganda Fide** with the conjoined **Church of the Re Magi**, and the aforementioned complex of the Palazzo di Spagna, also overlook the square. Opposite the Palazzo di Propaganda Fide is the **Column of the Immaculate Conception**, erected in the middle of the 19th century by Pius XI. The antique column in cipolin marble, set on a pedestal richly ornamented with statues and reliefs, receives the floral homages of the population on the 8th of December, the feast of the Immaculate Conception. At the center of the square is the Fontana della Barcaccia, set against the theatrical backdrop of the famous **Scalinata di Trinità dei Monti** (or the

66

Spanish Steps), which leads to the equally famous Piazza di Trinità dei Monti with the **Sallustian obelisk**, formerly in the Horti Sallustiani, at its center. This square is dominated by the bulk of the Church of Trinità dei Monti.

Fontana della Barcaccia - Perhaps the most congenial work by Pietro Bernini, father of the more famous Gian Lorenzo, this fountain (1627-29) stands at the center of the Piazza di Spagna and acts as a sort of fulcrum for the many buildings all around. It is a lively and brilliantly-conceived representation of a sinking boat leaking water at the stern and prow. The idea seems to have come from Pope Urban VII, who was struck by the sight of a boat that had sunk when the Tiber flooded.

Spanish Steps or Scalinata di Trinità dei Monti - The theatrical effect of these famous steps and their powerful evocative quality is part of the history of the image of the city. Built entirely in travertine by Francesco De Sanctis between 1723 and 1726, the Scalinata consists of twelve flights which widen and narrow in compact but varied stages in no way bound by rigid schemes, in line with rococo architectural concepts. The steps begin in Piazza di Spagna and rise to Piazza di Trinità dei Monti.

Church of Trinità dei Monti - One of the most impressive of the Franciscan churches in the city, Trinità dei Monti was begun in 1503 by Louis XII, but has been remodeled over the course of time. The sober

Below, the Fontana della Barcaccia at the center of Piazza di Spagna. On the right, a detail of the Scalinata di Trinità dei Monti (Spanish Steps).

facade, by Carlo Maderno, with a single order of pilasters and a wide columned portal, is surmounted by an attic with a large balustrade and is preceded by a **staircase** designed by Domenico Fontana (1587) and ornamented with capitals and antique bas-reliefs. The single-nave **interior** contains important works of art such as the fresco of *Scenes from the Life of Saint John the Baptist* by Naldini in the first chapel on the right and the justly-famous *Assumption* by Daniele da Volterra in the third chapel on the same side. In the second chapel on the left is another masterpiece by Daniele da Volterra, the *Deposition*, while the sixth chapel on the same side is home to *Isaiah and Daniel* (on the front of the arch) and the *Visi-*

Trinità dei Monti and the Spanish Steps rising to the church from the square.

tation by Perin del Vaga, the *Death of the Virgin* by Taddeo Zuccari, and the *Assumption* by Federico and Taddeo Zuccari. In the chapel to the left of the presbytery is the *Coronation of the Virgin*, another outstanding work by Federico Zuccari.

The cloister contains frescoes by various artists of *Scenes from the Life of Saint Francis of Paola*.

Piazza del Popolo - Piazza del Popolo, one of the most characteristic areas of Neoclassical Rome, is the child of Giuseppe Valadier's creative genius in the field of town planning and architecture. The original design dates to 1793.

Distinctive features of the square are the low exedrae defining its sides, topped by statues of the *Four Seasons*, and the two centrally-placed fountains, *Neptune and the Tritons* and *Rome between the Tiber and the Aniene Rivers*, that set off the obelisk. All the sculpture mentioned above dates to the first half of the 19th century and is the work of Gnaccarini, Laboureur, Stocchi, Baini, and Ceccarini.

Flaminian Obelisk - The obelisk that since 1589 has stood in the center of Piazza del Popolo is an exceptional legacy of classical Rome. Dating to 1200 BC, it was originally erected by the Egyptian pharaoh Rameses II in Heliopolis, opposite the Temple of the Sun. Augustus brought it to Rome and re-erected it in the Circus Maximus. Under Pope Sixtus V it was moved to its present site, and under Leo XII (early 19th century) it became the centerpiece of Valadier's fountains with their four basins and marble lions.

Church of Santa Maria di Montesanto - Together with its twin church of Santa Maria dei Miracoli, this is one of Bernini's small masterpieces, built in collaboration with Fontana for Monsignor Girolamo Gastaldi in the second half of the 17th century. A graceful tetrastyle **porch** decorated with marble statues precedes the church. The **interior**, on an original elliptical plan, contains various interesting works of art such as the *Virgin with Saint Francis*

Above, a view of the Spanish Steps in Piazza di Spagna. Below, the Flaminian Obelisk at the center of Piazza del Popolo.

69

and *Saint James the Greater* by the 17th-century master Carlo Maratta in the third chapel on the left, a 15th-century panel painting of the *Virgin of Montesanto* on the altar, and precious frescoes by Baciccia on the vault of the sacristy.

Church of Santa Maria dei Miracoli - The twin of the nearby Church of Santa Maria di Montesanto is also fruit of the collaboration between Bernini and Fontana. Like the other church, it is preceded by a theatrical tetrastyle **porch**, but unlike its twin, the **interior** is on a circular plan with two chapels on each side. The rich but not overpowering high altar is noteworthy, with the original sculptural group of the *Virgin and Four Angels* by Antonio Raggi (second half of the 17th century).

Santa Maria del Popolo - The first version of this sacred building dates to 1099, when it was decided to build a church financed by the people (hence its name) on the remains of the tombs of Rome's Domitia family. The church was, however, completely rebuilt in the second half of the 15th century, probably by Baccio Pontelli and Andrea Bregno. Bramante later lengthened the apse in linear perspective. The *facade* is divided into three bays by a lower order of pilaster strips: this brilliant solution, with

On these pages, the Church of Santa Maria del Popolo: above, a statue by Lorenzetto in the Chigi Chapel; below and right, details of the interior and the exterior of the church.

its perfectly symmetrical rhythm, makes Santa Maria del Popolo one of the most interesting Renaissance churches Rome. The Baroque **interior** on a Latin cross plan was remodeled by Bernini for Pope Alexander VII. The chapels of both aisles contain beautiful works, some of which are true masterpieces. The first chapel on the right has a delightful fresco of the *Adoration of the Child* by Pinturicchio over the altar. The second chapel on the same side, designed by Fontana in a medley of highly polished marbles, contains the *tombs of Cardinal Lorenzo Cybo and Cardinal Alderano*. The altarpiece with the *Immaculate Conception and Saints John the Evangelist, Gregory, John Chrysostom, and Augustine*, is by Carlo Maratta. A lovely marble sculpture of *Saint Catherine with Saint Vincent and Saint Anthony of Padova*, by the school of Bregno, decorates the altar in the fourth chapel. In the right transept is the *Visitation* by G. M. Morandi. In the **sacristy**, a marble altar by Bregno houses a 15th-century Sienese *Madonna*. The main chapel boasts a panel in Byzantine style, the *Madonna del Popolo*, which tradition ascribes to the hand of Saint Luke. Among the frescoes in the presbytery are the *Coronation of the Virgin*, the *Evangelists*, the *Sibyls*, and the *Fathers of the Church* by Pinturicchio. But the most celebrated among the many excellent works of art are in the first chapel of the left transept, where two of Caravaggio's most famous paintings, the *Conversion of Saint Paul* and the *Crucifixion of Saint Peter*, flank the altar, which is surmounted by the *Assumption* by Annibale Carracci. One of the major attractions of the left aisle is the **Chigi Chapel** built to plans by Raphael, who also prepared the cartoons for the mosaics in the dome. The chapel also contains frescoes by Salviati and, on the altar, the realistic *Birth of the Virgin* by Sebastiano del Piombo.

PANTHEON

Ara Pacis - Mausoleum of Augustus - *Piazza and Palazzo di Montecitorio* - **Palazzo and Galleria Doria Pamphili** - **Santa Maria sopra Minerva** - **Pantheon** - **San Luigi dei Francesi** - Palazzo Madama

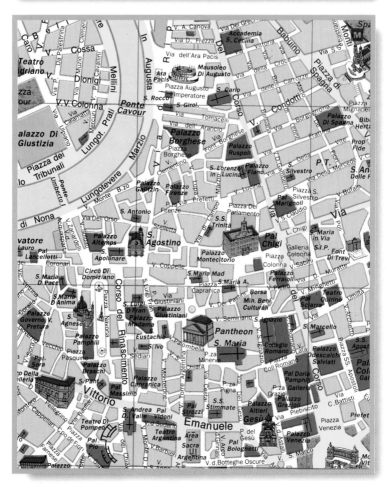

Ara Pacis - Coeval literary and epigraphical sources provide ample information as to the date of construction and the reasons underlying the creation of this extremely significant monument in Roman art. The *Res Gestae Divi Augusti*, emperor Augustus' official autobiography, and Ovid's *Fasti* inform us that the Roman Senate voted that an altar be erected in the Campus Martius to commemorate the return of Augustus from the campaigns in Spain and Gaul and to celebrate the *Pax Augustae*, Rome's new policies, and what the Romans hoped would be the beginning of a period of peace. The altar was begun on 4 July in 13 BC, near the Via Flaminia on property belonging to Agrippa, Augustus' general and a member of the imperial family by his marriage to Julia, the emperor's daughter. The *dedicatio* (that is, the inauguration ceremony upon completion of the work) was held on 30 January in 9 BC.

The discovery of the Ara Pacis dates to 1568, when nine of its sculpted blocks were found during construction of the Renaissance Palazzo Fiano (now Palazzo Almagià). In 1870, Von Duhn identified these marble fragments for the first time as remains of the famous monument. Systematic excavations begun in 1903 brought to light the supporting structures of the altar; the excavations were finally terminated, in 1937-38, on occasion of the Augustan bimillenial celebrations, and the altar was reconstructed in a pavilion built for this purpose next to the Mausoleum of Augustus, near the Tiber. At present, therefore, the Ara Pacis no longer occupies its original site and its orientation has also been changed, from east-west to north-south. The monument is composed of a rectangular marble enclosure on a podium (11.65 x 10.62 meters). It was originally accessed via a staircase, with two large doors (3.60 meters wide) that opened on the long sides and originally faced on the Via Flaminia and on the Campus Martius. The altar itself, set on a three-stepped podium, is inside the enclosure; on the west, five other steps permitted the priest to reach the top of the altar on which the sacrificial rites took place.

Details of the panels decorating the marble enclosure of the Ara Pacis and, below, a view of the monument.

73

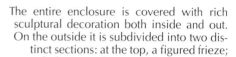

The entire enclosure is covered with rich sculptural decoration both inside and out. On the outside it is subdivided into two distinct sections: at the top, a figured frieze; below, a frieze with ornamental acanthus scroll motifs. The two major sections are separated by a meander band. These divisions are framed by pilaster strips, four at the corners and two near the doors, all decorated with "candelabra" of plant motifs. The pilasters support the entablature (completely rebuilt), which was originally probably crowned by acroteria.

The panels with mythical-allegorical scenes are on the longer sides of the enclosure, next to the doors. The two panels on the west side show scenes of the *Sacrifice of Aeneas to the Penates* (on the right) and the *Lupercal* (on the left), the grotto where the legendary she-wolf nursed the twins Remus and Romulus. The first scene is well preserved: Aeneas, *velato capite* and with the *sceptrum* in his left hand, is shown in the act of sacrificing the white sow with her 30 piglets to the Penates of Lavinium, who are represented by a small temple on the upper left.

The second scene has been almost entirely lost: all that remains is the shepherd Faustulus on the right and the god Mars on the left, besides some fragments of water plants that represent the banks of the Tiber.

In the two panels on the east side are, to the right, a fragment with the representation of Rome dressed as an Amazon, and to the left the nearly complete panel known as *Saturnia Tellus*. The personification of Italia at the center, a bountiful *seated female figure* with two children in her lap, is flanked by seminude nymphs symbolizing the other elements (water and air): the one on the right rides a sea monster, the one on the left flies on a swan. The landscape is also clearly delineated: to the right the ocean, at the center the earth and rocks populated by domestic animals

and flowering plants, and to the left the rivers, represented by reeds and a pitcher from which water is flowing. The scene is an allegory of Peace, which, thanks to Augustus, brings prosperity back to Italy, enriching the country with bountiful crops and herds.

The short sides contain the representation of a sacrificial procession, which while unified is organized in two distinct groups: one with the priests and the cult initiates, and one with all the members of the imperial family. The composition is closely bound to motives of protocol: in the first group, the conventional figures of priests and magistrates are arranged hierarchically according to their offices (*ordo sacerdotorum*); in the second, the members of the emperor's family, who are also more clearly characterized, are arranged in order of their claim to the throne according to the order of succession conceived by Augustus during the years in which the monument was being built.

The marble interior of the enclosure probably reproduces the temporary wooden fence (*templum*) erected for the ceremony held in 13 BC to dedicate the altar (*constitutio*). At the bottom is the fence of vertical laths; above, a motif of garlands with *paterae* and *bucrania* like those which hung on the actual fence. The side pieces of the altar inside the enclosure have survived; they are decorated with tendrils and rest on winged lion supports. A small, low-relief frieze, representing the annual sacrifice performed on the altar, runs all around both the inside and the outside of the *mensa* (table).

Mausoleum of Augustus - The dynastic tomb of the first emperor of Rome is a circular structure, 87 meters in diameter, consisting of a series of concentric walls in tufa connected by walls radiating out from the center. The first accessible chamber lies at the end of the long entrance corridor (*dromos*) which cuts through the structures described above. Two entrances in this wall lead to the annular corridor which rings the circular cella. The tomb of Augustus was here, in correspondence to the bronze statue of the emperor that stood at the top of the pier. The three niches of the cella contained other tombs of members of the Julian-Claudian dynasty.

Piazza di Montecitorio - The name of this slightly down-sloping square, one of the most representative sites of the bourgeois city, probably derives from the "Monte Accettorio," the meeting-place of the Roman centuries. At the center of the square is the **Obelisk of Psammetychus II**, dating to 594 BC. When it was brought to Rome from Heliopolis by Augustus, it was initially re-erected in the Campus Martius.

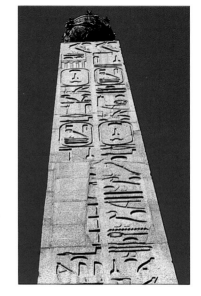

On the preceding page: a detail of the procession shown on the panels of the Ara Pacis and an aerial view of the Mausoleum of Augustus, the burial place of the members of the dynasty of Rome's first emperor.

Right: the Obelisk in Piazza di Montecitorio.

75

Palazzo di Montecitorio - Built along dignified Baroque lines, the palace was begun by Bernini but finished at the end of the 17th century by Fontana. It has been the seat of the House of Deputies since 1871.

Of particular note is the *facade*, on which Bernini succeeded in obtaining an effect of combined elegance and majesty by using a broken convex line with a recessed central body built in perspective.

In the ***interior*** (open to the public when Parliament is not in session) is the vast semicircular hall, dating to 1918, where so many political debates have taken place, and the immense *Library of the House of Deputies*, which contains some 400,000 volumes.

PALAZZO DORIA PAMPHILI AND GALLERIA

Today's palace, now the home of one of the richest and most prestigious art collections in the capital, originated as a primitive thirteenth-century building, the dwelling-place of the prelates of the adjacent church of Santa Maria in Via Lata. It was completely rebuilt in 1489 by Cardinal Giovanni Santoro to plans attributed to Bramante. The cardinal was soon forced, however, to relinquish his property to the duke of Urbino, Francesco Maria Della Rovere, nephew of Pope Julius II, who however was in residence only rarely. In 1573, one of his successors began a series of acquisitions of the surrounding properties which from then until the end of the century increased the surface area over which the coming expansion of the original building was to extend in the two centuries that followed. In 1601, after the enormous holding had passed to Cardinal Pietro Aldobrandini, construction of the two wings on the larger courtyard was begun. But in 1657, still under construction, the palace again changed hands, becoming the property of the Pamphili, the family of Camillo, the nephew of the then Pope Innocent

Piazza di Montecitorio with the facade of Palazzo Montecitorio and the Obelisk of Psammetychus II brought to Rome by Augustus.

Rest on the Journey into Egypt, *a masterpiece by Caravaggio, exhibited in the Galleria di Palazzo Doria Pamphili.*

X and husband of princess Olympia, the last descendant of the Aldo-brandini family. In 1659, taking their cue from the restructuring work then going on in Piazza del Collegio Romano, the facade of the palace facing on that square was completed in accordance with plans by Antonio Del Grande, a pupil of Borromini. The work on the Via Lata side continued in the years that followed, as did the decoration of the magnificent reception halls, in the Baroque style then very much in vogue. The Via del Corso side had to wait until 1730 before it was finally completed thanks to the intervention of Gabriele Valvassori, who in a little under three years created the highly-decorative *barrocchetto*-style facade and the monumental **Galleria** on a four-armed plan. It was here that the works of art in the family collection begun by Innocent X, which included his masterful portraits by Velasquez and by Bernini, were arranged. Further work on the palace was begun in the mid-1700s, following the passage of the property to the Doria Pamphili heirs, and it continued into the next century. At the same time, beginning in 1732 and for some decades thereafter, numerous artists and craftsmen were engaged in the decoration of the vast interiors. The first of these actions was the decoration of the ceiling of the gallery itself, frescoed by Milani with motifs inspired by the *Battle of the Giants* and the *Stories of Hercules*. The work continued into the apartments: the ceiling of the Sala del Trono was frescoed by Tommaso Agricola with the *Sacrifice of Iphigenia* and the ballroom was embellished with paintings by Nessi; the chapel was decorated, and in 1838 the grandiose Salone Aldobrandini was added to the Galleria. The latter space became the home of many works of art by great Italian and foreign masters, beginning with the original nucleus of the collection which included, among others, works by Caravaggio (for example, the celebrated *Rest on the Flight into Egypt*) and artists of the Emilian school (Parmigianino, Correggio). The Olimpia Aldobrandini inheritance added to this nucleus a number of masterpieces by painters of the Venetian school, including Titian, Tintoretto, Bellini and Bassano; it is instead to Cardinal Bernardo Pamphili that we owe the group of works by the Flemish masters; with the advent of the Doria family, the collection was also enriched by works by Sebastiano del Piombo, Bronzino, Lorenzo Lotto, and the so-called "primitive" painters.

Elephant of Piazza della Minerva - Considered one of Bernini's most delightful inventions, the elephant serves as the support for the Egyptian *obelisk* dating to the 6th century BC that formerly stood in the nearby *Isaeum Campense* or Temple of Isis. Sculpted by Ercole Ferrata in 1667, it is so small in relation to the column that it is popularly known as "Minerva's chick," even though the inscription on the base makes of it the symbol of a robust intellect capable of supporting great wisdom, the role assigned to the towering obelisk above.

Church of Santa Maria sopra Minerva - Built in the 8th century on the ruins of the temple of Minerva Chalcidicea, the church was rebuilt in 1280 in Gothic style and as such is the only true example of Gothic architecture remaining in Rome. Over the course of the centuries it was mercilessly remodeled and restored; the series of frequent interventions culminated in that of the 19th century, which disfigured the pure lines of the interior and succeeded in partially obliterating the original Gothic feeling. The 17th-century facade is simple but rather commonplace.

The stately *interior*, with its numerous chapels, consists of a spacious nave and two wide aisles. The compelling figure of *San Luigi Bertrando* by Baciccia stands on the altar in the second chapel of the right aisle; the luminous gold-ground *Annunciation* on the altar in the fifth chapel is by Antoniazzo Romano (1460); in the sixth chapel, the result of a collaborative effort by Giacomo della Porta and Carlo Maderno, the altar is adorned by the touching yet powerful *Last Supper* by Federico Barocci (1594); the seventh chapel has a fresco of *Christ Judge with Two Saints* by Melozzo da Forlì.

The famous Carafa Chapel in the right transept, with its graceful marble arch, is of particular note for the lovely frescoes by Filippino Lippi, who also painted the panel of the *Annunciation* on the altar. In the first chapel to the right is a splendid wooden *Crucifix* dating to the early 15th century. On the altar of the next chapel is an important late 17th-century paint-

Above, the obelisk in Piazza della Minerva and below, Bernini's elephant supporting the column.

ing of the *Madonna in Glory* with Saint Peter receiving into Heaven five new saints from Clement X's pontificate, by Carlo Maratta (1675), and in the lunette at the back a fresco of the mystical *Glory of the Holy Trinity* by Baciccia.
The chancel contains the splendid statue of the *Risen Christ* by Michelangelo. The relics of Saint Catherine of Siena are kept on the high altar; the figure of the reclining saint is by Isaia da Pisa. Behind the altar are the *funeral monuments of Clement VII and Leo X*, designed by Antonio da Sangallo. Mention should also be made of various funeral monuments in the left transept. Not far off is the entrance to the **sacristy**, behind which is a chapel built in the 17th century using the walls of the room in which Saint Catherine died. The atrium of the sacristy leads to the **Chapel of the Popes**

The Gothic nave of the Church of Santa Maria sopra Minerva.

and the 16th-century **cloister**, the vaults of which are covered with elaborate 17th- century frescoes.
The interior of the church also contains many tombs, including that of *Benedict XIII* at the head of the transept. In the left aisle (fifth, fourth, and third chapels) are still other tombs, including that of *Giovanni Vigevano* by Bernini (third chapel). Lastly, the first chapel contains the noteworthy *bust of Girolamo Bottigella*, attributed to Jacopo Sansovino.

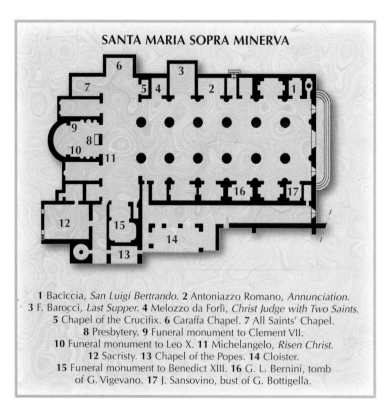

SANTA MARIA SOPRA MINERVA

1 Baciccia, *San Luigi Bertrando*. **2** Antoniazzo Romano, *Annunciation*.
3 F. Barocci, *Last Supper*. **4** Melozzo da Forlì, *Christ Judge with Two Saints*.
5 Chapel of the Crucifix. **6** Caraffa Chapel. **7** All Saints' Chapel.
8 Presbytery. **9** Funeral monument to Clement VII.
10 Funeral monument to Leo X. **11** Michelangelo, *Risen Christ*.
12 Sacristy. **13** Chapel of the Popes. **14** Cloister.
15 Funeral monument to Benedict XIII. **16** G. L. Bernini, tomb of G. Vigevano. **17** J. Sansovino, bust of G. Bottigella.

Aerial view of the Pantheon and Piazza della Rotonda. Below, the ruins of the Basilica of Neptune.

Pantheon.

Pantheon - Of all the buildings of ancient Rome, the Pantheon is the best preserved, thanks to its having been donated to Pope Boniface IV by the Byzantine emperor Phocas and later transformed into a church with the name of Santa Maria ad Martyres (609 AD).

The first building was erected in 27 BC by Marcus Vipsanius Agrippa, Augustus' faithful advisor, as part of the general urban improvement work targeting the central area of the Campus Martius, which had just then become his property. The temple was conceived for the glorification of the *gens* Julia and was called the Pantheon (*sanctissimum*): all the planetary divinities in addition to Mars and Venus, the protectors of Augustus' family, may have been honored here. Agrippa's building, as excavations carried out in the late 19th century have shown, was rectangular (19.82 x 43.76 meters) and faced south, not north as now. The facade was on the long side; it was preceded by a pronaos, in front of which was an open circular area paved in travertine. The temple was damaged in the fire of 80 AD and was restored by Domitian. It was again damaged by fire in Trajan's time, and was completely rebuilt by Hadrian between 118 and 128 AD in the form we still see today. This fact is confirmed by information supplied by a Latin historian - and also by the factory marks on the bricks, which bear the consular dates. The inscription on the architrave, *M(arcus) Agrippa L(uci) f(ilius) co(n)s(ul) tertium fecit*, was therefore placed there by Hadrian, who never put his own name on any of the monuments he built.

Hadrian's reconstruction profoundly modified the original building. The

facade was set facing north, the porch was set on the site occupied by the original temple, and the large rotunda was built over what was previously the open area in front of the temple. The facade of the large columned **porch** is still composed of eight columns in grey granite; behind the first, third, sixth and eighth columns of this row are set two red granite columns, in such a manner as to form three aisles; the central aisle, which is the widest, leads to the entrance. The side aisles end in two large niches destined for the statues of Agrippa and Augustus. The tympanum was decorated with a bronze crowned eagle, of which only the fix-holes still remain. The ceiling of the porch was also decorated in bronze, but the decorations were removed by Pope Urban VIII Barberini (whence the famous pasquinade, "*Quod non fecerunt Barbari, fecerunt Barberini*"). Behind the porch is a massive construction in brick, which joins the

Above, an unusual image of the interior of the Pantheon and its dome.

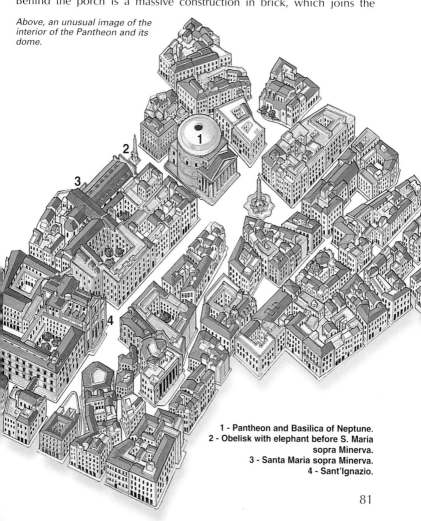

1 - Pantheon and Basilica of Neptune.
2 - Obelisk with elephant before S. Maria
sopra Minerva.
3 - Santa Maria sopra Minerva.
4 - Sant'Ignazio.

The facade of the Pantheon and, below, the exterior of San Luigi dei Francesi.
The church contains three celebrated works by Caravaggio.

porch and the **rotunda**, a gigantic cylinder with a wall that is six meters thick and divided into three superposed sectors marked externally by cornices. The wall lightens as it rises, and moreover is not always solid, being cut through by brick vaulting in various places. The height of the rotunda at the top of the dome is precisely that of its diameter (43.30 meters): the interior space is thus a perfect sphere. The **dome** is a masterpiece of engineering: it is the widest masonry dome ever raised and was cast in a single operation over an enormous wooden framework.

The **interior** of the building has six distyle niches at the sides and a semicircular exedra at the back; in between are eight small aediculae with alternating arched and triangular pediments. The dome is decorated with five tiers of hollow coffers that cover it completely except for a smooth band near the *oculus*, the circular opening (9 meters in diameter) that provides the only light to the interior.

Church of San Luigi dei Francesi - This church, construction of which began in 1518, was built for Cardinal Giulio de' Medici, the future Pope Clement VII. It was finished in 1589 by Fontana.

The **facade**, perhaps by Giacomo della Porta, is divided into five bays by pilaster strips. The lower level has three portals and two niches with statues, while a large central balcony with niches and statues animates the upper level.

In the **interior**, with a nave and two aisles, are five chapels on either side in which are concentrated so many universally-acknowledged masterpieces of art that the church is on a par with any museum.

The second chapel in the right aisle contains the splendid *Scenes from the Life of Saint Cecilia* frescoed by Domenichino (1616-17); on the altar stands *Saint Cecilia*, a perfect copy by Guido Reni of Raphael's painting of the saint. On the altar of the fourth chapel is the *Oath of Clovis* by

Martirio di San Matteo *by Caravaggio, in San Luigi dei Francesi.*
Below, the facade of Palazzo Madama, where the Italian Senate meets.

Jacopino Del Conte. The *Assumption*, a warm and colorful painting by Francesco Bassano, decorates the high altar of the church.

Three basic works in the development of Baroque painting are in the fifth chapel of the left aisle: Caravaggio's paintings of *Saint Matthew and the Angel* (on the altar), the *Vocation of Saint Matthew* (left) and the *Martyrdom of Saint Matthew* (right), all of great emotional intensity and all painted between 1597 and 1602. In the third chapel, on the left, are Giacinto Gemignani's delicate *Scenes from the Life of Saint Louis.*

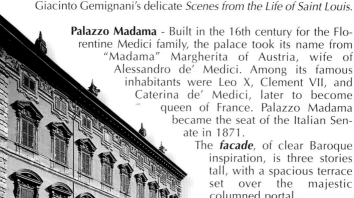

Palazzo Madama - Built in the 16th century for the Florentine Medici family, the palace took its name from "Madama" Margherita of Austria, wife of Alessandro de' Medici. Among its famous inhabitants were Leo X, Clement VII, and Caterina de' Medici, later to become queen of France. Palazzo Madama became the seat of the Italian Senate in 1871.

The **facade**, of clear Baroque inspiration, is three stories tall, with a spacious terrace set over the majestic columned portal.

Of note in the **interior** are the vast Hall of Honor, with its 19th-century frescoes by Cesare Maccari, and the well-stocked **Library**, which contains 450,000 volumes and thousands of incunabula, manuscripts and statues.

PIAZZA NAVONA

**Piazza Navona - Sant'Agnese in Agone -
Santa Maria in Vallicella - Palazzo Altemps -** Museo Barracco -
Sant'Andrea della Valle - Campo dei Fiori - Galleria Spada

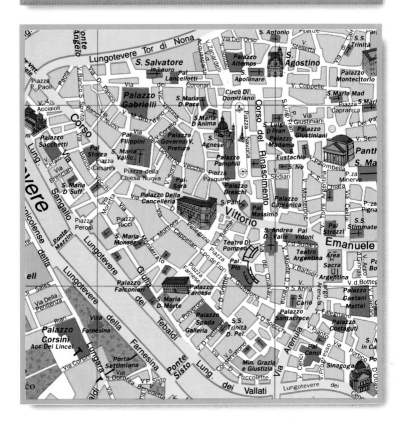

Piazza Navona - This square, the most famous of Baroque Rome, covers the site of Domitian's stadium. The name would seem to derive from a popular corruption of the term for the competitive (*in agone*) games that were held here in Roman times. From Domitian onward, the stadium was used almost exclusively for sports events, including the famous regatta held in August, in which the participants wore the colors of the nobles and the civic clergy. Today, the square hosts the Christmas market of the *Befana* from mid-December to Twelfth Night. But the real attraction is Gian Lorenzo Bernini's famous **Fontana dei Fiumi** (Fountain of the Four Rivers - 1651), which won for the artist the admiration and protection of the then-pope Innocent X. The rivers represented in the fountain are the *Danube*, the *Ganges*, the *Nile*, and the *Rio de la Plata*. They are arranged on a steep rocky crag from which a Roman obelisk, taken from the Circus of Maxentius, rises daringly into the air. Aligned with the Fountain of the Four Rivers are the *Fountain of the Moor*, at the south end in front of the *Palazzo Pamphili*, and the *Fountain of Neptune*, formerly "of the Calderari," at the northern end of the square.

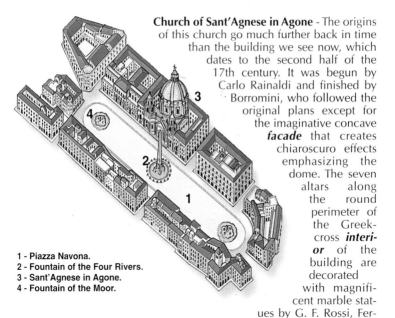

Church of Sant'Agnese in Agone - The origins of this church go much further back in time than the building we see now, which dates to the second half of the 17th century. It was begun by Carlo Rainaldi and finished by Borromini, who followed the original plans except for the imaginative concave *facade* that creates chiaroscuro effects emphasizing the dome. The seven altars along the round perimeter of the Greek-cross *interior* of the building are decorated with magnificent marble statues by G. F. Rossi, Ferrata, Raggi, and Campi. The fresco in the dome of the *Glory of Paradise*, with its free interpretation of the theme, was begun by the 17th-century painter Ciro Ferri and finished by his follower S. Corbellini. The charming allegorical paintings in the pendentives are by Baciccia.

1 - Piazza Navona.
2 - Fountain of the Four Rivers.
3 - Sant'Agnese in Agone.
4 - Fountain of the Moor.

Church of Santa Maria in Vallicella (also known as Chiesa Nuova) - Begun in the second half of the 16th century, this church was completed in the early years of the following century with the fine *facade* with its two orders of pilasters strips. The *interior*, with a nave and two side aisles, is sumptuously decorated and contains many outstanding works such as the fresco in the barrel vault celebrating the *Vision of Saint Philip Neri* (who during the construction of the church saw it saved from collapse by the Virgin) by Pietro da Cortona, who also painted the figures of the *Four Prophets* (Isaiah, Jeremiah, Ezekiel, Daniel) in the pendentives

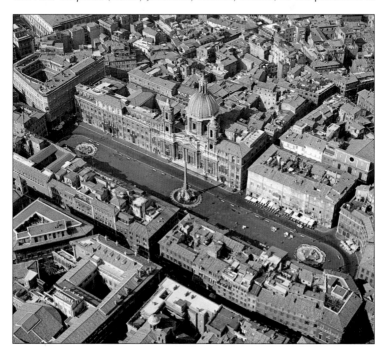

of the dome, the *Triumph of the Holy Trinity* in the vault of the dome, and the *Assumption of the Virgin with Saints* in the apse. The first chapel on the right is home to a *Crucifixion* with the Virgin, the Magdalen and Saint John the Evangelist, by Scipione Pulzone; on the altar in the transept is the *Coronation of the Virgin* by the painter known as the Cavalier d'Arpino; on the altar in the Spada family chapel is a painting of the *Madonna with Saints Charles Borromeo and Ignatius* by Carlo Maratta. There are also three paintings by Rubens: the superb *Madonna and Angels* in the apse is flanked by *Saints Domitilla, Nereus and Achilleus* (on the right) and *Saints Gregory, Maurus, and Papias* (on the left). The *Presentation of the Virgin in the Temple* in the left transept is by Federico Barocci. The transept gives access to the elegant **sacristy**, where there is a marble group of *Saint Philip Neri and an Angel* by Algardi and the ceiling fresco by Pietro da Cortona depicting the *Angels with the Instruments of the Passion*. On the altar of the sacristy chapel is an important painting by Guercino, *Saint Philip Neri in Adoration*. Stairs lead from the sacristy to the Rooms of Saint. Philip in which are found a painting of *Saint Philip Neri* by Guido Reni and the *Ecstasy of Saint Philip* by Pietro da Cortona. Lastly, the fourth chapel in the left aisle contains a *Visitation* by Barocci.

On these pages, three details of the Fontana dei Fiumi in Piazza Navona.

PALAZZO ALTEMPS

It was Count Girolamo Riaro, nephew of Pope Sixtus IV and the husband of Caterina Sforza, who in the late 15th century commissioned the architect Baldassare Peruzzi to build a massive palace with a simple Renaissance facade and a Doric-style courtyard adorned with ancient statues. The work continued even after the palace passed into the hands of the cardinal of Volterra, Francesco Soderini, and in 1568 to Cardinal Marco Sittico Altemps. The later charged Martino Longhi the Elder, who is also the author of the tall panoramic tower with its loggia on the roof and belvedere, with completion of the construction. Cardinal Altemps revealed himself as a great collector of ancient art, and in this activity he was favored by his friendship with Pope Clement VII, who he had promoted as candidate to the papacy. As a sign of his gratitude, Clement VII presented the Altemps family with a precious relic: the body of his far-off predecessor Saint Anicetus. This relic, a unique case of private burial of a pope, was moved to the palace chapel, frescoed with scenes of his life and of his martyrdom by Ottavio Leoni and Pomarancio. The precious **Altemps Collection** of ancient statuary suffered a quite different fate. It was broken up in the eighteenth and nineteenth centuries, when the palace became the property of the Spanish Sacred College, and only 16 pieces survived; these are today on display in the building, now a section of the **Museo Nazionale Romano** inaugurated in December 1997, together with two analogous collections: the **Boncompagni Ludovisi Collection** and the **Mattei Collection**, transferred here from the Museo delle Terme. The former of these, the largest and the most prestigious, was begun by Cardinal Ludovico Ludovisi, nephew of Gregory XV, who collected examples of ancient statuary to adorn his villa built around 1621 between the Pincio and the Quirinale on the site of the ancient Horti Sallustiani. Other statues came to light during the work for construction of the villa; the collection thus acquired the so-called *Acrolito* and the *Galatian Killing his Wife* (found together with the *Dying Galatian*, which is now in the Musei Capitolini) and later there were added the *Ares*, the *Athena*, and the *Large Ludovisi Sarcophagus*. Sculptors of the caliber of Bernini and Algardi were involved in the restoration and integration of these priceless marbles; with their master's touch they returned statues like the *Hermes Loghios*, the *Dadophoros* and the *Bathing Aphrodite* to their original splendor.

The villa later passed into the hands of Giambattista Boncompagni, who opened the collection to the public (which at the time included such figures as Goethe and Winckelmann). In the nineteenth century, following the discovery of the *Ludovisi Throne* and other sculptures, the collection totaled 339 pieces. It was scattered following the demolition of the villa and was acquired only in part by the State in 1901.

In the oval, a relief with the helmed head of the god Mars, on exhibit in Palazzo Altemps.

Oratorio dei Filippini - A delightful example of Borromini's Baroque architecture, the oratory consists of various richly decorated rooms and is the seat of the ***Archivio Storico Capitolino***, the ***Biblioteca Romana***, the ***Biblioteca Vallicelliana***, the ***Società Romana di Storia Patria***, and the ***Istituto Storico Italiano per il Medioevo***.

Corso Vittorio Emmanuele II - This great artery was built after the proclamation of Rome as capital and was opened to traffic in 1881. At least in part, Corso Vittorio Emmanuele II retraces the route of the old Papal Way; it links some of the most distinctive districts of Rome, including the Pigna, Sant'Eustachio, the Parione, and the Ponte neighborhoods.

A general view of Piazza Navona with Sant'Agnese in Agone and the fountains. Above, the exterior of the Museo Barracco, or Piccola Farnesina.

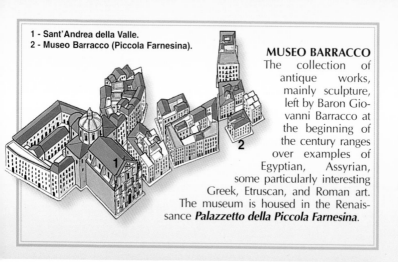

1 - Sant'Andrea della Valle.
2 - Museo Barracco (Piccola Farnesina).

MUSEO BARRACCO

The collection of antique works, mainly sculpture, left by Baron Giovanni Barracco at the beginning of the century ranges over examples of Egyptian, Assyrian, some particularly interesting Greek, Etruscan, and Roman art. The museum is housed in the Renaissance *Palazzetto della Piccola Farnesina*.

Church of Sant'Andrea della Valle - Construction of this grandiose edifice, to plans by Francesco Grimaldi and Giacomo Della Porta, began in 1591. In the first two decades of the 17th century, Maderno crowned the structure with the splendid dome. The powerful facade (built somewhat later by Rainaldi) is in travertine and presents two tiers of columns with numerous niches containing statues: the angel sculpted by Ferrari is particularly striking. The huge single nave is lined on both sides by large chapels that contain significant art. In the first chapel on the right is a high relief marble altar of the *Holy Family* by Raggi (1675); the second chapel (probably designed by Giacomo Della Porta) has four black marble arches on the walls, which contain the mortal remains of Piero Strozzi's children, and, at the altar, a *Pietà* with bronze copies of the statues of *Leah* and *Rachel* by Michelangelo in San Pietro in Vincoli. Right afterwards, at the back of the right wall over the last bay before the transept, is the *tomb of Pope Pius III Piccolomini* (Francesco Todeschini Piccolomini), sculpted by Ferrucci. The dome is frescoed with an imaginative and theatrical *Glory of Paradise* (1621-25) by Lanfranco, who also painted the *Saint Andrew* at the altar in the right transept. Domenichino frescoed luminous scenes in the apse and the sanctuary (1624-28): *Saints Peter and Andrew Being Shown the Savior* by Saint John the Baptist, the *Calling of the Saint Andrew and Saint Peter*, *Saint Andrew Led to his Death*, the *Flagellation of Saint Andrew*, and *Saint Andrew Received into Heaven*. The large frescoes (1650-1651) on the corner walls of the apse depicting the crucifixion and burial of Saint Andrew are by Mattia Preti. Once past the left transept we encounter the tomb of another Piccolomini pope: Pius II (Enea Silvio Piccolomini). Lastly, the first chapel on the left side contains the mystical altarpiece of the *Assumption*, by Passignano, and various lovely sculptures including *Saint Martha* by Francesco Mochi, the *Baptist* by Pietro Bernini, *Saint John the Evangelist* by Ambrogio Bonvicino, and the two *putti* on the pediments of the two side doors, one by Pietro and the other by Gian Lorenzo Bernini.

Piazza del Campo dei Fiori - This busy square, particularly crowded when the colorful market is held, was once the melancholy site of capital executions. At the beginning of the piazza a late 19th-century fountain, the exact copy of the original 16th-century fountain that was moved to Piazza della Chiesa Nuova, lends an air of grace to the busy milieu. At the center of the square stands the *monument to Giordano Bruno* sculpted in the late 19th-century by E. Ferrari: it was in Campo de' Fiori that the philosopher was burned alive as a heretic in February of 1600.

GALLERIA SPADA
The very facade of this palace, today the home of the Council of State and one of the most important art museums in the city, surprises the visitor, with its architectural affiatus and the imaginative design of the decoration. Some of the most farseeing architects of the time, first and foremost Bartolomeo Baronio, who was followed by Giulio Mazzoni, were involved in the construction of this singular building, commissioned in the mid-16th century by Cardinal Girolamo Capodiferro. To Mazzoni we owe the interesting decoration of the courtyard and the facade, which consists in four superimposed orders which, starting from the first floor, alternate three rows of windows of differing sizes and a complex decorative apparatus with a simple, flat facing. The facade at the first floor level features eight niches containing the statues of illustrious figures in the history of ancient Rome: Trajan, Pompey, Quintus Fabius Maximus, Romulus, Numa Pompilio, Marcellus, Caesar and

Augustus; at the mezzanine level above, instead, is a series
of garlands with cherubs and caryatids and medallions
depicting a dog standing near a burning column and a scroll with a Latin
motto, the emblem of Cardinal Capodiferro. On the last floor, crowning
the building, the windows alternate with eight panels bearing inscriptions
relative to the exploits of the eight historical figures that appear in the niches on the *piano nobile*. Mazzoni employed the same extraordinary imag-
inativeness in the decoration of the courtyard, which is adorned with elegant reliefs of a *Battle of Centaurs* and *hunting
scenes,* as well as statues of the *Olympian gods.*
Following the death of Cardinal Capodiferro, in 1559 the building
passed to his mother

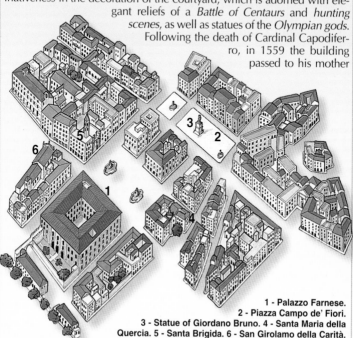

1 - **Palazzo Farnese.**
2 - **Piazza Campo de' Fiori.**
3 - **Statue of Giordano Bruno.** 4 - **Santa Maria della
Quercia.** 5 - **Santa Brigida.** 6 - **San Girolamo della Carità.**

and his nephew Pietro Paolo Mignanelli and then, in 1632, to Cardinal
Francesco Spada, who commissioned Borromini to carry out renovation.
Borromini, in collaboration with Maruscelli and Della Greca, made a
number of fantastic modifications to the original structure: the most sen-
sational was to create the so-called Galleria Prospettica, a corridor nine
meters in length that thanks to peculiar architectural sleights of hand
appears instead to be 37 meters long. Borromini, in developing an original idea by the Augustinian friar Giovanni Maria di Bitonto, in fact created a singular play of perspective by building a slightly inclined floor with
a series of arches and columns that decrease in size and height from the
near to the far end of the corridor so as to create the illusion of greater
length. The illusion is so effective that the statue of Mercury set at the end
of the gallery as the focus of the perspective, seems much larger than it
actually is. The Galleria Spada, which contains the works of art collected
by Cardinal Bernardino Spada, is instead of a completely different nature.
Here, works by the most important painters of the sev-
enteenth century are exhibited in accordance with
the tried-and-true criterion of the seventeenth-century
private picture gallery: Titian, Mattia Preti, Baciccia,
Guercino, Guido Reni, Annibale Caracci, Rubens,
Solimena, and Orazio and Artemisia Gentileschi are
only a few of the artists represented here.

*On the facing page: above, the facade of Sant'Andrea
della Valle; below, the monument to Giordano Bruno at
the center of Piazza Campo de' Fiori.*

*Right: a Madonna on the corner of a building in Campo
de' Fiori.*

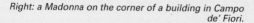

91

ISOLA TIBERINA AND
SANTA MARIA IN COSMEDIN

Porticus of Octavia - Synagogue - Theater of Marcellus - **Isola Tiberina** - Forum Boarium - **Santa Maria in Cosmedin** - Bocca della Verità - Arch of Janus - **Circus Maximus**

Below, the exterior of the Porticus of Octavia in the Campus Martius.

Porticus of Octavia - The Porticus of Octavia is situated in the Campus Martius, north of the Theater of Marcellus and the Circus Flaminius (of which nothing remains today), on the site of the earlier Porticus Metellii.

The complex, built by Augustus between 33 and 23 BC and dedicated to his sister Octavia, was destroyed by the fire of 80 AD and restored by Domitian. A second reconstruction was undertaken by Septimius Severus after another fire in 191 AD. The remains we see today are those of the latter version, but our information about the ground plan is provided by the *Forma Urbis* of Severian date.

The building, which is rectangular in plan and measures 119 x 132 meters, had porticoes of two rows of columns on the long sides and two entrance propylaea at the center of colonnades on the short sides. Inside were the temples of Jupiter Stator and Juno Regina. The former was a *peripteros sine postico* (that is, with colonnades on three sides and semicolumns on the back); the latter prostyle, with six columns on the front and three at the sides.

Augustus also erected the Curia Octaviae, an apsidal building in the Porticus behind the two temples, and the Greek and Latin libraries.

The Porticus of Octavia was also a real museum: the works exhibited included 34 bronze equestrian statues by Lysippos representing Alexander the Great with his horsemen at the Battle of Granicus, taken from a sanctuary in Macedonia, and a bronze statue of Cornelia, the mother of the Gracchi, of which the base remains. The parts of the complex that are still visible and in good condition include the propylaeum on the south side, which projected inwards and outwards with two facades consisting of four Corinthian columns topped by pediments, with an inscription on the architrave celebrating the Severian restoration. Two columns of the external facade are still standing, while the other two were replaced in the Middle Ages by an arch.

Synagogue - The Synagogue, or Israelite Temple, stands on Via del Portico di Ottavia, along the Tiber. Like other Italian synagogues, it is characterized by a style that can be best classified as "exotic revival," in this case Assyrian-Babylonian. The building terminates in a large aluminum

dome, a clear indication of its belonging to the early twentieth century; in fact, the Synagogue was designed by the architects Armanni and Costa and built in 1904. As the presence of a Synagogue would indicate, the area in which it stands was once occupied by the Jewish ghetto. From the Pons Fabricius (or "of the Quattro Capi"), the neighborhood spread out from the Tiber to encompass various streets in this part of the city, some of which still exist and some not, to its other boundary along part of the Theater of Marcellus, which was however outside the enclosure. Pope Paul IV Carafa had the area enclosed in 1556; the wall was torn down in 1887. But many of Rome's Jewish families stayed in their homes and continued to live in this part of the city.

Synagogue.

Two images of Rome's synagogue: on the right, the facade on the Tiber; below, a view from above.

Theater of Marcellus - The project for the so-called Theater of Marcellus dates to Caesar's time, but the building was finished only in 13 BC by Augustus, who officially dedicated it in the name of his nephew Marcellus, his first designated heir, who died prematurely in 23 BC.
In the 13th century, the building was occupied by the noble Savelli family; in the 18th century it passed to the Orsinis. The refined Renaissance

palace that occupies the third floor of the exterior facade of the cavea is the work of the architect Baldassarre Peruzzi.
The theater must have been a massive construction. The front was provided with a facade of 41 arches, framed by semicolumns, on three levels. The first two floors are Doric and Ionic; the third, of which nothing remains, must have been an attic closed by Corinthian pilasters. The facade was originally 32.60 meters in height. The inner passageways and the radial walls of the *cunei* are built of *opus quadratum* in tufa stone through the first ten meters' depth and in *opus caementicium* with an *opus reticulatum* facing in the interior.
It has been calculated that the cavea (129.80 meters diameter) held between

Below, the Theater of Marcellus; above, a detail of one of the half columns framing the arches.

Facing page, below: the remains of Ponte Rotto.

15,000 and 20,000 spectators, making it the largest theater in Rome as far as audience capacity was concerned.

Beyond the orchestra (37 meters diameter) was the stage, of which nothing remains, although we know it was flanked on both sides by apsed halls, of which a pier and a column of one are still standing. Behind the stage was a large semicircular exedra with two small temples. The decoration of the building was also distinguished by the richness of its decoration, an idea of which is still lent by the Doric frieze on the lower order.

Isola Tiberina - According to an old written tradition, the small island in the Tiber, now known as the Isola Tiberina, was formed when the grain that had been harvested in the Campus Martius (the private property of the Tarquinii) was thrown into the river after the expulsion of the last Etruscan king of this line from Rome.

The first important building erected on the island, the temple of Aesculapius, dates to 291 BC. Although nothing remains today of the original

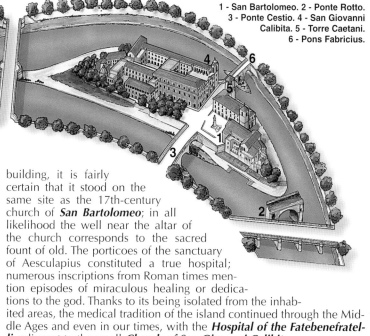

1 - San Bartolomeo. 2 - Ponte Rotto. 3 - Ponte Cestio. 4 - San Giovanni Calibita. 5 - Torre Caetani. 6 - Pons Fabricius.

building, it is fairly certain that it stood on the same site as the 17th-century church of **San Bartolomeo**; in all likelihood the well near the altar of the church corresponds to the sacred fount of old. The porticoes of the sanctuary of Aesculapius constituted a true hospital; numerous inscriptions from Roman times mention episodes of miraculous healing or dedications to the god. Thanks to its being isolated from the inhabited areas, the medical tradition of the island continued through the Middle Ages and even in our times, with the **Hospital of the Fatebenefratelli**, adjacent to the small **Church of San Giovanni Calibita**.

In antiquity, the island was joined to the city by two bridges.

The bridge that still today connects the island to the left bank, near the Theater of Marcellus, is the ancient **Pons Fabricius**. It is 62 meters long and 5.50 meters wide; the two wide, slightly flattened arches have twin spans of 24.50 meters and spring from a massive central pier pierced by a small arch that serves to relieve the pressure of the water on the structure during floods.

The other bridge, by which the island communicates with Trastevere, is no longer the original one. The ancient **Pons Cestius** was built in the first

century BC, perhaps by the praetor of 44 BC, that same C. Cestius to whom the famous funeral monument in the shape of a pyramid is dedicated. The bridge was restored in 370 AD by the emperor Valentinian I. It was torn down and partially rebuilt between 1888 and 1892.

The unique form of the Isola Tiberina, in the shape of an elongated

boat, together with the remembrance of the ship which had brought the serpent of Aesculapius to Rome gave rise to an odd architectural adaptation of the site which probably dates to the first century AD, when the easternmost point of the island was turned into the prow of a trireme. Downstream of the Isola Tiberina are the haunting ruins of the so-called **Ponte Rotto**, a bridge built on the remains of the ancient Roman *Pons Aemilius* of 179 BC. Some would date its origins to the 6th century BC, on the basis of its embankments. The span still standing in midstream dates to the late 16th century, although the pylons on which it rests are still those of the Roman bridge.

Forum Boarium - The so-called Forum Boarium covered most of the plain between the Tiber and the group of hills nearest the river (Capitoline, Palatine and Aventine). The area was of enormous importance in the early development of the city of Rome, since it was here that the two principal trade routes in ancient central Italy crossed: the river Tiber, which was at the time navigable, and the north-south route from Etruria to Campania. There was an easy ford downstream from the Isola Tiberi-

Above, a detail of the Church of San Bartolomeo; center, a view of Vico Jugario in the Forum Holitorium; below, Pons Cestio with San Bartolomeo and the Isola Tiberina in the background.

na at the spot where Rome's first bridge, the Pons Sublicius, was built. The city's first trading port (*Portus Tiberinus*) was installed in the bend of the river between the Forum Boarium (the cattle market) and the Forum Holitorium (the legume and vegetable market).

The ancient monuments still visible in this area include two exceptionally well preserved temples, which lie fairly close together in what is now Piazza Bocca della Verità on the site of the old Forum Boarium. The first of these structures is known as the **Temple of Fortuna Virilis**, but should instead be identified as the Temple of Portunus, an ancient tutelary deity of the port. The building stood very close to the *Portus Tiberinus*, just outside the *Porta Flumentana*, and may have been built as early as the period of the Etruscan kings. It was obviously restored more that once; its present aspect dates to a restoration of the 1st century BC. The temple stands on a podium in rubblework faced with slabs of travertine. The temple is Ionic pseudoperipteral in style, with four columns on the facade and with long sides comprising two columns and five semicolumns against the longitudinal walls of the cella. The walls of the building are built completely of tufa stone from Aniene, while the columns, the bases and the capitals of the semicolumns are in travertine. The entire structure was stuccoed. The original cornice, on which the lions are still visible, is exceptional.

The second temple is the circular structure erroneously called the **Temple of Vesta**. It was, instead, as was proved by the discovery of a block inscribed with topographical data, the Temple of Hercules Victor mentioned in literary sources. The temple was founded in the late 2nd century BC by a Roman merchant who had made his fortune in oil. He had it built near the trading port, and dedicated it to Hercules, the patron god of the corporation of the *olearii*. The temple is a round peripteral building with twenty Corinthian columns, standing on a stepped *crepidoma*; the circular cella opened to the east; the entablature has been completely lost. The entire temple was built in Pentelic marble, probably by the Greek architect Hermodoros of Salamina, who had various commissions in Rome in the second half of the 2nd century BC.

The Isola Tiberina in the scale model of ancient Rome in the Museo della Civiltà Romana.

Church of Santa Maria in Cosmedin - The Church of Santa Maria in Cosmedin was built in the 6th century near the temples of Hercules and of Ceres, on the remains of a large porticoed hall dating to the Flavian period. The name derives from the fact that the church had been turned over to Greeks who had escaped the iconoclastic persecution, and who were probably responsible for its decoration (the word *cosmedin* may refer to these "ornaments"). The *Schola Graeca*, as the church was also called, was restored by Nicholas I in the 9th century and by Gelasius II and Calixtus II in 12th, when the women's galleries were walled up (and lost) and the church acquired a new porch with a central vestibule. In the 18th century, Giuseppe Sardi adorned the **facade** with rich decorations, but the "period restoration" carried out by Giovenale in the late 19th century brought the appearance of the church back into line with that of the tall Romanesque **bell tower**. The **interior**, which had undergone frequent

remodeling over the centuries, was also restored to its original 8th-century form, with some concessions to 12th-century style. The church is thus a building on a typical basilica ground plan with a nave and two aisles separated by piers and reused antique columns, and terminating in three apses. The *Chapel of the Choir* (with the *Virgin and Child* of the 15th century Roman School) and the **sacristy**, access to which is from the right aisle, were later additions to the actual basilica. The architectural decoration, also strictly in keeping with the original style, includes the paschal *candlestick*, the *bishop's cathedra*, the *baldacchino* over the high *altar*, and the monolithic altar in red granite. The **crypt**, which consists of three rooms and a small apse, is built

Above, the interior of Santa Maria in Cosmedin; left, a detail of the mosaic of the Adoration of the Magi.

into the foundations of the Flavian hall. Only a part of what we see is original, since most of the structures have undergone massive and repeated restoration.

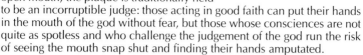

Bocca della Verità - At the back of the left side of the portico of the church of Santa Maria in Cosmedin is a large stone disk representing the frowning face of a river god, commonly known as the Bocca della Verità or "Mouth of Truth." Although it is actually an antique drain cover carved in the form of a mask with an open mouth, the plaque is traditionally held to be an incorruptible judge: those acting in good faith can put their hands in the mouth of the god without fear, but those whose consciences are not quite as spotless and who challenge the judgement of the god run the risk of seeing the mouth snap shut and finding their hands amputated.

Arch of Janus - This wide, four-sided marble arch that stands between the Velabrum and the Forum Boarium can be identified with that *arcus divi Constantini* mentioned in the *Regionarii* of Constantine's time as being in Region XI. Fragments of the dedicatory inscription from the arch, walled in the facade and interior of the Church of San Giorgio in Velabro, lead us to believe that the arch was probably erected in honor of Constantine by Constantius II, on occasion of his visit to Rome in about 356 AD.
The conventional name of Arch of Janus derives from the term *ianus* (from the patron god of gateways) used to designate covered passageways, arcades and arches.
It measures 12 meters per side and is 16 meters high. The four piers, faced with marble slabs (in part reused), stand on molded plinths. Above the plinths, the two outer faces of each pier have two rows of semicircular

Above, the great stone disk known as the Bocca della Verità. Below, the pavement of Santa Maria in Cosmedin.

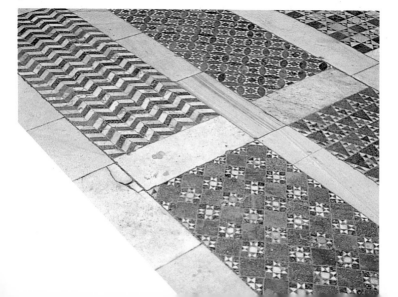

niches with shell-shaped conchae designed to accommodate statues; the two rows are separated by a cornice. Originally, they were probably framed by small columns which in the lower row rested on the cornice of the plinth and in the upper row rested on the cornice at the height of the opening. The arches are all round and develop into barrel vaults, which at their crossing form a cross vault ceiling with brick ribbing. The attic, of brick faced with marble, was torn down in 1827 because it was held to be a medieval addition.

The predilection for facades with niches framed by small columns on corbels is typical of the 4th century AD, and for this reason the Arch of Janus can be compared with the north apse of the Basilica of Maxentius, with Maxentius' 307 AD remodeling of the Temple of Venus and Rome, with the facade of Diocletian's palace in Split, and with the modifications made by Diocletian to the interior of the Curia.

Circus Maximus - Today, only the lay of the land, much higher than the first arena, betrays the form of the original structure. For a long time the circus was entirely of wood; the painted wood *carceres*, or the starting gates for the chariot races, and the central

Circus Maximus.

spina that covered and channeled the stream that ran through the valley, and around which the race was run, were built in 329 BC.

In 174 BC, the censors Fulvius Flaccus and Postumius Albinus had the *carceres* rebuilt in masonry, and placed seven stone eggs along the spina as markers for the number of circuits the chariots had run. In 33 BC, Agrippa had bronze dolphins set up for the same purpose. Caesar used the Circus for hunts, besides for competitions. The *pulvinar*, a sacred box reserved for the tutelary gods of the games, was added by Augustus on the side toward the Palatine; in 10 BC, the emperor had the obelisk of Rameses II, brought to Rome from Heliopolis, placed on the *spina*. Pope Sixtus V transferred the 23.70 meter high obelisk to Piazza del Popolo in 1587.

Claudius took a hand in restoration of the circus following a fire in 36 AD: he had the *carceres* rebuilt in marble and had the *metae* (the "goal posts," or conical extremes of the spina) covered in gilded bronze. The Circus was once more destroyed in the fire of 64 AD. Nero rebuilt it and increased the number of seats. Another fire under Domitian ravaged the construction; this time, rebuilding was completed by Trajan. Restoration work was carried out under Constantine; Constantius II embellished the spina with a second obelisk, that of Thutmosis II, which came from Thebes and was even higher than the first (32.50 meters). Sixtus V moved Thutmosis' obelisk as well, to Piazza San Giovanni in Laterano in 1587. The Circus measured 600 x 200 meters and had a capacity of 320,000 spectators. The most important of the events held there were the chariot races during the first week of September on occasion of the *Ludi Romani*, games which opened with a religious procession in which the highest religious and civil authorities of the city took part.

CASTEL SANT'ANGELO

Palazzo di Giustizia - **Castel Sant'Angelo** -
Via della Conciliazione

Aerial view of Ponte Sant'Angelo that provided access to Hadrian's Mausoleum.

Palazzo di Giustizia - Built between 1889 and 1910 to designs by Guglielmo Calderini, the building is characterized by the fact that the three-story central block is higher than those on either side, as well as by its imposing dimensions. The architecture is also set off by typical examples of monumental sculpture like the great *Quadriga* by Ettore Ximenes that crowns the principal block and the enormous statues (almost the equivalent of the ancient colossi) of the *Jurists* on the entrance ramps and the group with *Justice*, *Strength* and *Law* on the central portal.

Above, the facade of the Palazzo di Giustizia.

Castel Sant'Angelo - The massive fortress overlooking the Tiber and known as Castel Sant'Angelo was originally the mausoleum of the emperor Hadrian, designed and ordered built by Hadrian himself in 130 AD as his final resting place and that of all the members of the Antonine dynasty. The mausoleum was built on a square plan with the entrance in the form of a triumphal arch that gave access, through a long corridor and a capacious vestibule (still visible), to the overlying structures, which consisted in a gigantic cylindrical drum 65 meters in diameter surmounted by a square tower on which stood the gilded bronze sculptural group of a quadriga driven by the emperor in the guise of Helios, the sun god. The overall aspect of the construction was that of an immense tumulus grave, of Etruscan derivation and built on the model of the Mausoleum of Augustus, in which the main cylindrical

1 - Castel Sant'Angelo
(Hadrian's Mausoleum).
2 - Ponte Sant'Angelo.
3 - Ponte Vittorio Emanuele II.

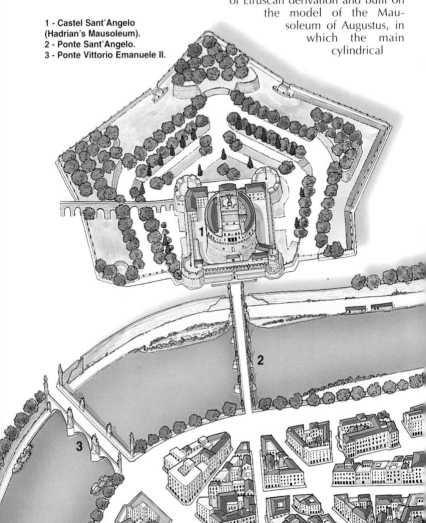

Castel Sant'Angelo from the bridge of the same name; below, the bronze statue of the Archangel Michael on the summit of the fortress.

portion of the structure was topped by a cone of earth planted in cypress and holm-oak. The sepulchral chamber at the center of the mausoleum, which housed the cinerary urns of the emperor and his family members and later those of all his successors up to Caracalla, was reached through a helicoidal gallery, the structure of which is still recognizable today despite later drastic remodeling. Even under Aurelian, in fact, the Hadrian's Mausoleum, while still preserving its role as a place of burial, had become part of the defensive system created to defend Ponte Helios, today's **Ponte Sant'Angelo**, which performed the function of access ramp to the mausoleum. In the meantime, certain of the structures had been torn down and the materials reused for construction of new buildings: the Parian marble blocks that sheathed the exterior disappeared, as did the colossal bronze peacocks, now in the Cortile del Belvedere in the Vatican, and the marble columns of the imperial sacellum, used in Saint Paul's Basilica. In about 520, Theodoric, who had for a short while moved the capital of his kingdom to Rome, transformed the building into a state prison, a role it was destined to play until 1901 (among others, Cellini and Cagliostro were held prisoners here). He also made it a fortress, to which use it was consecrated at the time of the Gothic War that bloodied Rome for a lengthy period. Some decades after the end of the conflict, in 590, the plague descended to afflict the city. Saint Gregory the Great was pope at

the time; one day, as he crossed the bridge in front of the mausoleum, he saw at the summit of the conical roof an angel sheathing a flaming sword, which he took as a sign that the epidemic would soon cease. From that moment on the mausoleum/fortress took the name of Castel Sant'Angelo, but only later, in 1544, was the episode commemorated with the installation of a marble statue of the *Archangel Michael* by Raffaello da Montelupo in the place the apparition had been seen. The original angel was replaced in 1752 by the bronze copy by Verschaffelt.

During the Middle Ages, the fortress became especially important for defense of the Vatican, above all from the ninth century, when Pope Leo IV made it an integral part of that system of walls that delimited the area known as the "Leonine City" and that connected it to many other buildings, including the nearby Vatican Palace. In the 13th century, under Pope Nicholas III, an overhead corridor was added along this stretch of the walls. Known as the "Passetto" or the Borgo Corridor, it was restructured and perfected in the following centuries to permit the popes to reach Castel Sant'Angelo (certainly a much safer place than the nearby palace) quickly in case of danger; the corridor was also used for secretly conducting prelates or nobles suspected of crimes into the prisons in the fortress. As part of the actions targeting improvement of the defens-

Views of the interior of Castel Sant'Angelo.

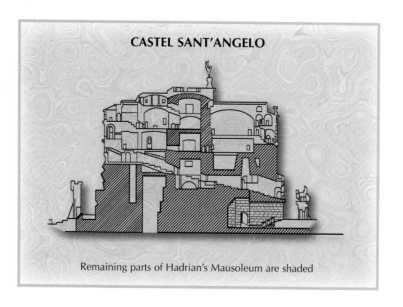

CASTEL SANT'ANGELO

Remaining parts of Hadrian's Mausoleum are shaded

es of the Leonine City carried out in the late 15th century, the first pope of the modern age, Alexander VI, had Giuliano da Sangallo reinforce the castle with construction of a four-sided surrounding with four octagonal corner towers named for the four evangelists, a series of new bastions, and a wide moat. A few years later, under Julius II, the marble loggia overlooking the Tiber was added; Paul III, fearing a Turkish invasion of the coasts of Latium, commissioned Antonio Sangallo the Younger to completely restore the defensive installations and to enlarge the papal apartments in the castle. The rooms were decorated by Perin del Vaga and his studio in the mid-sixteenth century with cycles of frescoes inspired by the history of the Church, as in the Sala Paolina (or Sala del Consiglio), and by figures from classical mythology, as in the rooms known as the Camera del Perseo and the Camera di Amore and Psyche. But for the most part, Castel Sant'Angelo still conserves the character of a fortress built for defense, with its armed bastions complete with batteries of cannon, the Armory of Clement X built by Bernini and later transformed into the Chapel of the Condannati (prisoners awaiting execution in the Courtyard of the Angel) the so-called "Oliare," large rooms and silos used to store foodstuffs for use in case of siege, and the parapet walk, which still today offers the visitor a full view of the Vatican and indeed a goodly portion of the city of Rome.

Via della Conciliazione - This broad prospective thoroughfare leading to the majestic Saint Peter's Basilica was created in 1937; its construction forced demolition of a great part of the old and characteristic group of buildings known as the Spina dei Borghi. A number of very interesting buildings face onto this great thoroughfare, the name of which celebrates the reconciliation between the Italian State and the Church. The 15th-century *Palazzo dei Penitenzieri*, built by Baccio Pontelli for cardinal Domenico della Rovere, has two tiers of cross-paned windows on the facade; of the large rooms inside, one is believed to have been frescoed by Pinturicchio. *Palazzo Torlonia*, dating to not much later, has a wide Renaissance facade, probably by Andrea Bregno, and a delightful courtyard with arcaded porticoes on square piers, decorated with statues. The Church of **Santa Maria in Traspontina**, begun by Sallustio Peruzzi and continued by Mascherino, has a spacious facade with two levels of pilasters; in it there open three large portals as well as niches and windows. The Latin-cross, single-nave interior has fine chapels on either side. In the first chapel on the right is a *Saint Barbara* by the Cavalier d'Arpino, and on the altar of the fifth chapel on the same side, a *Saint Albert* by Pomarancio.

Visited Here

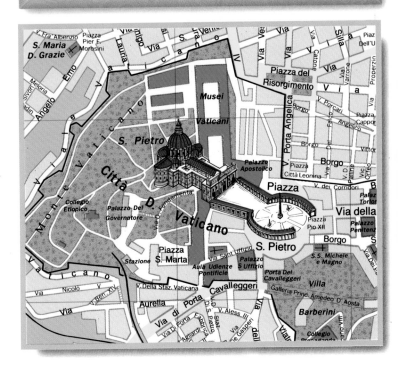

VATICAN CITY

Piazza San Pietro (Saint Peter's Square) - **Basilica di San Pietro in Vaticano (Saint Peter's Basilica)** - Vatican Grottoes - **Vatican Palaces** - **Vatican Museums** - **Raphael Rooms** - Raphael's Loggia - **Sistine Chapel** - Pinacoteca Vaticana

Vatican City - Vatican City lies between Monte Mario to the north and the Janiculum to the south. In Roman times, the area now covered by the small Vatican State was called the *Ager Vaticanus* and was occupied by a circus and by Nero's gardens. Since 1929, the year in which the Lateran Treaty was stipulated between the Holy See and the Italian State, Vatican City has been an independent sovereign state. The boundaries of this state, with a population that can be numbered in the hundreds, are defined by Via Porta Angelica, Piazza del Risorgimento, Via Leone IV, Viale Vaticano, Via della Sagrestia, and Piazza San Pietro. In addition to being the head of the Apostolic Roman Catholic Church, the pope has full legislative, executive and judiciary powers. Vatican City is completely independent of the Italian state, even though the two maintain extremely friendly relations. The Vatican prints its own stamps and has its own railroad station and a well-known Italian-language newspaper, the *Osservatore Romano*, which is distributed throughout Italy. The city also has its own security service (once called the "pontifical carabinieri") and a real police force: the famous "Swiss Guards" who since the early 16th cen-

Above, the insignia of the patron of the arts Pope Alexander VII, on the upper level of Bernini's colonnade in Saint Peter's Square.

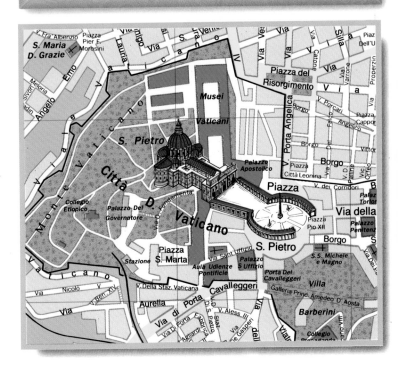

106

tury have protected the person of the pope and still wear the uniforms that were probably designed by Michelangelo.
Despite its small size, the Vatican is perhaps the world's single richest repository of works of the fine arts and architecture.

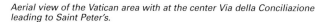

Piazza San Pietro (Saint Peter's Square) - A sacred setting, uniquely evocative and imbued with profound religious and symbolic connotations: Saint Peter's is perhaps the most famous square in the world. Since the Middle Ages it has welcomed and been a gathering place for countless multitudes of pilgrims come to visit Saint Peter's Basilica, the center of Christianity, offering a vital space for the functions of the religious life of the city. The square was built over a part of the ancient Vatican Circus (or Nero's Circus, though actually built by Caligula), of which there remains the so-called **Vatican Obelisk**, transported here in 37 BC from Alexandria, where it decorated Caesar's Forum. Called in medieval times the *aguglia*, it stood at length beside the basilica, until 1596, when Sixtus V ordered Carlo Maderno to move it to its present site. In 1613, Paul V bid the same Maderno build a **fountain** to its right; half a century later, a "twin" fountain by Carlo Fontana, placed symmetrically with respect to the first, was added. Again under Sixtus V, the original bronze globe that topped the obelisk (today in the Capitoline Museums) and that was believed to contain the ashes of Caesar was replaced with that pope's family emblem, the mountains and the star, topped by a crucifix containing a fragment of the Holy Cross of Christ's Crucifixion. In the mid-17th century, when the monumental work of rebuilding Saint Peter's Basilica was well-delineated, attention naturally shifted to the square before it. The fervent activity then being concluded provided the impetus for the sumptuous design of the square, which was built by Gian Lorenzo Bernini between 1656 and 1667. The triumphant spectacular feeling that through the genius of the Baroque architect and sculptor emerged in the execution of this immense masterpiece was not entirely dictated by artistic considerations; the design was also imbued with profound symbolic significance, to the point that the entire opus may be interpreted as a monumental allegory. The great portico that branches out from the facade of the basilica to form two hemicycles delineated by a double row of Tuscan columns supporting an entablature animated by a procession of statues of saints and the immense coats of arms of Alexander VII, under whose pontificate the opus was realized, is a symbolic embrace by the Church that would welcome and protect all the faithful of the world in this and in the next life. The vast elliptical space (240 meters in width), so theatrically defined by the two

Aerial view of the Vatican area with at the center Via della Conciliazione leading to Saint Peter's.

Saint Peter's Square and Basilica.

Saint Peter's Basilica.

hemicycles, is possessed of many symbolic references. Arisen as the last forum of Rome and dedicated to Christianity, it owes its form to that of the circuses of the ancient *Urbe*, and in particular to the Colosseum: the square may thus be said to play the role of historical *trait-d'union* between the early Church, persecuted in the figures of the martyrs who in the amphitheaters were put to death, and the glory of the Church triumphant, in which Christ and the saints portrayed in the statues are participants. But the elliptical form is also evocative of the Firmament, in which according to the theory of Copernicus, coeval with construction of the square, the planets describe such orbits, and of the Universe, understood as the space-time dimension in which the obelisk, which stands at the geometrical center of the ellipse and is the gnomon of an immense sundial, symbolizes the sun itself and alludes to the central figure of the pope, the Vicar of Christ on Earth.

Basilica di San Pietro in Vaticano (Saint Peter's Basilica) - In the classical period, Nero's Circus stood on what is now the site of Saint Peter's, between the Tiber, the Janiculum, and the Vatican hill. Saint Peter, the Prince of the Apostles, was martyred and then buried here in 64 AD. Pope Anacletus had a small *ad corpus* basilica, or a simple shrine, built here. In 324, the emperor Constantine replaced the presumably modest shrine with a true basilica, similar to many other churches built in Rome in that period. The original Saint Peter's was completed in 349 by Constantius, son of Constantine, and over the centuries was embellished and renovated by donations and the restoration work carried out by the popes and munificent princes. It was in Constantine's basilica that Charlemagne received the crown from the hands of Leo III in 800; Lothair, Louis II, and Frederick III were also crowned emperors after him. Even so, a thousand years after its foundation, Saint Peter's was falling into ruin. In 1452, Pope Nicholas V, on the advice of Leon Battista Alberti, appointed Bernardo Rossellino to renovate and enlarge the Basilica to the latter's plan. Various parts of the building were torn down and work on the new tribune was started, but soon abandoned when Nicholas V died in 1455. Work was not resumed until 1506, under Pope Julius II della Rovere, and this time the planned intervention was radical. Most of the original church was dismantled by Bramante (who earned himself the title of *maestro ruinante*), who intended building a "modern" building in the Classical style, from the ground up, on a Greek-cross plan inspired by the Pantheon. Various architects and works supervisors - Fra' Giocondo, Raphael, Giuliano da Sangallo, Baldassarre Peruzzi, and Antonio da Sangallo the Younger - succeeded each other until about the middle of the century until finally, in 1547, Michelangelo was appointed by Paul III. Needless to say, Michelangelo followed his own interpretation of Bramante's plan: he modified and simplified it in part, and designed a soaring dome (originally hemispherical) to crown the renovated basilica. Michelangelo was succeeded by Vignola, Pirro Ligorio, Giacomo Della Porta, and Domenico Fontana, all of whom interpreted Michelangelo's ideas quite faithfully. Then, under Paul V, it was decided to expand the basilica and return to the Latin cruciform plan. With this in mind, the architect Carlo Maderno added three chapels to each side of the building and brought the nave as far as the present facade, the building of which was entrusted to him when he won an important competition. Work on the facade was begun in November of 1607 and terminated in 1614, after having absorbed mountains of "travertine from Tivoli."

This **facade**, of truly grandiose proportions, is based on use of the giant Corinthian order, with columns and pilasters that on the ground floor frame a large central porch with an arch on either side (the one on the left, the so-called *Arch of the*

View from above of Saint Peter's Square and Via della Conciliazione.

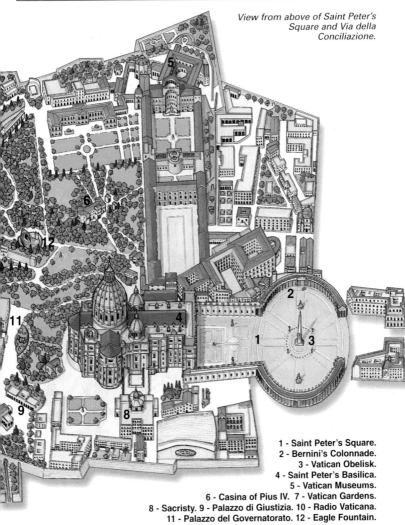

1 - Saint Peter's Square.
2 - Bernini's Colonnade.
3 - Vatican Obelisk.
4 - Saint Peter's Basilica.
5 - Vatican Museums.
6 - Casina of Pius IV. 7 - Vatican Gardens.
8 - Sacristy. 9 - Palazzo di Giustizia. 10 - Radio Vaticana.
11 - Palazzo del Governatorato. 12 - Eagle Fountain.

Bells, leads to Vatican City proper) and, above, a row of nine balconies. The crowning element is an attic surmounted by a balustrade which supports thirteen enormous statues, representing *Christ, Saint John the Baptist* and all of the *Apostles* except Saint Peter. Above everything, partially masked by the facade, looms **Michelangelo's** magnificent **dome** with its strong ribbing, and, emerging from the front but to the sides, the "minor" domes of the Gregorian and the Clementine chapels by Giacomo Barozzi da Vignola. After the death of Carlo Maderno in 1629, the next director of works was Gian Lorenzo Bernini, who left his unmistakable mark on the building: the prevalently Baroque character it now displays was his doing. It is sufficient to mention the decorative transformation of the nave and the aisles, the erection of the justly-famous bronze *Baldacchino* (begun in 1624 and inaugurated on Saint Peter's Day in 1633) over the Papal Altar, the decoration of the piers of the dome with four large statues, and, of course, the placing of the *Throne of Saint Peter* at the back of the apse. This is one of Bernini's most sumptuous inventions, a truly marvelous machine built around the old wooden chair which a pious tradition says was used by the apostle Peter. The layout of Saint Peter's Square, once more by Bernini, also dates to the papacy of Alexander VII (who financed the works for the throne). It was instead under Clement X that the architect designed and built the small round temple which is the tabernacle of the Chapel of the Sacrament. Any number of chapels, all splendid in one way or the other, line the perimeter of Saint Peter's Basilica: to begin with, the **Chapel of the Pietà**, named after Michelangelo's famous marble sculpture of the *Pietà* made between 1499 and 1500, when the artist was still a young man, for Cardinal Jean de Bilhères. After the **Chapel of Saint Sebastian** (which contains Francesco Messina's *Monument to Pope Pius XII*) comes the better-known **Chapel of the Holy Sacra-**

The facade of Saint Peter's. Facing page: above, the exterior of the grandiose dome by Michelangelo; below, the interior of the dome.

PAVLVS·V·BVRGHESIVS·ROMANVS·PONT·MAX·A

ment, with the *tabernacle* by Bernini and the elaborate bronze railings designed by Borromini; next is the **Gregorian Chapel**, a late 16th-century work completed by Giacomo della Porta and heavily decorated with mosaics and precious marbles; the **Colonna Chapel**, with its astounding marble altarpiece of *Leo the Great Halting Attila* by Algardi and the *tombs* of many popes named for the saint - Leo II, III, IV, XII; the Clementine Chapel, named after Pope Clement VIII, built for him by Giacomo della Porta, which houses the mortal remains of Saint Gregory the Great; also by Della Porta, the sumptuous **Chapel of the Choir**, decorated with gilded stuccoes; finally, the **Chapel of the Presentation**, with the recent *Monument to Pope John XXIII* by Emilio Greco.

Saint Peter's Basilica infact contains a whole collection of famous monuments, from Michelangelo's *Pietà* to the venerated 13th-century effigy of *Saint Peter* shown in the act of blessing, to Bernini's *funeral monument to Pope Urban VIII*, the analogous *funeral monument to Pope Paul III*, by Guglielmo Della Porta, the *bronze tomb* created by Antonio Pollaiolo for Pope Innocent VIII and which was originally in the old Saint Peter's, and the Neoclassical *Stuart Monument* by Canova.

Brief mention must also be made of the *baptismal font*, in porphyry, that was once part of a classical sarcophagus (later used as the sepulcher for Otto II) and was adapted to its present use by Carlo Fontana.

The great **sacristy** rises before the left transept. As large as a church, and in fact originally conceived as an independent building, the sacristy consists of the **Sagrestia Comune** on an octagonal central plan, the so-called **Sacristy of the Canons**, and the **Chapter Hall**. It was all designed by the Roman architect Carlo Marchionni at the behest of Pius VI, who laid the first stone in 1776.

Annexed to the basilica is the **Museo della Fabbrica di San Pietro**, or Historical Artistic Museum, which includes the *Treasury of Saint Peter's*. It was designed by Giovan Battista Giovenale and contains what remains of the enormous artistic patrimony of the church which was repeatedly broken up and carried off during the Saracen raids, the Sack of Rome in 1527, and the Napoleonic confiscations.

went Here

The interior of Saint Peter's Basilica. Below, the majestic nave; right, Bernini's bronze Baldacchino.

Details of the interior of the basilica: above, the bronze statue of Saint Peter *attributed to Arnolfo di Cambio; top right, Bernini's* Monument to Alexander VII; *bottom right, the* Tomb of Saint Peter *containing the mortal remains of the apostle. Below, Michelangelo's* Pietà, *in the first chapel to the right entering the basilica.*

Vatican Grottoes - The grottoes, situated under the nave of Saint Peter's Basilica, contain the tombs of many popes, as well as early Christian sarcophagi, architectural fragments and various monuments from the Basilica. The area embraces two sections, known as the "New Grottoes" and the "Old Grottoes."

New Grottoes. At the beginning of our tour is a finely-executed 8th-century mosaic of the *Madonna Enthroned with the Child and Two Worshipers*. There follow a number of chapels: the *Chapel of Saints Cyril and Methodius*; the *Polish Chapel*; the *Chapel of San Columbanus*; the *Lithuanian Chapel*; the *Chapel of the Partorienti*, with on the altar a 15th-century fresco of the *Madonna and Child* attributed to Melozzo da Forlì; the *Chapel of the Bocciata* with a 14th-century fresco of the *Madonna and Child* over the altar; and the four chapels corresponding to the statues of the pilasters - *Veronica, Saint Andrew, Saint Longinus,* and *Saint Helena*. Facing *Saint Peter's Chapel*, or the *Clementine Chapel*, richly decorated with paintings and stuccowork attributed to G. B. Maini (18th century), is the *tomb of Pope Pius XII Pacelli*. Next is a series of *statues of the apostles* sculpted by Matteo del Pollaiolo, Giovanni Dalmata, and Mino da Fiesole.

Old Grottoes. The itinerary begins with an estimable 15th-century high relief of the *Madonna Enthroned with the Child and Saints Peter and Paul* by Isaia da Pisa; next is the quite linear structure of the *tomb of Pope Pius VI*, the *tomb of Pope John XXIII*, the "Good Pope," under a 15th-century relief of the *Virgin and Child*. Following, on the left, is the *tomb of Queen Christina of Sweden*, while on the right is the *tomb of Queen Carlotta of Savoy*. Then come the *tombs of Popes Marcellus II, Innocent IX, and Julius III*. The Old Grottoes stretch on and on, but the rest of the area is not open to the public.

Saw This 115

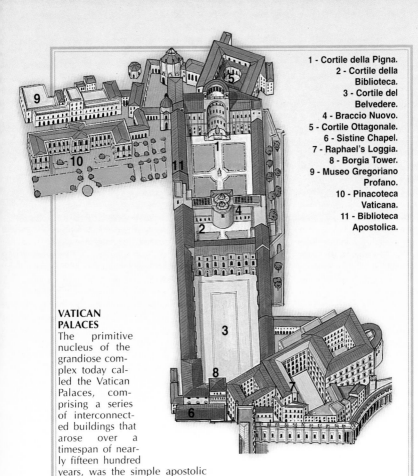

1 - Cortile della Pigna.
2 - Cortile della Biblioteca.
3 - Cortile del Belvedere.
4 - Braccio Nuovo.
5 - Cortile Ottagonale.
6 - Sistine Chapel.
7 - Raphael's Loggia.
8 - Borgia Tower.
9 - Museo Gregoriano Profano.
10 - Pinacoteca Vaticana.
11 - Biblioteca Apostolica.

VATICAN PALACES

The primitive nucleus of the grandiose complex today called the Vatican Palaces, comprising a series of interconnected buildings that arose over a timespan of nearly fifteen hundred years, was the simple apostolic residence built by Pope Symmachus in the early sixth century. This building, of which no visible trace remains today, since it was progressively transformed and encompassed into later buildings, was initially only a temporary abode for the popes (who at the time resided on a stable basis in Palazzo del Laterano) during their visits to the Basilica of Saint Peter, to which it was adjacent.

The small papal palace was later enlarged and grew in importance, to the point that in the 9th and 10th centuries it hosted the emperors Charlemagne and Otto I, who came to Rome for their coronation ceremonies in the Vatican basilica. The site had in fact been made extremely secure by the raising of the sturdy circle of walls ordered by Leo IV as protection for the space in which both the basilica and the papal residence arose; the area thus delimited took the name of Città Leonina. Nevertheless, the course taken by history was such that in the following centuries the "city" progressively fell into a state of abandon, until extensive restoration work became necessary. This began only in the twelfth century under Eugenius II and Celestine III. During the thirteenth century, it was thought to further enlarge the structure, with the aim of transforming it into the permanent residence of the popes. The project, the most fervent supporter of which was Pope Innocent III, was dictated above all by the site's position, which was better defensible thanks to the presence of the walls of the Città Leonina and the proximity of Castel Sant' Angelo, to which the apostolic palace was linked at the end of the century through the so-called **Passetto** or **Borgo Corridor** built by order of Nicholas III. It was, however, not until the following century that popes resided in the Vatican on a stable basis. On 17 January 1377, Gregory XI, the first pope to return to Rome following the period spent in exile by the highest ecclesiastical orders of the Church in Avignon, took up residence in the Vatican and proclaimed it the permanent seat of the papacy. For the rest of the 14th and all through the 15th century, the complex underwent a seemingly endless series of actions targeting the transformation and enlargement of the existing structures and construction of new buildings. The plan for a new **Vatican Palace** took form under Nicholas V, who in 1450 enlarged the papal palace and transferred his court there.

By incorporating the fourteenth-century buildings, he gave rise to a grandiose building on a quadrangular plan that developed around the **Cortile del Pappagallo**. The building consisted of many rooms, in the decoration of which there participated the greatest masters of the time, including Andrea del Castagno and Piero della Francesca. The new palace also had its chapel, today called the **Chapel of Nicholas V**, frescoed by Beato Angelico with *Scenes from the Lives of Saints Stephen and Laurence.* On the ground floor, many of the rooms overlooking the courtyard became the primitive nucleus of the Vatican Library founded by the same pope in 1451. Twenty or so years later, Sixtus IV ordered renovation and entrusted decoration of the rooms to Melozzo da Forlì and Ghirlandaio. In 1473, Sixtus IV also commissioned Giovanni De' Dolci to build a chapel for the papal ceremonies, which took his name: the **Sistine Chapel**.

The decoration of its interior was carried out by artists of the Tuscan and Umbrian schools, notably Botticelli, Pinturicchio and Perugino, who in the period 1481-1483 adorned it with the *Life of Moses* and the *Life of Christ.* The building begun under Nicholas V was completed only by Alexander VI Borgia, who in the late 1400s had built what are today called the **Borgia Apartments**, composed of six rooms, three in the apostolic residence itself and three in the **Borgia Tower**. The decoration of this section was entrusted to Pinturicchio and his school. The various rooms take their names from the frescoes: in the Sybilline Room, the Umbrian artist and his disciples painted the figures of the *sibyls* and the *prophets* that announced the advent of the Messiah; the decoration of the Room of the Creed instead centers on the profession of the Christian faith, with the figures of *prophets* and *apostles* carrying the articles of the faith; in the Liberal Arts Room, Antonio da Viterbo painted the *Arts of the Trivium* (*Grammar, Rhetoric, and Logic*) and of the *Quadrivium* (*Geometry, Arithmetic, Music, Astronomy*) in panels decorated with the heraldic emblems of the Borgia family; the Saints' Room, a masterpiece by Pinturicchio, is decorated with scenes from the lives of the saints and martyrs of the Church; the Room of the Mysteries of the Faith was also decorated by Pinturicchio and his disciples; the Pontiffs' Room was completely restructured following its collapse in 1500 and decorated with stuccos and frescoes by Giovanni da Udine and Perin del Vaga. Before the work ordered by Alexander VI, in the years 1484-1492, Pope Innocent VIII had commissioned Giacomo da Pietrasanta to build what is now called the **Palazzetto del Belvedere** in the highest part of the Belvedere valley but aligned with the Vatican Palace, as a place of rest and meditation in the green cornice of the slopes of the Vatican hill.

And this was the way things stood when Julius II ascended the papal throne in 1503: two palaces about 300 meters distance the one from the other, which to Julius' energetic eye simply begged to be united to form a single complex. The Della Rovere pope charged Bramante, at the time superintendent of the construction

The Apollo del Belvedere *in the Gabinetto di Apollo near the Cortile Ottagonale.*

work for the rebuilding of Saint Peter's Basilica, with carrying out this operation. The architect from the Marches region thus designed two extremely long **Galleries** with porticoes overhead (completed under Pius IV and Gregory XIII and later reserved for the Musei Vaticani) to link the two buildings. There was thus created an enormous central courtyard called the **Cortile del Belvedere**. The internal facade of the Palazzetto was modified through construction of a tiered exedra, transformed in the mid-1500s by Pirro Ligorio into an enormous niche that was long believed (erroneously) to be the work of Bramante. By Bramante's hand, instead, was **Saint Damasus' Court**, born from the enlargement of the Palazzo Vaticano and distinguished by three superposed orders of arches completed by Raphael after the death of Bramante in 1514, and by frescoes by Raphael and his followers, among whom Giulio Romano, Perin del Vaga and Polidoro da Caravaggio. Twelve of the thirteen vaulted bays that make up this harmonious, airy arched corridor called **Raphael's Loggia** were decorated with *Scenes from the Old Testament*, while the thirteenth shows episodes taken from the *New Testament*. Raphael also decorated a number of rooms in the interior of the Palazzo Vaticano, now called the **Raphael Rooms** in his honor, which Julius II has previously entrusted to the hand of other artists of great value such as Lorenzo Lotto, Perugino and Sodoma. In the same period, Julius II commissioned Michelangelo to decorate the **Sistine Chapel**; between 1508 and 1512 he frescoed the ceiling and the lunettes above the windows. For the former, the great Tuscan artist chose subjects taken from the Old Testament, and in particular from the Book of Genesis, all turning on the central episode of the **Creation of Adam**, while in the lunettes he painted the **Ancestors of Christ**, the figures of the Hebrew families awaiting His Coming. The work begun under Julius II continued through the papacy of his successor, Leo X, who definitively affixed the seal of the Florentine Renaissance to the structures of the Vatican complex. Between 1534 and 1549, under Pope Paul III Farnese, the Sistine Chapel was completed with that immense masterpiece by Michelangelo entitled the **Last Judgement**, built around the figure of the Christ of the elect and of the damned. The pope also wanted to create another reserved place of worship besides the Sistine Chapel, which had become the seat of the conclaves, and so in 1540 he charged Antonio da Sangallo the Younger with the building of what is today called the **Pauline Chapel**. It is home to the last two of the great frescoes by Michelangelo, the *Conversion of Saint Paul* and the *Crucifixion of Saint Peter*. The same year, Sangallo began construction of the so-called **Sala Regia**, decorated by many artists including Perin del Vaga, Daniele da Volterra and Vasari, who worked in the chapel after its completion, in 1573.

Paul III's successors down through Sixtus V dedicated their energies to restoration and remodeling, almost entirely under the direction of Pirro Ligorio; the activity culminated under Gregory XIII with the construction of the east-facing wing of the Vatican Palace along the side of Saint Damasus' Court.

The enlargement of the parts of the palace facing the Borgo and Saint Peter's Square was instead the result of restructuring work ordered by Sixtus V, who

The exterior of the building that houses the Pinacoteca Vaticana.

between 1587 and 1588 had Bramante's Cortile del Belvedere cut almost in half by commissioning Fontana to erect the across its length the wing of the **Biblioteca Apostolica Vaticana**, to which he transferred the Vatican's rich collection of manuscripts, engravings, maps, codices, incunabula and prints, previously housed in the ground-floor rooms of the Borgia Apartments.

Two distinct courtyards were thus formed: the first, up against the Vatican Palace, that kept the denomination **Cortile del Belvedere**, and a second, under Innocent VIII's Palazzetto, that took the name of **Cortile della Pigna** after the ancient Roman fountain in the form of a bronze *"pine cone,"* discovered near the Baths of Agrippa and the Temple of Isis and Serapis near Santa Maria sopra Minerva, that was installed on the landing of the stairs to the Palazzetto; it is flanked by two *peacocks*, likewise in bronze, that are thought to be part of the decoration of the Hadrian's Mausoleum. In the 1600s, the complex of apostolic buildings thus defined underwent the first series interventions sponsored by Clement VIII, to whom we owe the further enlargement of the Vatican Palace with the creation of the **Sala del Concistoro**, completed in 1603, and the so-called **Sala Clementina**, used as the antechamber for papal audiences. A second round of works was promoted by Urban VIII, who commissioned Bernini to design the **Scala Regia**, completed under Alexander VII, and the **Sala Ducale**. The latest modifications to the Vatican palaces in order of time regard mainly their transformation into a museum complex. This sort of intervention began in the late 18th century, at a time when interest in archaeology and the Classical antiquities was very high.

Thus the restructuring of the existing buildings and the construction of new structures again changed the face of the complex, at least to a certain extent: the Palazzetto del Belvedere was enlarged and transformed into the Museo Pio-Clementino, one of Bramante's Galleries was restructured to make it a suitable home for the Museo Chiaramonti, and the Etruscan and Egyptian museums were founded. Notable among these actions is that by Pope Pius VII: in 1817, in order to create a place for certain of the works in the collection of classical antiquities, he commissioned the architect Raffaele Stern to build the **Braccio Nuovo**, a gallery running parallel to the wing of the Biblioteca Apostolica Vaticana. This construction further divided the Cortile del Belvedere, creating a third space known as the **Cortile della Biblioteca**. In the second half of the 19th century, under Pope Pius IX, one wing of Raphael's Loggia was completed and called the **Loggia di Pio IX**; the same pope also ordered construction, in 1860, of the **Scala Pia** that leads to the Borgo Corridor. And restructuring continued into the 20th century: Pius XI enlarged the rooms destined to house the Pinacoteca Vaticana, and in 1932 ordered the monumental entrance to the Musei Vaticani; John XXIII and Paul VI, in the 1960s and 1970s, created new structures that now host the Palazzo del Laterano collections.

Detail of the relief of the Good Shepherd and harvest scenes on an early-Christian sarcophagus in the Vatican Museums.

VATICAN MUSEUMS

From the very first, the complex that is today called the Palazzi Vaticani and that is the result of a long process of construction and transformation has hosted splendid collections of art assembled by the various popes. The supreme pontiffs also enriched the collections by patronizing the arts and employed entire generations of Italian and foreign artists in the creation of masterpieces on commission. The many collections, from those of Greek, Roman, Etruscan and Egyptian antiquities to those of books and paintings (the latter now in the celebrated **Pinacoteca Vaticana**) slowly filled the available rooms, halls and galleries as they were built - and in many cases provided the impetus for their construction. The arrangement of the collections has changed over the centuries in relation both to the increase in available space and to changes in the criteria in vogue for the organization and cataloging of works in museums. And the buildings gradually became museums to all effects; the first step in this direction was taken in the latter half of the eighteenth century by Clement XIV, who transformed the Palazzetto del Belvedere into the museum that following the reorganization ordered by Clement's successor Pius VI took the name of **Museo Pio-Clementino**. In the first half of the following century, that passion for archaeology and antiquity that was a hallmark of Neoclassical taste induced two popes, Pius VII and Gregory XVI, to create one of the cardinal institutions of the Vatican museum complex: the former was responsible for the foundation of the **Museo Chiaramonti**, to the decoration of which even Canova contributed and for which the so-called Braccio Nuovo was expressly built in 1816; the latter, instead, organized the **Museo Gregoriano Etrusco** and the **Museo Gregoriano Egizio** in seventeen rooms. Later on in the nineteenth century, Pope Leo XIII, to whom we owe restoration of numerous of the myriad parts making up the Vatican complex, opened to the public many rooms which theretofore had been reserved for the pope and the highest members of the ecclesiastical hierarchy. The first such revelation was the Borgia Apartments, the rooms of which later became the seat of the **Collection of Modern Religious Art** inaugurated by Pope Paul VI in 1973. The creation of new museums went on all through the twentieth century: John XXIII had both the **Museo Missionario-Etnologico**, instituted in 1926 to house the material exhibited at the Missionary Exhibit of the 1925 Jubilee, and the **Museo Pio Cristiano**, founded in 1854 by Pius IX to organize the paintings, inscriptions, reliefs and sculptures from the catacombs and the ancient Roman basilicas, moved to the Vatican from their original rooms in the San Giovanni in Laterano complex.

MUSEO GREGORIANO EGIZIO

The collection of Egyptian antiquities was organized in 1839 at the behest of Pope Gregory XVI, but Pius VII had already begun this interesting collection at the beginning of the century. Today the museum, although it cannot compare to the Egyptian museums in Cairo, Florence, Paris, Turin, Berlin or London, houses an important group of finds in its ten rooms. Of particular note are two colossal statues of the *goddess Sekhmet* (1408-1372 BC), a splendid colossal statue of the *queen Thuya* (1280 BC), the head of the pharaoh *Mentuhotep* (2054-2008 BC), three large statues of *Ptolemy II* (285-274 BC) as well as mummies from various periods, funerary urns, anthropoid sarcophagi, and basalt statuettes of naophoroi (priest bearing a small temple).
Some of the rooms of the Egyptian Museum offer fine views of the **Cortile della Pigna**.

MUSEO PIO-CLEMENTINO

In 1771, Clement XIV organized the first of the Vatican museums, when in the rooms of the Palazzetto del Belvedere he installed the primitive Renaissance nucleus of the collection of antique statuary theretofore preserved in the **Cortile Ottagonale** designed by Bramante and enlarged by Michelangelo Simonetti in 1773. Pope Clement's successor Pius VI further enlarged the collection and expanded the space occupied by the museum into other parts of the Vatican complex. Close by the Cortile Ottagonale, in what is called the **Gabinetto di Apollo**, stands one of the sculptures that most aroused the interest of scholars of antiquities, such as Winckelmann and Goethe: the celebrated *Apollo del Belvedere*, a fascinating work attributed to Leocares and discovered in the 1400s near the church of San Pietro in Vincoli. The **Gabinetto dell'Apoxyomenos** owes its name to another masterpiece of ancient sculpture, a Roman copy of a work by Lysippos of an athlete scraping the sweat from his body, unearthed in the mid-1800s in Trastevere. The **Gabinetto del Laocoonte** is instead the home of the sculptural group found in the 1500s in Nero's Domus Aurea and inspired by the famous episode of the Trojan War in which the priest Laocoön and his sons are strangled by two serpents sent by Athena after the failure of the Trojan horse hoax, revealed by the priest. The work enormously influenced the art of the late Renaissance, above all that of Michelangelo. The **Gabinetto dell'Hermes** owes its name to a copy, dating to the time of Hadrian, of a statue by Praxiteles portraying the god in the guise of psychopompos; that is, the conductor of the souls of the dead on their journey to the afterworld. The statue that lends its name to the **Gabinetto del Perseo** is, instead, of Neoclassical matrix; it was sculpted in 1800 by Antonio Canova and was inspired by the *Apollo del Belvedere*. Pius VI commissioned the **Sala degli Animali** of Michelangelo Simonetti in 1776: here were laid out exhibits of sculptures and fragments of Roman mosaics having animals as their subjects. The most famous piece in this highly singular collection is the Roman copy of Skopas' statue portraying Meleager with a dog and the head of a wild boar. Innocent VIII enlarged the Palazzetto with the aim of creating new exhibit spaces, among which the **Galleria delle Statue**, to provide a home for many noteworthy sculptural works such as the *Sleeping Ariadne*, the *Resting Satyr* and the *Barberini Candelabra*. Besides the Sala degli Animali mentioned above, Simonetti also built other rooms, in which he used perspective effects to exalt the works of art they contain. This is the case of the **Sala delle Muse**, home to the celebrated *Belvedere Torso* that inspired Michelangelo's nudes in the Sistine Chapel, of the **Sala Rotonda**, where we find the *Otricoli Jupiter* and the colossal gilded bronze statue of *Hercules*, of the **Sala a Croce Greca**, custodian of the *sarcophagus of Constantia*, Constantine's daughter, and that of *Saint Helena*, the emperor's mother, and of the **Gabinetto delle Maschere**, home to the famous *Venus of Cnidos*. Clement XIV had previously readapted certain rooms in the building to host the collections; this is the case of the **Galleria dei Busti**, which exhibits examples of imperial Roman lapidary portraiture among the world's most famous; for example, the busts of *Caracalla*, of *Caesar*, and of *Augustus*.

The Crux Vaticana, *in the Treasury of Saint Peter's. It is a reliquary set with precious stones, dating to the second half of the 6th century, donated by the emperor of Byzantium Justin II. On the arms of the cross is the dedication to the emperor and his wife Sophia.*

MUSEO CHIARAMONTI

The **Museo Chiaramonti**, founded by order of Pius VII (Barnaba Chiaramonti) in the early 1800s and laid out by Antonio Canova, was arranged in the first portion of the eastern gallery designed by Bramante to link the Palazzetto del Belvedere with the Palazzo Vaticano, and was then extended into the **Galleria Lapidaria**, created to provide a home for the Vatican's profuse collection of inscriptions on stone, and into the **Braccio Nuovo**, built expressly to house the works which were excluded from the spaces offered by the other galleries. In a space decorated in strict accordance with the canons of Neoclassical art, the first section of the museum presents various exhibits of Roman statuary of Greek inspiration: gods of Olympus, like the statue of *Athena*, a copy of a Greek original by the school of Myron, alternate with portrayals of mythical heroes, like the *Hercules with his Son Telephos*, and portraits of figures of Roman times, such as that of a *priest of Isis*, also known as *Scipio Africanus*, or the anonymous *male head* veiled in the typical garb of the ritual sacrifices. The Galleria Lapidaria, accessible only for reasons of study, instead offers a sweeping panorama of pagan and Christian inscriptions, most of which come from necropoli and catacombs. The collection, begun by Clement XIV for the famous epigraphist Gaetano Marini, was augmented by Pius VI and Pius VII. The Braccio Nuovo, built by Stern in 1817 across the Cortile Belvedere and parallel to the

*Two celebrated frescoes by Raphael in the Stanza della Segnatura: above,
The* School of Athens; *below,* The Dispute of the Blessed Sacraments.

gallery of the Biblioteca Apostolica, is another wide and luminous gallery interrupted at its center by a vast hall with an apse, in which are placed a number of
masterpieces of Roman statuary. Of special note among these is the so-called
Augustus of Prima Porta, showing the emperor, wearing a finely-engraved suit of
armor, in the act of haranguing his subjects and with a cherub, the symbol of
Venus, protector goddess of the *gens* Julia, at his feet; the statue of the *Nile*, which
together with that representing the *Tiber* (now in the Louvre) adorned the Temple
of Isis and Serapis and was discovered in the early 1500s near Santa Maria sopra
Minerva; and the celebrated *Doryphoros*, a copy of the bronze original by Polycleitus, with its perfect and harmonious proportions.

GALLERY OF THE CANDELABRA

This room is named after the marble *candelabra* placed to the sides of the arches along the long corridor. The vaults were frescoed by Torti and Seitz in the
19th century.
The Gallery contains major works of art from the Classical period, including a
splendid *Sleeping Satyr*, a *Boy Playing with Nuts*, the 2nd-century *Diana of the
Ephesians*, an exquisite *sarcophagus* with the *Slaughter of the Niobids*, a charming statue of an *Old Fisherman* and a 3rd-century BC *Fighting Persian*, both by
artists of the Pergamene School, and other interesting works of this period.

MUSEO GREGORIANO ETRUSCO

In the first half of the nineteenth century, interest in Etruscan studies and investigation of the Italic populations of the pre-Roman era led to the organization of a campaign of systematic excavations, many of which were conducted at sites in the Papal State of the time in areas such as Cerveteri, Tarquinia, Vulci, and Veii. The finds were cataloged and arranged in a museum instituted especially for that purpose in 1837 by Gregory XVI; the collection later grew by donations and other acquisitions. The layout of the museum begins with series of interesting *funerary urns* documenting the Iron Age civilizations in Etruria and Latium. A complete tomb has been reassembled from the material found in the *Regolini-Galassi Tomb* to show what normally accompanied the dead; objects in bronze, ceramic and bucchero vases (bucchero was a typically Etruscan black clay mixture), and finely-worked gold pieces. The museum also contains exquisite examples of the urns in which the Etruscans preserved the ashes of their dead: that called the *Calabresi Urn*, dating from the 7th century BC, is outstanding. The *Mars di Todi* is instead a precious illustration of the heights reached by this culture in the art of bronze casting. But the major attraction of the museum is its collection of ceramics, containing vases of various types, either decorated with figures or simply crafted in one-tone clay, and in particular the superb **Benedetto Guglielmi Collection** that which brings together interesting ancient black- and red-figured vases.

GALLERY OF TAPESTRIES

Of particular note among the numerous tapestries kept here are those of the so-called *New School*, woven in the manufactory of Pieter van Aelst in Brussels from cartoons by Raphael's pupils. These ten masterpieces were exhibited for the first time in the Sistine Chapel in 1531.

GALLERY OF MAPS

In this 16th-century room, 120 meters in length, are displayed *40 maps* (eight of them on the two short sides of the gallery) of various regions of Italy and the territories that belonged to the Church. Antonio Danti was commissioned by Pope Gregory XIII to paint them in 1580-1583 to cartoons by his brother Ignazio Danti, a well-known cosmographer and architect.

ROOMS OF PIUS V

The **Gallery of Pius V**, decorated with late-15th and 16th century tapestries from the workshops of Tournai and Brussels, respectively, leads to the two **Rooms of Pius V** and the **chapel** reserved for the members of the Pope's family. The chapel is dedicated to Saint Michael, and decorated with frescoes in the vault (Federico Zuccari) and above the altar (Giorgio Vasari).

RAPHAEL ROOMS

The master began frescoing what are now known as the **Stanze di Raffaello** (Raphael Rooms) in 1509. The work, which continued into the following years under Leo X, revolves around themes that celebrate the power of Faith and the Church. The first room to be frescoed was the Stanza della Segnatura, or Signature Room, called thus because it was here that the pope signed official documents; Raphael's sure touch gleams from all the frescoes in this magnifi-

The Expulsion of Heliodorus from the Temple, *a splendid work by Raphael that lends it name to the Room of Heliodorus.*

cent room, from the *Dispute of the Blessed Sacraments*, depicting the glorification of the Eucharist, to the *School of Athens*, where within a grandiose architectural frame the wise men and the philosophers of ancient times are set side by side with the seigneurs and the artists of the Renaissance cultural scene, all gathered around the figures of Plato and Aristotle, and to the *Parnassus*, an allegorical celebration of the arts impersonated by the mythological figures of the Muses and the pagan gods. In the alternating medallions and panels of the ceiling, almost as though to offer a symbolic compendium of the frescoes on the walls below, Raphael painted a number of allegorical representations of the Sciences and the Arts (*Theology, Justice, Philosophy, Poetry, Astronomy*) together with emblematic episodes referred to them (*Adam and Eve*, the *Judgement of Solomon, Apollo and Marsyas*). Between 1512 and 1514, Raphael worked on the decoration of the Room of Heliodorus, where he frescoed historical episodes in accordance with an iconographic program dictated by Julius II: *Leo I Halting Attila*, alluding to the Battle of Ravenna in 1512 at which the future Leo X defeated the French; the *Miracle at Bolsena*, illustrating the institution of the Corpus Domini by Urban IV and also calling to mind the vow made by Julius II before the siege of Bologna; the biblical episode of the *Expulsion of Heliodorus from the Temple*, which refers to the pope's struggle against the enemies of the Church; and finally the *Liberation of Saint Peter*, alluding to the liberation of Leo X, who was imprisoned following the Battle of Ravenna. The next two years were dedicated to the Room of the Fire in the Borgo, which takes its name from the principal fresco, *The Borgo Fire of 847 AD,* inspired by the figure of Leo IV who quenched the fire by making the sign of the Cross. This fresco and the other three in the room (the *Battle of Ostia*, the *Oath of Leo III*, the *Coronation of Charlemagne*), executed almost entirely by Raphael's pupils under the strict guidance of the master, make specific reference to the illustrious predecessors of Leo X, during whose pontificate the room was decorated, who bore his same name.

The Sala dei Palafrenieri also contained wall paintings by Raphael, which were destroyed and later replaced by other frescoes ordered by Gregory XIII in the late 1500s. The decoration of the Hall of Constantine, instead, is certainly the work of one of Raphael's most important followers, Giulio Romano. Following the death of the master he led a team of artists who illustrated in fresco episodes from the life of Constantine: the *Baptism of Constantine*, the *Battle of the Milvian Bridge*, the *Apparition of the Cross*, and *Constantine's Donation*.

RAPHAEL'S LOGGIA

One of the most significant corners in the entire Vatican palace complex, the lovely, airy loggia was begun by Bramante but terminated by Raphael in about 1518. Twelve of the 13 bays with pavilion vaults (an inspired architectural solution) are frescoed with scenes from the *Old Testament*, while the last is decorated with stories of the *New Testament*.

The frescoes, all exhibiting an extreme freshness and an imaginative use of perspective, are the work of some of Raphael's most illustrious pupils, such as Giulio Romano, Polidoro da Caravaggio, Giovanni da Udine, Perin del Vaga, Pellegrino Aretusi da Modena, and Vincenzo da San Gimignano.

COLLECTION OF MODERN RELIGIOUS ART

The rooms of the **Borgia Apartment**, where the popes resided until 1507, were adapted in the early nineteenth century to host the Pinacoteca Vaticana and later housed a section of the Biblioteca Apostolica. It was Paul VI who in 1973 finally decided that these and other spaces within the Vatican, for a total of fifty rooms, should be renovated to accommodate the many works of modern and contemporary art donated to the Vatican by artists and collectors from every corner of the globe and all depictions of religious subjects or illustrations of episodes from the Bible and the Gospels.

The collection, which soon became one of the world's most prestigious in the sector, includes masterpieces by such Italian painters as Modigliani, De Pisis, Manzù, Carrà, Morandi, Guttuso, Sironi, Rosai, Cagli, Fontana, Marini, Purificato, De Chirico, Balla, and Boccioni, as well as by such foreign masters as Matisse, Rodin, Dalì, Chagall, Klee, Utrillo, Kokoschka, Picasso, Kandinsky, and Braque.

(SISTINE CHAPEL)

Between 1475 and 1481, under Pope Sixtus IV Della Rovere, Giovannino de' Dolci built what may be called the "Chapel of Chapels" to plans by Baccio Pontelli. Architecturally, the Sistine Chapel is a spacious rectangular hall with a barrel vault, divided into two unequal parts by a splendid marble *transenna* or screen by Mino da Fiesole, Giovanni Dalmata and Andrea Bregno. The same artists also made the *Cantoria*.

But the chief attractions of the Sistine Chapel are of course its frescoes, particularly those by Michelangelo on the walls and vault. Michelangelo's marvelous paintings postdate those covering the wall facing the altar and the two side walls, painted during the pontificate of Sixtus IV (between 1481 and 1483) by Perugino, Pinturicchio, Luca Signorelli, Cosimo Rosselli, Domenico Ghirlandaio, and Botticelli. At that time the vault was blue and strewn with stars, and so it remained until Julius II commissioned Michelangelo to redecorate the vast surface.

One of the figures frescoed on the ceiling of the Sistine Chapel.

The back wall of the Sistine Chapel with Michelangelo's masterful fresco of the Last Judgement.

Saw This ↑

MICHELANGELO IN THE SISTINE CHAPEL

Michelangelo, the famed master of the Sistine Chapel, completed his frescoes in two phases: the period between 1508 and 1512 was employed in painting the vaults under commission by Pope Julius II, whereas his other masterpiece, the *Last Judgement*, was commissioned by Pope Paul III (Alessandro Farnese) for the back wall of the chapel nearly a quarter of a century later. These two frescoes, which together cover a surface of approximately 800 square meters, represent perhaps the greatest artistic achievement of all time.

Beginning from the rear left, the frescoes around the vault are of *Jeremiah*, meditating; the *Persian Sibyl*, reading; *Ezekiel*, holding a scroll as he listens to an angel; the *Erythraean Sibyl*, consulting a book; *Joel*, reading a papyrus; *Zachariah*, consulting a book; the *Delphic Sibyl*, unwinding a scroll; *Isaiah*, in meditation with a book in his hand; the *Cumaean Sibyl*, opening a book; *Daniel*, writing; the *Libyan Sibyl*, turning to pick up a book; and lastly *Jonah*, in ecstasy at the moment of his exit from the whale's belly. Above these

twelve figures, softly rendered nudes support festoons and medallions. In the center, nine pictures depict the stories of the Genesis. Beginning from the one above the altar, they are: God dividing the light from the darkness, God creating the sun, the moon, and plant life, God dividing the waters and the land and creating the fishes and the birds, the incredibly famous *Creation of Adam*, the *Creation of Eve* from Adam's rib, the *Temptation* and the *Expulsion of Adam and Eve* from the Garden of Eden, the *Flood*, and the *Drunkenness of Noah*. The spandrels at the sides
of the vault contain depictions of other Old Testament stories: *Judith and Holophernes*, *David and Goliath*, the *Punishment of Haman*, and the *Brazen Serpent*. The lunettes over the windows contain equally splendid frescoes of the *Ancestors of Christ*.

Twenty-five years later, between 1536 and 1541, Michelangelo returned to the Sistine Chapel, this time under the papacy of Paul III Farnese. His great new fresco of the *Last Judgement* covers the whole back wall of the Sistine Chapel; it is so large that two of Perugino's earlier frescoes had to be destroyed and two large arched windows walled up.

THE RESTORATION OF THE SISTINE CHAPEL

The contribution of a prominent Japanese broadcaster, the Nippon Television Network Corporation, which used high tech methods to film each single detail of the work, made it possible to undertake the restoration of Michelangelo's great frescoes in the Sistine Chapel.

The results surprised scholars and in part reopened the question of the interpretation of the master's great works. Prior to restoration, criticism had centered on discussion of Michelangelo's somber tones and his introspective search for color. As a result of the restoration the true colors of the works, darkened by time and other causes, have emerged from under layers of candle smoke and are once more revealed in their original brilliance and light, more "modern" and striking than ever. This "rediscovered" Michelangelo, the painter of the Sistine chapel, thus reaffirmed himself as an artist possessed of such mastery as to leave his audience breathless, even after almost five centuries.

The technicians involved in the restoration also had the opportunity to experience first-hand the uncomfortable position in which Michelangelo had to work: a physical strain that could only have compounded the creative and intellectual effort made by this great genius in painting his masterpiece.

BIBLIOTECA APOSTOLICA VATICANA

Founded in 1475, much of the library was decorated by painters of the caliber of Melozzo da Forlì, Antoniazzo Romano, and Domenico and Davide Ghirlandaio. In the 16th century, Domenico Fontana enlarged it by building a new structure above the dividing stairs of the Cortile del Belvedere. The library contains an inestimable treasure in manuscripts, printed books and codices: 7000 incunabula, more than 60,000 manuscripts, 100,000 prints and maps, 800,000 printed works, and 100,000 separate autographs and thousands of document files. The Vatican Library collections occupy splendidly decorated rooms.

PINACOTECA VATICANA

This exceptional collection of paintings, founded by Pope Pius VI, is one of the most prestigious in the world and boasts masterpieces of undeniable beauty that span an arc of time from the 12th through the 18th centuries. Although deprived of the many works transported to France in the late 1700s following the Treaty of Tolentino and recovered only in part about twenty years later thanks to the efforts of Canova, the picture gallery grew over the years to incorporate other papal collections in part from the sacristy of Saint Peter's and in part from the summer residence of the popes in Castel Gandolfo. The works are arranged in chronological order, beginning with the "primitives." This part of the collection contains panels of enormous value such as the *Mary Magdalen* by Veneziano, the *Madonna with Child* by Vitale da Bologna, the *Saint Francis* by Giunta Pisano and the *Last Judgement* by Friars Giovanni and Niccolò, a precious panel of the Roman Benedictine milieu dat-

Two of Michelangelo's frescoes on the ceiling of the Sistine Chapel, following restoration: Original Sin *and, below, the* Creation of Adam.

The recent restoration of the ceiling of the Sixtine Chapel revealed Michelangelo's colors in all their original splendor.

ed to the late 11th or the early 12th century. The *Scenes from the Life of Saint Stephen* by Bernardo Daddi lead into the following section, which is dedicated to Gothic painting and centers mainly on Giotto and his followers. Works by the great Tuscan master include the *Stefaneschi Polyptych*, commissioned during Giotto's Roman sojourn by Cardinal Stefaneschi for one of the altars of the old Saint Peter's Basilica. This splendid altarpiece is accompanied by such beautiful paintings as Simone Martini's *Redeemer*, the *Madonna del Magnificat* by Daddi, and the *Nativity* by Giovanni di Paolo. Beato Angelico's stay in Rome is evinced by such highly evocative works as the *Scenes from the Life of Saint Niccolò di Bari* and the *Stigmata of Saint Francis*, in delicate counterpoint to works by Filippo Lippi and Benozzo Gozzoli. Two indicative examples of the activity of Melozzo da Forlì are to be found in the fragments of the fresco that once decorated the apse of Santi Apostoli with a depiction of the *Ascension*, destroyed in the 1700s, and the colossal mural painting that embellished the first seat of the Biblioteca Apostolica; it is a work dating from the second half of the 15th century illustrating *Sixtus IV Appointing Bartolomeo Sacchi Prefect of the Library*. Melozzo

ushers the visitor on toward a more mature phase of 15th-century painting, in which alongside works by foreign masters such as Lucas Cranach, the author of a dramatic *Pietà* in typical Nordic tones, we find the *polyptychs* by Carlo and Vittorio Crivelli.

But it is the Umbrian school that triumphs, with its evocative Renaissance works like the *Coronation of Maria* by Pinturicchio and Perugino's *Virgin with Child and Four Saints*. These paintings in turn provide a sort of introduction to the section dedicated to Raphael, which contains some of the finest of his works.

Of particular note is the *Transfiguration*, the last works by the master from Urbino, commissioned in 1517 by Giulio de' Medici, then cardinal and the future Clement VII; the *Madonna di Foligno*, painted for Sigismondo Conti, Julius II's personal secretary, and finally the ten *Tapestries*, created in 1515-1516 by Flemish weavers after Raphael's cartoons, which once hung in the Sistine Chapel on occasion of the conclaves and the most solemn ceremonies. Another great master, Leonardo, is also represented here, with the sketch for a painting of *Saint Jerome*. This particularly significant work reveals interesting facets of the chiaroscuro techniques

131

and the compositional methods used by Leonardo. The 16th-century section also contains a great number of paintings of the Venetian school, among which the intense *Portrait of the Doge Nicolò Marcello* by Titian and works by Veronese. The consequence of the evolution of painting in the 1500s was inevitably the interesting works of the Tuscan and Roman Mannerist schools, represented here by Vasari (*The Martyrdom of Saint Stephen*), Caracci (*The Sacrifice of Isaac*) and by the Cavalier d'Arpino (*Annunciation*).

The works of some of the greatest exponents of the Baroque revolution are also exhibited here: first and foremost the *Deposition* by Caravaggio, painted in the very first years of the 17th century, but also paintings by Guido Reni (*The Crucifixion of Saint Peter*) and Domenichino (*The Communion of Saint Jerome*). Fascinating rooms are dedicated to the work of Italian artists active in Rome, such as Pietro da Cortona, Orazio Gentileschi, and Baciccia, but also to foreign masters like Poussin, Van Dyck and Rubens. The portion of the museum specifically concerned with 19th-century painting contains a number of surprising works by Giuseppe Maria Crespi, Giaquinto, and Donato Creti.

MUSEO GREGORIANO PROFANO

The original nucleus of the museum, which was initially located in the Palazzo del Laterano, dates from the first half of the nineteenth century. It was in fact Pope Gregory XVI who began systematic arrangement of the many Greek and Roman finds unearthed during the course of the archaeological excavations conducted in the territory of the former Papal State. In 1970, the extensive collection was transferred to the Vatican spaces built especially for the occasion by order of Pope John XXIII by the architects Fausto and Lucio Passarelli. The museum is divided into five sections containing to Greek sculpture and works exemplary of the various phases in the development of Roman sculptural art, from that of copying and adapting the Greek models to independent production in the Imperial Age and late antiquity. Among the most important works of Greek origin are the *fragments of sculptures from the Parthenon* and the *head of Athena*, a celebrated expression of the art of Magna Graecia. For a long time, the influence of Greek and Hellenistic art was fundamental in the evolution of Roman art; this was especially true in the field of sculpture, which moved its first steps by copying ancient models. This is the case of the statues of *Marsyas* and of *Athena*, reproductions of the renowned bronze group cast by Myron in 460 BC that stood at the entrance to the Athens acropolis, and of the *Chiaramonti Niobe*, inspired by a famous sculptural group attributed to Skopas. In the late republican era and the first years of the empire, Roman sculpture began to strike out on its own, above all in the sector of portraiture, with both full-figure *statues* and *busts* of famous personages and the emperors and their family members. Many reliefs, like that of the *Vicomagistri Altar*, representing a sacrificial procession, also stand precious witness to the unfolding of religious and civil life in Roman society. Funerary art, which revealed itself especially prodigious in the production of *sarcophagi* (to which the museum dedicates an entire section) sheds much light on the myths of ancient times (*Adonis*, *Oedipus*, *Phaedra*, etc.) through the reliefs that constitute the decoration of the coffins. Oriental myths and reliefs pervade the examples of 2nd-and 3rd-century Roman Art exhibited in the last section, including the fine *Mithrasn Slaying the Bull*.

MUSEO PIO CRISTIANO

Founded in 1854 by Pius IX, this museum boasts a rich collection of objects found in catacombs and ancient basilicas. Among the most important are the 4th-century *sarcophagi* with scenes inspired by the Old and New Testaments, a rare and splendid 3rd-century sculpture entitled the *Good Shepherd*, and the famous *inscription on the tombstone of Bishop Aubercius*, who lived in Marcus Aurelius' time.

MUSEO MISSIONARIO-ETNOLOGICO

The museum was founded in 1926 by Pius XI in the Palazzo del Laterano and in the 1950s was transferred to its present site by Pope John XXIII. This rare collection of material was put together by missionaries in Asia, Africa, and South America. The museum offers the opportunity to discover objects used in the homes and in the civil and above all religious lives of these peoples. One portion of the collection, containing cult objects and small stone figures of divinities, is of more strictly philosophical and religious interest, while another, more strictly ethnographical portion is mostly reserved for the use of scholars and experts.

VATICAN GARDENS
The gardens cover an extensive area reaching from the Vatican buildings to the walls of the Città Leonina. The gardens are among the most famous green spaces in the world, and although planned in various stages they have changed little since the 16th-17th centuries. The complex and fascinating geometry of the formal Italian garden is here interpreted through use of large and small boxwood hedges with avenues and flowerbeds, often laid out in labyrinthine designs, and is set off by theatrically-placed decorative sculptures and constructions such as the artificial grottos, nooks of mystery and abstraction proposed in accordance with the concepts that inspired the architects of the time to represent symbolic places.

CASINA OF PIUS IV
Although it bears the name of Pope Pius IV, this highly imaginative building, consisting of two structures facing each other over a small square, was actually commissioned from the architect Pirro Ligorio by Paul IV. Inside the larger building are frescoes by Barocci, Federico Zuccari and Santi di Tito.

Detail of a lunette in the Sistine Chapel, following restoration.

JANICULUM

Church of Sant'Onofrio - **Janiculum Hill** - Fontana dell'Acqua Paola - Villa Sciarra - **San Pietro in Montorio**

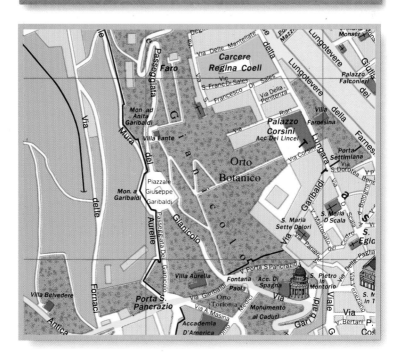

Below, the Victory Lighthouse on the Janiculum hill.

Church of Sant'Onofrio - The church, dating to the first half of the 15th century, is preceded by an arched portico that is simple and rhythmic in its design. The lunette over the entrance portal contains a fresco of the *Madonna and Child* by Claudio Ridolfi. The single-nave **interior** has side chapels which house quite interesting paintings, such as those of the *Annunciation*, by Antoniazzo Romano, in the pendentives of the vault in the first chapel. Over the altar in the second chapel is the *Madonna of Loreto* by Agostino Carracci, while the third chapel on the left contains the *Portrait of Cardinal Sega* by Domenichino. The numerous frescoes in the apse are attributed to Baldassare Peruzzi.

Janiculum Hill - This narrow, green-clad hill, which rises between Saint Peter's and the Trastevere, derives its name from the cult of the god Janus to whom the whole area was once dedicated. The long peaceful route that runs along the ridge is famous for its splendid panoramas of the

134

city and for its natural beauty.

Along our itinerary - which we will think of as beginning at the Church of Sant' Onofrio - we find the historical *oak of Tasso*, now partially destroyed by a bolt of lightning, under which the great poet is said to have sat in meditation; somewhat further on, the esplanade with the **Victory Lighthouse**, erected in 1911 by the Italian residents of Argentina on occasion of the Roman Exposition, which in the evening casts tricolor rays of light on the landscape below.

In **Piazzale Anita Garibaldi** is the equestrian monument to this heroine by the sculptor Mario Rutelli (1932); the mortal remains of Anita Ribeiro Garibaldi, brought from Nice, are inhumed in the base. Almost opposite the monument, looking out on the urban panorama, is the 16th-century **Villa Turini-Lante-Helbig**, now the seat of the Finnish Academy and the Finnish embassy to the Holy See.

Piazzale Garibaldi is a stupendous observation point over the city, with its esplanade dominated by the imposing monument erected in 1895 by the sculptor Emanuele Gallori. On the pedestal of the equestrian statue of the Hero of Two Worlds are two high reliefs depicting Garibaldi's battles and two allegories, one of *America* and the other of *Europe*.

Further on, near Porta S. Pancrazio, is a facade known as the **House of Michelangelo**. Saved during the 19th-century demolition of the building in which Michelangelo lived in Macel de' Corvi, it was reused here to conceal a water reservoir.

Numerous herms in the various avenues on the hill keep alive the memory of the heroic commitment of those who fought with Garibaldi.

Fontana dell'Acqua Paola - This monumental fountain, on which Domenico Fontana collaborated, was built between 1610 and 1612 for Pope Paul V. A large semicircular basin with a triumphal arch under splendid granite columns recites a prologue to the fountain; a pleasant garden stretches out behind.

Villa Sciarra - The 15th-century building, which once belonged to the noble Sciarra family, was donated to the city in 1932 by an its last owner, an American matron. It is surrounded by a splendid public park in which eighteenth-century fountains, statues and marble reliefs are framed by luxuriant vegetation.

Church of San Pietro in Montorio - The construction of this splendid religious complex dates to the 9th century. It was dedicated to Saint Peter on the erroneous supposition that the saint was crucified here.

From top to bottom: the equestrian monument and tomb of the heroine Anita Ribiero, Garibaldi's wife, the monument to Giuseppe Garibaldi in the square of the same name, and the Fontana dell'Acqua Paola.

Most of the building was remodeled in the late 15th century and also underwent rather heavy-handed restoration in 1849.

The **facade**, in Renaissance style, is sober and elegant with no trace of weightiness. Probably designed by the school of Bregno, it is on two floors with corner pilasters and a large Gothic rose window at the center. The mighty portal, reached via a double flight of stairs, is also quite impressive.

The single-nave **interior** has four chapels at the two sides and two larger chapels that form the transept.

Particularly striking, in the first chapel on the right, is the famous *Flagellation of Christ* by Sebastiano del Piombo, thought by some to be from drawings by Michelangelo (1518); in the second, Pomarancio's *Madonna della Lettera* on the altar; in the third, the *Annunciation*, the *Presentation* and the *Immaculate Conception* by Cerruti. In the fourth chapel, designed by Vasari, are the noteworthy tombs of Antonio and Fabiano del Monte with reclining figures sculpted by Bartolomeo Ammannati. In the fifth chapel on the left, designed by Daniele da Volterra, is the *Baptism of Christ* by the same artist; in the fourth, the dramatic altarpiece of the *Deposition* by Dirck van Baburen, a follower of Caravaggio; in the third, a *Saint Anne Enthroned* and a *Madonna and Child*, undisputed masterpieces by Antoniazzo Romano; in the second chapel, designed by Bernini, is a beautiful high relief by F. Baratta.

A small masterpiece by Bramante stands to the right of the church - the **Tempietto of San Pietro in Montorio**. This circular building has 16 Doric columns that surround the cella to form an ambulacrum. It is one of the most significant examples of early Renaissance architecture and marks the transition from the 15th-century forms to the new architectural ideas that were to distinguish the following century. A statue of *Saint Peter* (early 16th century) stands at the altar in the remarkably tasteful **interior**. The richly decorated crypt is also interesting; in it is a large hole, which legend recounts to be that left by the shaft of the cross on which Saint Peter was crucified.

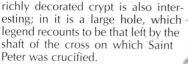

Bramante's beautiful Tempietto of San Pietro in Montorio.

TRASTEVERE

Santa Cecilia in Trastevere -
Basilica of Santa Maria in Trastevere -
Palazzo Corsini alla Lungara - Galleria Corsini -
Villa Farnesina - Ponte Sisto

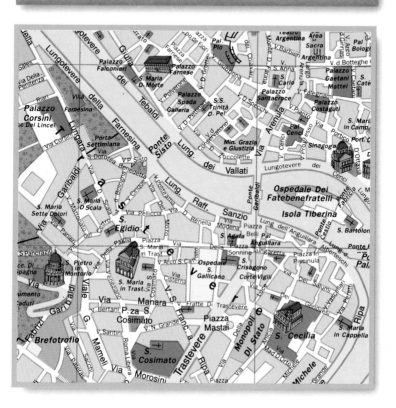

Palazzetto Anguillara and Tower - This complex dates to the 13th century. The year in which the building was severely damaged in an earthquake, 1538, signaled the beginning of its gradual decay (for the people it soon became the "*Palazzaccio*"), which was not arrested until the early 20th century when it became the property of the city of Rome. Restoration, involving considerable restructuring and not only conservative actions, has unfortunately altered much of the original architectural design.

The marble plaque of an ancient votive offering; below, a view of the courtyard and the portico of Santa Cecilia in Trastevere.

Church of Santa Cecilia in Trastevere -
The origins of this church, which stands at the back of a spacious courtyard, date back to the 5th century, when it was built on the remains of a Roman house said by some to be that of Saint Valerian, a martyred Roman patrician. The rococo *facade*, with its polished lines, harmonizes well with the sober Romanesque **bell tower**. The 18th-century *interior*, with a nave and two

Santa Cecilia in Trastevere with its lovely Romanesque bell-tower.

aisles, is home to with a praiseworthy fresco of the *Apotheosis of Saint Cecilia*, by Sebastiano Conca, in the vault. In the vestibule is the *monument to Cardinal N. Fonteguerri*, a rare work by Mino da Fiesole (1500). The church also conserves two canvases by Guido Reni, the *Decapitation of Saint Cecilia* and *Saint Cecilia and Saint Valerian*, in the former *calidarium* of the Roman structure at the end of a corridor, frescoed by Brill and Pomarancio, that leads off the first chapel in the vestibule. At the center of the presbytery is a *marble ciborium*, a 13th-century masterpiece by Arnolfo di Cambio. It is supported by four black and white columns, with trilobate arches, tympanums and spires, and decorated with statues of angels. Also of note are the *marble statue of Saint Cecilia* by Maderno (under the altar in the presbytery), and the *mosaic of Paschal I* in the semidome of the apse.

A detail of the Last Judgement *by Pietro Cavallini in the Church of Santa Cecilia.*

Santa Maria in Trastevere - Possibly founded around 221 AD by Saint Calixtus (or so at least legend would have it), the church was completely rebuilt at the dawn of the second millennium and again restructured in the 18th century by Pope Clement XI. The simple 12th-century *facade* is splendid, with its three arched windows and fine mosaics from the same period. A Romanesque *bell tower*, lightened at the top by various aediculae, stands to one side of the church. The spacious *interior* is on a basilica plan, with a nave separated from the two aisles by ancient granite columns. The Virgin of the *Assumption* by Domenichino gazes down sweetly from the ceiling and an impressive *marble tabernacle* by Mino del Reame stands at the beginning of the nave. Among the many works that decorate the right aisle is the excellent *Flight into Egypt*, a successful synthesis of forceful coloring and melodious narration by Carlo Maratta, on the left wall. In the apse, at the height of the windows, are various outstanding mosaics by Cavallini narrating *Scenes*

Santa Maria in Trastevere: above, the interior with the nave and the mosaic-decorated apse; center, the episcopal throne and a detail of Cavallini's mosaic of the Presentation in the Temple; *below, a view of the facade.*

from the Life of the Virgin. To the right and left of the apse are the *funeral monuments* of Cardinal Osio and of Roberto Altemps, duke of Wales (mid-16th century), and on the left wall at the back of the transept that of Cardinal Pietro Stefaneschi, a 15th-century work by Magister Paulus.

Church of Santa Maria della Scala - The design of this church is by Francesco da Volterra, although the actual construction work was carried out in the late 16th century by O. Mascherino. The *facade* consists of two superimposed levels broken by pilasters and displays an interesting play of light and shade. The extremely ornate Latin-cross *interior* expands into chapels on either side. Among the most interesting works contained in the church are, in the first chapel on the right, the *Beheading of Saint John the Baptist,* a rare work by Gherardo delle Notti, and in the apse several paintings by Luca de La Haye, also known as

The access corridor to the vestibule of the Galleria Nazionale di Arte Antica in Palazzo Corsini.

Luca Fiammingo: the *Baptism of Christ,* the *Wedding at Cana,* the *Communion of the Apostles,* and the *Ascension.* On the altar in the second chapel on the left is the mystical *Death of the Virgin* by C. Saraceni.

PALAZZO CORSINI ALLA LUNGARA AND GALLERIA CORSINI

The palace was originally a suburban villa built for Cardinal Raffaello Riario, nephew of Sixtus IV, on Via della Lungara (at the time Via Santa). The street linked the building with the Foro Boario area and with San Giorgio al Velabro, of which church the cardinal was the prelate. Construction work begun in the late 15th century continued under Julius II with the enlargement of the original structure. By the 17th century, the villa consisted of a main building with only nine windows on two floors and secondary facade overlooking the gardens (today's **Orto Botanico**) that rose with the hill to the **Casino dei Quattro Venti**, probably built for the Riario family by Mattia De' Rossi; it was destroyed in 1849 during the struggles for Italian unity. The palace knew one of its moments of greatest importance when from 1659 onward it hosted queen Christina of Sweden, who having collected around herself a conspicuous court of men of letters and artists, founded the first Roman Academy. Following her death in 1689, the institute took the name of Arcadia, and the meeting place moved to the nearby Bosco Parrasio on the slopes of the Janiculum.

The year 1736 marked a turning point in the life of the building. It was purchased by the Corsini family following Lorenzo Corsini's election as Pope Clement XII and chosen as the Roman residence of the noble Florentine family, who transferred their well-stocked library and precious art collection here. Ferdinando Fuga was charged with enlarging and restructuring the villa, and when the scaffolding came down it had been transformed into a three-story palace with 21 windows. Fuga also designed the **facade**, which already tended toward Neoclassical essentiality with its massive stone pilaster strips and crowning balustrade, and a carriageable vestibule with a monumental staircase. The Corsini family also took a particular interest in the gardens, which they enhanced with new plants, statues and plays of water. But above all, they were great collectors of art and of books, beginning with that Cardinal Neri, nephew of Pope Clement XII, who set aside the two new wings built by Fuga as the homes of the Biblioteca Corsini and the **Galleria Corsini**. The latter, which is still structured as though it were a private picture gallery, contains mostly works that mark the transition from the Baroque to Classicism, juxtaposing in an ideal artistic itinerary Caravaggio's *Saint John the Baptist* and the works of his most illustrious followers (Orazio Gentileschi, Gerard Seghers, etc.) with the works of eighteenth-century painters of Classical and Neoclassical inspiration (Maratta, Panini, Batoni). The Galleria also contains many works by Neapolitan artists and by the so-called "primitives" (Andrea di Cione, Beato Angelico), added to the collection in the 1800s.

Villa Farnesina - Probably the most significant example of a Renaissance villa in Rome, Villa Farnesina was commissioned from Baldassarre Peruzzi by Agostino Chigi and decorated by the greatest names in Roman painting of the time, from Raphael to Giulio Romano, Sodoma, Sebastiano del Piombo, and Peruzzi himself, who was an excellent painter. The two-story **facade** overlooking the garden, with pilasters, is splendid. The **interior** is subdivided into numerous rooms, each of which is uniquely decorated with frescoes. The first is the **galleria**, with the fable of *Cupid and Psyche* painted by Raphael and his followers in the vault; next comes the *saletta*, with a frieze painted by Peruzzi; in another vast room is the famous fresco of *Galatea* by Raphael, as well as paintings by Peruzzi (the *Constellations* on the ceiling) and Sebastiano del Piombo (*Head of a Youth*, scenes from the *Metamorphoses*, and *Polyphemus* in the lunettes). In a room adjacent to the **Salone delle Prospettive** on the upper floor is the *Wedding of Alessandro and Rossana* by Sodoma - perhaps his best work.

Gabinetto Nazionale delle Stampe - This collection, housed in the Villa Farnesina, dates to the end of the 19th century. It consists of a great number of prints and drawings by Italian and foreign artists who were active between the 15th century and modern times. Of particular note is the drawings collection of the 16th, 17th and 18th centuries, one of the richest in the world.

Ponte Sisto - The bridge, thought to have been designed and built by Baccio Pontelli, dates to 1474; it replaced the ancient Roman bridge erected under Marcus Aurelius. The name derives from Pope Sixtus IV, under whom it was built and who probably commissioned it from the architect. This splendidly designed span on four arches is one of the most interesting examples of this architectural genre to be found in the capital.

Ponte Sisto, built under Pope Sixtus IV in 1474.

SAN GIOVANNI IN LATERANO

Porta Maggiore -
Santa Croce in Gerusalemme - Scala Santa -
Baptistery of Saint John - **Basilica of San Giovanni in Laterano**

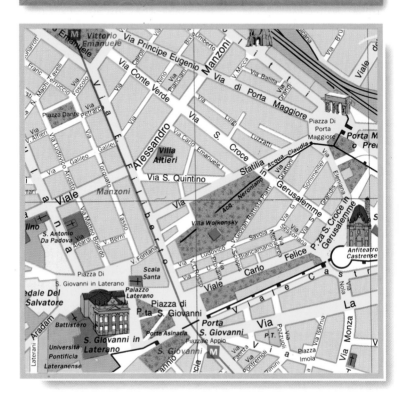

Porta Maggiore - One of the most monumental remains of Imperial Rome has given its name to the piazza that came into being around it. Known also as Porta Prenestina, this gate was built in the year 52 AD by the emperor Claudius, and was the point of origin of two roads, one of which led to Prenestre and the other to Labici. Architecturally, the gate consists of two openings with arches flanked by robust piers and aediculae.

Church of Santa Croce in Gerusalemme - According to tradition, this church was built by Saint Helena, Constantine's mother, and the composite name would date to after the 4th century, when the name of the Holy Cross was added to that of *Sancta Hierusalem*. It was here that the pope, during a fascinating ritual, showed the worshipers the golden rose, the symbol of the delights reserved for them in the perennial garden of the mystical celestial Jerusalem. As far as the site is concerned, the building rose next to the *Sessorianum*, or imperial palace, and may even have been that part of it derived from the enlargement of the chapel in which Helena had placed the fragment of the miraculous True Cross she discovered on Calvary Hill. This explains the three names by which the church is mentioned in historical sources: *Sessoriana* (from the imperial palace), *Hierusalem* (since it was a place consecrated to the mysteries of Redemption), and *Heleniana* (after its august founder).

Two Vatican councils met within its walls, convoked in 433 by Sixtus III and in 502 by Saint Symmachus. The various reigning popes in the centuries that followed continuously tended to and restored the building:

142

Gregory III restructured the roof, which had been destroyed, Benedict VII had the adjacent monastery built, and Leo X, Alexander II, Lucius II and Eugenius III all carried out work of one kind or another. Innocent II made a pilgrimage there (barefoot it is said) to beseech God, in this Roman *Hierusalem*, for victory over the Saracens. Abandoned during the "Avignon captivity," Santa Croce was restored in 1370 by Urban V, who spent the enormous sum of three thousand gold florins; about a hundred and twenty years later (1492) Cardinal Consalvo Mendoza began new restorations, which remained famous because during the works the relic of the True Cross (hidden in the arch of the tribune and consisting of a corroded wooden tablet with three lines of a trilingual inscription - in Latin, Greek and Hebrew - reading "*Jesus Nazarenus Rex Judaeorum*") was found.

Despite these restorations, the building maintained its original form at least up to the time of Benedict XIV when, after the main facade and the porch had been torn down, the architects Pietro Passalacqua and Domenico Gregorini raised the present facade with the annexed portico. It was also then that the hill known as "Monte Cipollaro" was leveled, because it obstructed the view of the church from the direction of the Lateran as well as making it difficult to accede to the church from that side. Passalacqua and Gregorini's prospective **exterior** is a play of concavities and convexities, broken by an order of Corinthian pilasters and concluding in the center in a large curvilinear tympanum with the papal insignia. Further up, a *fastigium* inserted into the attic, as animated as the rest of the facade, supports the statues of Saints Helena, Luke, Matthew, John the Evangelist, and Constantine. The Romanesque **bell tower** erected in 1144 under Lucius II contrasts with this pleasantly busy front.

Due to the radical restoration actions to which the church has been subjected over the centuries, the only original elements remaining in the **interior** are the ground plan, part of the vertical structures (for example, only eight of the twelve columns which once stood in the nave are left), and the magnificent Cosmatesque pavement. The decoration (including the architectural members) instead follows the chronological and stylistic development in the history of design, since work was almost continuously in progress in the building and on the whole was not destructive. Mention can be made of the large *Triumph of the Cross* by Corrado Giaquinto, a pupil of Sebastiano Conca da Molfetta, that was added to the decoration of the already ornate ceiling, or the particularly effective fresco, painted in the vault in the apse, of *Scenes of the Terrestrial Jerusalem*. The latter work was commissioned by Cardinal Carvajalo (whose funeral monument also stands in the church) around the turn of the 15th century; it was formerly attributed to Pinturicchio but is now considered to be by Antonio Aquilii, better known as Antoniazzo Romano. Lastly, at the center of the large curve of the apse is the "*marble machine in honor of the Holy Sacrament*," which dates to 1536. It was originally meant to be an altarpiece but was later converted into a funeral monument for Cardinal Francisco Quiñones (d. 1540), the confessor of Charles V, who seems to have commissioned it from Jacopo Tatti (otherwise known as Sansovino). But Sansovino apparently made only the two statues of *David* and *Solomon* in the side niches.

Porta San Giovanni - One of the most interesting of the Renaissance gates of Rome, this portal was built by Jacopo del Duca for Pope Gregory XIII. The original structure has a monumental gateway with pilaster strips in high-relief rusticated masonry at the sides. Popular belief attributes esoteric, magical powers to the interesting Moor's head in the keystone.

Piazza di San Giovanni in Laterano - This vast square, of ancient origin, is lined with many soberly elegant buildings including the massive Palazzo del Laterano and the graceful Baptistery of Saint John or the Church of San Giovanni in Fonte. More or less at the center of the square is a slender Egyptian obelisk in red granite, all of 47 meters high: dating to the 15th century BC, it was brought to Rome in 357 by Constantius II, son of Constantine, and set up in the Circus Maximus; in 1587, Sixtus V had it moved here by Fontana. The fountain at its base dates to the early 17th century.

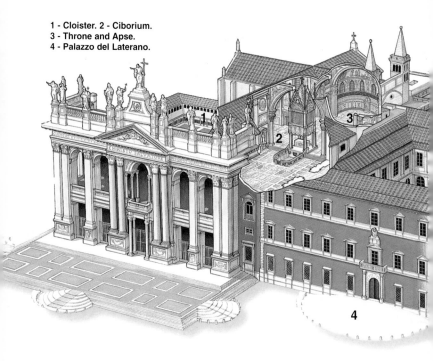

1 - Cloister. 2 - Ciborium.
3 - Throne and Apse.
4 - Palazzo del Laterano.

Above, a cutaway view of the Basilica of San Giovanni in Laterano; below, the Scala Santa.

Scala Santa - The Palazzo del Sancta Sanctorum owes its name to the fact that was originally designed to contain, or incorporate, the **Popes' Chapel** (or *Sancta Sanctorum*). Pope Sixtus V commissioned the palace from the architect Domenico Fontana, who built it in 1585-1590. The Chapel was originally part of a building known as the "Patriarchio" (7th - 8th centuries) that at the time housed the papal court. The name of "Scala Santa" derives from the erroneous identification of one of the staircases of the Patriarchio as the flight of stairs in Pilate's *Praetorium* ascended by Christ when he was judged by Pilate. Nowadays, the term *Sancta Sanctorum* is used to indicate the **Chapel of Saint Laurence**, overflowing with relics and at the same time a true jewel of Cosmatesque art with its *tabernacles* along the walls and its mosaic *ceiling*.

Palazzo del Laterano - Built for Sixtus V by the architect Domenico Fontana on the site of the ancient Patriarchio, the residence of the Popes from Constantine until the papacy was transferred to Avignon (1305). The magnificent palace, on which work began in 1586, was conceived as a summer residence for the papal court, which was then moved to the Quirinal. The building has a square ground plan; the **facade** was inspired by that of the Palazzo Farnese, but does not succeed in expressing the same power. The light-filled **loggia-belvedere** with its columns is nevertheless particularly lovely.

Baptistery of Saint John - Originally raised by Constantine, the baptistery was completely reconstructed a number of times; the building we see today dates to the 17th century. It is also known as San Giovanni in Fonte or in Laterano. The structure is that of the prototype Christian baptistery, with an octagonal floor plan centering on eight porphyry columns. The works of art decorating the walls include the canvas of *Scenes from the Life of Saint John the Baptist* by Andrea Sacchi, frescoes by Carlo Maratta, and the *Destruction of the Idols* by A. Camassei and G. Gemignani. Among the many chapels, mention must be made of the Chapel of Saint John the Baptist, with the original bronze doors, the Chapel of San Venantius, with 7th-century mosaics, and the Chapel of Saint John the Evangelist, with the bronze doors of 1196. In the right apse are two canvases of note: a *Madonna* by Sassoferrato and, above all, a *Saint Philip Neri* by Guido Reni.

Basilica of San Giovanni in Laterano - Originally built by Constantine, plundered by the Genseric's Vandals, frequently sacked, damaged by the earthquake of 896 and various fires - for most of its existence, the Basilica of San Giovanni in Laterano has been the object of reconstruction and restoration. Among the artists who participated in these works were Giovanni di Stefano di Francesco Borromini, who renovated it for Innocent X, and Alessandro Galilei, who redid the facade in 1735. The **exterior** of the Cathedral of Rome is characterized by the monumental architecture of the giant Corinthian order used by Galilei and the projecting central portion of the facade. The balustrade above the attic supports the colossal statues of *Christ*, Saints *John the Baptist* and *John the Evangelist,* and the *Doctors of the Church*. There are five entrances (the last to the right is known as the "Porta Santa" and is opened only in Jubilee years), each surmounted by a loggia. The statue of *Emperor Constantine* was brought here from the Baths of Diocletian.

The majestic **interior** is a Latin cross with a nave and two aisles on either side. The original antique columns have been encased in robust piers, while grooved pilasters support a splendid entablature and above it a

The facade of San Giovanni in Laterano; above, one of the statues that decorated the nave of the basilica. On the following pages: an aerial view of the Lateran complex with the Basilica of San Giovanni in Laterano and the Palazzo del Laterano.

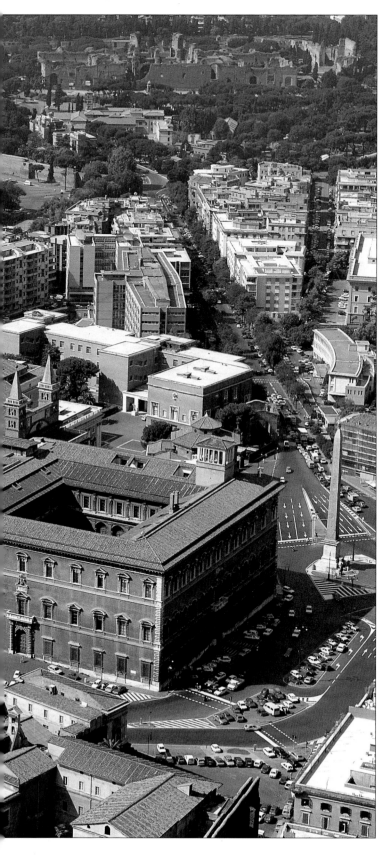

sumptuous *ceiling* said to have been designed by Pirro Ligorio. Along the walls are ranged the figures of *Prophets*, *Saints*, and *Apostles* designed by Borromini but executed by his followers in the 18th century. At the crossing of the transept, the visitor unexpectedly finds himself at the Gothic heart of the Basilica before the *baldacchino* by Giovanni di Stefano, at the top of which are the silver reliquaries enclose the precious relics of the heads of Saints Peter and Paul. Another of Saint Peter's relics, the rough wooden altar table on which the apostle is said to have celebrated mass in the catacombs, is preserved in the papal altar. A double flight of stairs leads to the subterranean *burial chamber of Martin V*, with its well-known *tomb slab* by Simone Ghini probably sculpted under Donatello's supervision. The great conch of the apse at the back of the Basilica is covered with mosaics dating to the 4th, 6th, and 13th centuries (note, in particu-

The nave with its beautiful floor.

Right, the rich wooden ceiling and, below, a view of the presbytery.

lar, the figures of the *Apostles* signed by Jacopo Torriti). Above the organ, a large 19th-century fresco by Francesco Grandi depicts episodes concerning the *Founding and Construction of the Basilica*. The decoration of the transept also deals with analogous subjects (including the *Conversion of Constantine*); it was completely restored during the pontificate of Clement VIII by the architect Giovanni della Porta and the painter known as the Cavalier d'Arpino. Under the Cavalier d'Arpino's fresco of the *Ascension of Christ* is the gilded bronze pediment, supported by antique bronze columns, that protects the altar of the *Chapel of the Holy Sacrament* designed for Clement VIII by Pietro Paolo Olivieri and supporting a precious *ciborium*. Among the many other chapels built in various periods as further decoration for the basilica are the **Colonna Chapel**, also know as the *Choir Chapel*, by Girolamo Rainaldi (1570-1655); the **Chapel of the Crucifixion**, which preserves a fragment of the presumed *Funeral Monument of Nicholas IV* attributed to Adeodato di Cosma (13th century); the **Chapel of Massimo**, by Giacomo della Porta; the **Torlonia Chapel**, quite different from that preceding it and splendidly decorated in neo-Renaissance style by the architect Raimondi (1850); and the architecturally-complete and self-sufficient **Corsini Chapel**, built on the Greek-cross plan by Alessandro Galilei for Clement XII. A corridor leads to the **Old Sacristy**, with the *Annunciation* by Venusti and a *Saint John the Evangelist* by the Cavalier d'Arpino, and to the **New Sacristy**, with a 15th-century *Annunciation* of the Tuscan school. In the nearby Cosmatesque Cloister, a 13th-century work by Vassalletto, are visible remains of the most ancient portion of the Basilica.

SAN PIETRO IN VINCOLI

Church of the Santi Quattro Coronati - Basilica of San Clemente -
"Ludus Magnus" - Parco Oppio - **Domus Aurea** -
Basilica of San Pietro in Vincoli

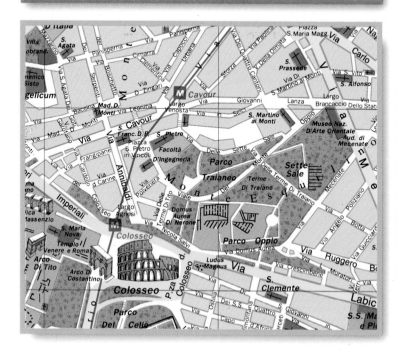

Church of the Santi Quattro Coronati - Historical references to the Santi Coronati mention two groups of martyrs whose glorious vicissitudes seem to center around the Greek demigod of medicine, Asklepios, worshiped in Rome as Aesculapius in a sanctuary situated on the Isola Tiberina. The first group consists of five Christian stone cutters and sculptors who were martyred in the quarries of Pannonia after they refused to sculpt the statue of Aesculapius, while the other four are identified as being four Roman soldiers called *cornicularii*, members of Diocletian's guard, who were cast to the dogs because they had refused to sacrifice to the idol of the same Aesculapius. The ambiguity of the tradition is due to the fact that at a certain point the bodies of the Pannonian martyrs were transported to Rome and buried in a cemetery, *ad duos lauros*, where the remains of the *cornicularii* had already been buried thanks to the pious intervention of Saint Sebastian, who had gathered up their remains after their martyrdom.

The site now occupied by the Church of the Santi Coronati was once called *caput Africae* and hosted a *sacellum* to Diana; Fra' Giocondo, Baldassarre Peruzzi, and Jacopo Sansovino measured and sketched a considerable quantity of archaeological material found scattered throughout the area.
As far as the basilica itself is concerned, three successive construction

phases can be identified: the first, early-Christian (4th century) phase, is attributed to Pope Saint Miltiades; a second phase, between 847 and 855, came under Pope Leo IV, formerly the titular cardinal of the church, who totally renovated it; and a third phase, after the destruction wreaked by Robert Guiscard's Norman troops in 1084, during which Pope Paschal II in practice changed even the general layout of the church, shortened it, and consecrated it anew in 1110.

Radical restoration was also undertaken under Alfonso Cariglio, titular cardinal under Martin V (1417-31); there followed work commissioned by the Infante of Portugal, who was also titular cardinal of the church and who provided it with a new ceiling and new vaults over the aisles and considerably reduced the women's galleries. Still further remodeling, once more in part destructive since it involved elimination of the apse decoration dating to the time of Paschal II, was carried out in 1632 by Cardinal Garsia Millini. It was not until 1912 that the first real preservative restoration, promoted by Cardinal Respighi and directed by Antonio Muñoz, was begun on the Santi Coronati.

Situated at the back of two **courtyards** and enclosed by the walls of the adjacent convent (which dates to the period in which Innocent II assigned the basilica to the Benedictines of Sassovivo), the church of Santi Quattro Coronati is now tripartite with eight granite columns, vaulting over the side aisles, and a flat wooden ceiling over the nave; the pavement is in Cosmatesque marble-work. Two flights of stairs under the altar of Saint Sebastian lead to the small **crypt** with the sacred relics of Sebastian himself and of the *cornicularii* Severus, Severinus, Carpophorus, and Victorinus. The present presbytery, reached from the transept via two steps, is delimited by the curve of the apse, a rather unusual situation which testifies to the adaptation performed following the destruction of the original sanctuary.

The interior decoration is distinguished by the work of Giovanni da San Giovanni in the apse; alternating with the three windows that admit light are two tiers of paintings that depict the **Lives** of the two groups of Saints (the four *cornicularii* and the other five), while the central altarpiece shows the *Glory of Martyrdom* referred to both groups.

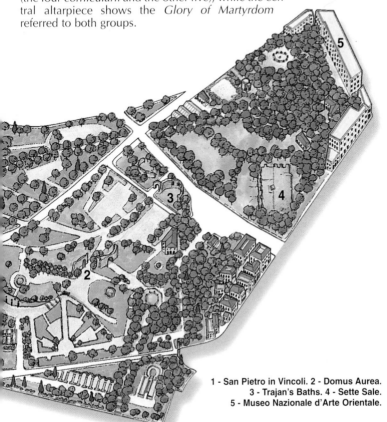

1 - San Pietro in Vincoli. 2 - Domus Aurea.
3 - Trajan's Baths. 4 - Sette Sale.
5 - Museo Nazionale d'Arte Orientale.

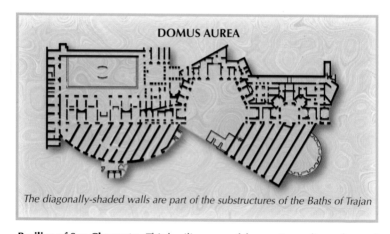

DOMUS AUREA

The diagonally-shaded walls are part of the substructures of the Baths of Trajan

Basilica of San Clemente - This basilica, one of the most grandiose places of worship in the city, dates to 385 AD. It was destroyed in the 11th century by the Normans led by Robert Guiscard, who however rebuilt it on what remained of the structure that had been razed, The result was the superposition of two churches. The ***Upper Basilica***, considerably remodeled early in the 18th century, consists of a four-sided portico at the back of which is the church (both dating to the 12th century) with a not-very-successful Baroque ***facade***. The ***interior***, also remodeled in the 18th century, still conserves echoes of its medieval origins, with two rows of seven columns in marble and granite separating the nave from the aisles. The nave is embellished with ceiling frescos, mostly by G. Chiari. Chiari is also responsible for the decoration of the walls, assisted by Sebastiano Conca. Also of particular note is the *Schola Cantorum*, dating to the 12th century, almost at the end of the nave. The large mosaic in the apse, a masterpiece by the Roman artists of the 12th century, depicts the *Triumph of the Cross*. In the first chapel in the right aisle are *Scenes from the Life of Saint Dominic* by Sebastiano Conca; in the first chapel of the left aisle, a splendid 15th-century fresco cycle by Masolino da Panicale; and in the rear chapel, a delicate *Our Lady of the Rosary* by Sebastiano Conca. The Lower Basilica consists of one huge room. The narthex is decorated with 11th- and 12th-century frescoes of the *Miracle of Saint Clement*. In the nave in the interior, frescoes of *Scenes from the Life of Christ* dating to the middle of the 9th century are still legible.

"Ludus Magnus" - What we see today are the remains of the most famous barracks for the gladiators (the others were the *Ludus Gallicus*, the *Ludus Dacicus*, and the *Ludus Matutinus*). Careful investigation has made an exact reconstruction possible. The building consisted of a three-story main structure on a rectangular ground plan, in which the gladiators were housed; at the center, perfectly in keeping with the Roman's rational, sober concept of functional architecture, was a porticoed court repeating the plan of the building as a whole. A small amphitheater, where the gladiators trained, was set in the middle of the court.

Parco Oppio - The park is a veritable botanical treasure chest containing more than 2500 varieties of roses, which when in bloom transform the area into a large variegated spot of color. This naturalistic ambience of rare beauty harmonizes wonderfully with the archaeological remains dating to Roman times: the monumental *entrance to the Domus Aurea*, the haunting *remains of the Baths*, and a *fountain* decorated with groups of amphoras.

Domus Aurea - In the early years of his reign, Nero had the *Domus Transitoria* built as his personal residence, with the aim, as the name of the dwelling ("house of passage") indicates, of joining the imperial properties on the Palatine and Esquiline hills. After the fire of 64 AD had destroyed most of it, the emperor began construction of another grandiose complex in its stead. It took the name of Domus Aurea ("Golden House"), and the name itself is an indication of the magnificence of its design.

The complex occupied an area of about 100 hectares stretching from the

Palatine to the Esquiline, the Caelian, and the Oppian hills, made available by the expropriation of numerous public and private buildings destroyed or damaged in the fire. The Domus Aurea was designed by the architects Severus and Celerus and decorated by the painter Fabullus; it was also embellished with a great number of statues pillaged from Greece.

Literary sources, notably Suetonius, tell us it was built like a villa, featuring many sumptuous pavilions separated from each other by extensive woods and luxuriant groves full of animals, both wild and domestic, and with gardens, fountains, and ornamental waterworks. The entire complex was centered around a large artificial lake ("like an ocean," in the words of Suetonius) which lay in the valley where the Colosseum was later to rise. A colossal bronze statue (over thirty meters high) of Nero in the guise of the sun god stood in the vestibule.

The architects had invented all sorts of extravagant refinements for the emperor's pleasure. The ceilings of the banquet halls were made of mobile ivory plaques so that flowers and perfume could be showered down on the guests; the most important of these halls was round and rotated with the movement of the earth. The baths were supplied with sea water and sulphurous water. But what particularly offended public opinion of the time was the enormous extension of a layout that provided living quarters for a single individual only, even if he was the emperor, and the fact that it rose in the heart of the city, and covered a large part of it.

All that remains of the entire complex of the Domus Aurea is a pavilion on the Oppian hill that survived because it was encased in the foundations of Trajan's Baths after its destruction by fire in 104 AD. This sector consists of two architecturally distinct parts showing a marked incoherency in the ground plan at the line along which the irregular rooms meet.

Only a small part of the pictorial decoration of these rooms has survived but it suffices to give us an idea of the splendor of the whole and the high level achieved by the painter whom tradition has identified as Fabullus. Some of the surviving rooms take their names from the paintings: the **Room of the Owl's Vault** was once the large central hall, the **Room of the Black Vault** the alcove of the chamber to the east, and the **Room of the Yellow Vault** a smaller room communicating with it. The apsed room to the east also still has remnants of decoration.

These paintings, rediscovered in the 15th century, were the source of inspiration for a group of Renaissance artists who created a decorative genre which went by the name of "grotesques," from the word *grotte* they used to designate the rooms of the Domus Aurea. The names of the members of this group, scratched on the stucco, are still legible; one of these early defacers of ancient monuments was Raphael, who with his followers used this new style in the decoration of the Vatican loggia.

The remains give us no more than a partial idea of what Nero's monumental project was like. The fine marble and anything else valuable it contained were already removed in antiquity. We can only try to imagine what sophisticated baroque illusions and plays of perspective it incorporated, since the remains were used as a substructure for Trajan's Baths.

MUSEO NAZIONALE D'ARTE ORIENTALE

Founded in 1957, this museum contains a superb collection of Oriental art from countries ranging from Iran east to Japan. The many objects exhibited came to the museum through donations, exchanges and, above all, from the excavations carried out by the ISMEO (Istituto Studi Medio-Orientali), which has its headquarters, as does the museum, in the historical Palazzo Brancaccio. The many works on exhibit include protohistoric bronzes from Iran, zoomorphic vases from the Caspian region dating to between 1200 and 800 BC, some interesting finds from Mohammedan Iran, pieces from China, Japan and Korea such as ritual bronzes of the Shang period (14th - 12th centuries BC) and bronze Buddhas (386-534 AD), objects from India, Nepal, the Asian Southeast and Tibet, such as a terracotta plaque of Sunga tradition (1st century BC), and two rare terracottas from Java.

Basilica of San Pietro in Vincoli - This basilica stands on the slope of the Esquiline hill overlooking the plain where the Capitoline, Palatine, and Caelian hills run together. The church owes its name to a legend concerning Eudocia, wife of Theodosius II, emperor of the Eastern Empire, who is said to have found, during a pilgrimage to Jerusalem, the chains used to bind the apostle Peter. Part of these chains remained in Constantinople, but some of the links were sent to Rome to Eudocia's daughter, who in turn presented them to the pope. And then came the miracle. While Leo I the Great was holding them, the links were miraculously welded together with other links said to come from the same holy chain and already venerated in Rome. Be that as it may, San Pietro in Vincoli does not appear to have been consecrated by Leo I but by his predecessor, Sixtus III, who was pope from 432 to 440. Moreover, the present building, the one which was consecrated by whichever pope, was preceded by another church of a different name. Excavations have revealed the remains of an apsed hall with a single nave and a "pierced" presbytery dating to the third century. This construction stood on the area covered by the church built in the mid-5th century and "modern" for its times, in which the simple straight hall was replaced by a three-aisle structure with a transept. Perhaps the best known and most incisive restorations of the Basilica are the so-called Roverian restorations, promulgated by Cardinal Francesco Della Rovere (later Pope Sixtus IV) and above all Cardinal Giuliano Della Rovere, who became titular cardinal of San Pietro in Vincoli in December 1471. These restorations, which were finished in 1475 for the Jubilee, would seem to have been planned and directed by the architect Baccio Pontelli, to whom is also attributed the project for the renovation of the palace annexed to the Basilica and the adjoining Cloister, which were however not finished until the time of Julius II.

The *tomb of Julius II* was completed around 1540, after numberless vicissitudes. The contract that Michelangelo signed with the executors of the pope's will, dated 6 May 1513, stipulated twenty-eight figures and three reliefs, all to be placed in a suitable architectural setting. The entire project was to be finished in seven years time at a total cost of 16,500 gold ducats. But as time went by, the project kept shrinking in scope (the successive stages of design are witnessed by contracts of 1516 and 1532) until the final agreement between the artist and the heirs provided for only three statues by Michelangelo and three by Raffaello da Montelupo. Of the entire project, all that now remains in San Pietro in Vincoli is the famous *Moses*, seated between *Rachel* (or the Contemplative Life) and *Leah* (or the Active Life); even the mortal remains of Julius II were wretchedly lost during the ill-omened sack of Rome in 1527.

The old early-Christian basilica, already heavily restored, was even further modified in the second half of the 16th century. An additional structure added above the portico ended up concealing the windows so that new ones had to be opened. In 1705, Francesco Fontana, son of Carlo, was commissioned by Giovan Battista Pamphili to build a wooden vault to screen the trussed timber beams of the roof; sixty years later, the interior of the portal was framed by an aedicula and the basilica was repaved in brick, an action which raised the level of the floor by about ten centimeters. The last major modification represents a pivotal element in the present aspect of the church: it was made by Vespignani, who worked in the area of the presbytery and replaced the Baroque altar with a typical open *ciborium* preceded by a *confessio*.

The exterior of San Pietro in Vincoli; on the facing page, Moses *by Michelangelo.*

On the following pages: Moses, *part of the funeral monument created by Michelangelo for Julius II in the Basilica of San Pietro in Vincoli, Saint Peter's chains under the altar, and the nave of San Martino ai Monti.*

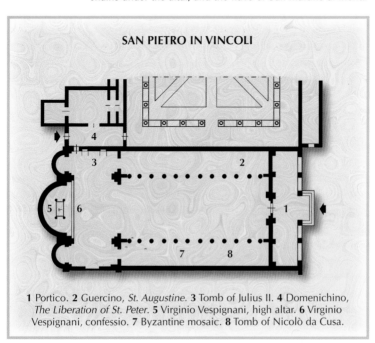

SAN PIETRO IN VINCOLI

1 Portico. **2** Guercino, *St. Augustine.* **3** Tomb of Julius II. **4** Domenichino, *The Liberation of St. Peter.* **5** Virginio Vespignani, high altar. **6** Virginio Vespignani, confessio. **7** Byzantine mosaic. **8** Tomb of Nicolò da Cusa.

155

SANTA MARIA MAGGIORE

Basilica of Santa Maria Maggiore - Santa Pudenziana -
Santa Maria degli Angeli - **Baths of Diocletian -**
San Lorenzo fuori le Mura - Museo Nazionale Romano

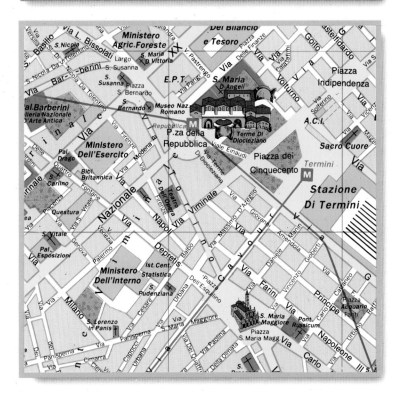

Santa Maria Maggiore.

Basilica of Santa Maria Maggiore - In August of 352 AD, snow miraculously fell on the Esquiline hill, and in it Pope Liberius traced the perimeter of the first church on the site, popularly called Santa Maria della Neve (Our Lady of the Snow). The present Church of Santa Maria Maggiore was completely rebuilt by Sixtus III (432-440) after the Council of Ephesus. The basilica was neither restored nor rebuilt until the 12th century, when Eugene III had a portico built for the facade, much like those still standing in San Lorenzo fuori le Mura or in San Giorgio al Velabro. At the end of the 13th century, Nicholas IV promoted the renovation of the apse. Only in the 18th century did Clement XII, after having demolished the old portico, entrust the creation of a new facade to Ferdinando Fuga.

Now giving the impression of being squeezed between the two tall flanking buildings (dating to the 17th and 18th centuries), the facade is preceded by a vast flight of steps and features a portico with an architrave on the ground floor and a loggia with arches above; the whole is crowned by a balustrade which curiously extends on either side of the facade to define the twin palaces at the sides. Rich sculptural decoration runs along the front and under the portico, while the loggia of the upper floor, dating to the 13th century, still preserves the mosaic decoration of the older facade. The ***interior*** is on a tripartite basilica plan with forty Ionic columns supporting an entablature with a mosaic frieze. The coffered ceiling is commonly attributed to Giuliano da Sangallo, while, as to be expected, the pavement is in Cosmatesque marblework, although much of it was restored under Benedict XIV. An old tradition says that the rich decoration of the ceiling was made with the first gold that came from America, donated to the basilica by its illustrious protectors the kings of Spain.

On the facing page, an aerial view of Rome in which the impressive Santa Maria Maggiore is clearly visible. Below, a view of the facade of the basilica.

The chapels that branch off from the aisles date mostly to the 16th century. Of particular note are the **Sistine Chapel**, on a Greek-cross plan with a cupola, by Domenico Fontana, and the **Pauline Chapel**, like the former in plan but built for Pope Paul V Borghese by Flaminio Ponzio. Lastly, the right aisle shelters the **Baptistery**, also designed by Flaminio Ponzio, into which Valadier set a porphyry baptismal font.

Church of Santa Pudenziana - The earliest references to the *Ecclesia Pudentiana* date to the 4th century AD. It is said that the house of the senator Pudens, a member of the family of the *Acilii Glabriones*, was situated on the ancient *Vicus Patricius* (later Via Urbana) that separated the Viminale from the Esquiline, and that during his sojourn in Rome the apostle Peter was a guest for all of seven years in this luxurious mansion.
The first restoration was conducted in the 5th century under Pope Innocent I; after this time, other works were carried out in the 8th, 11th and 13th centuries, under

Above, the colonnade and the mosaics of the nave of Santa Maria Maggiore; below, details of the apsidal mosaics of the Virgin by Jacopo Torriti: Dormitio Virginis *above and the* Coronation of the Virgin *below.*

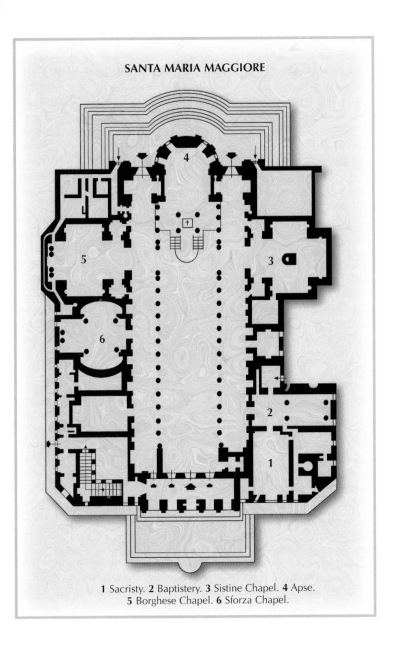

SANTA MARIA MAGGIORE

1 Sacristy. **2** Baptistery. **3** Sistine Chapel. **4** Apse.
5 Borghese Chapel. **6** Sforza Chapel.

popes Hadrian I, Gregory VI and Innocent III.

The last in the series of great restorations of the church was the transformation and remodeling begun in 1588 by Cardinal Caetani that gave the structure its present aspect. A description of old nevertheless testifies to its original forms.

In the **interior** of Santa Pudenziana, the left aisle has several noteworthy points of interest, beginning with the **chapel** dedicated to the apostle Peter, who is said to have officiated on the site for seven years. The chapel, which had already undergone restoration by the priest Massimo and been decorated with mosaics by the late 4th century, is in effect the historical and religious center of the church. Other legendary places of worship in the same aisle are the *well* in which Saint Pudentiana interred the bodies of at least three thousand martyrs, and the **Caetani Chapel**, adorned with precious "arancio antico" and "lumachella" marbles. The

The mosaic in the apse of Santa Pudenziana.

mosaics were executed on cartoons by Federico Zuccari and the relief of the *Adoration of the Magi* is by Pier Paolo Oliviero.

Lastly, mention must also be made of the mosaic (restored in 1831-32) in the conch of the apse, depicting *Christ Imparting the Blessing* and holding in His left hand an open book with written on it: *"Dominus Conservator Ecclesiae Pudentianae"* to the eternal glory of the merciful saint after whom the church was named.

Piazza dell'Esedra - Piazza della Repubblica, or dell'Esedra, is undoubtedly the most prestigious and magnificent of the city squares that were reorganized after Italy became a nation. Framed by two large, porticoed, late 19th-century *palazzi* that curve around the piazza, at the center is the *Fountain of the Naiads* created in 1885 by Alessandro Guerrieri. The fountain has a wide circular basin decorated with four bronze groups of nymphs; the center sculpture of *Glaucus Struggling with a Fish* is the work of Mario Rutelli (1912).

Church of Santa Maria degli Angeli - This church was designed by Michelangelo and was incorporated into the ancient hall of the *tepidarium* of the Baths of Diocletian. It was remodeled in the mid-18th century. The *facade* is bare and straightforward, not in the least affected.

The Greek-cross *interior* is interesting for the unusual architectural development of the space: the transverse arms are connected to the vestibule by means of an inspired solution making use of a double passageway. The church contains numerous monuments and objects of art worthy of note. In the entrance vestibule are many *funeral monuments*, such as that dedicated to the great painter Salvador Rosa, or that of that other famous 17th-century master, Carlo Maratta, which he himself designed. The lovely *Christ on the Cross* by Daniele da Volterra is at the altar; on the right side of the cross aisle are four large altarpieces by Ricciolini (*Crucifixion of Saint Peter*), Tremollière (*The Fall of Simon Magus*), Muziano (*The Sermon of Saint Jerome*), and Mancini (*Saint Peter Raising Tabitha from the Dead*). On the left side are four other large altarpieces by Pietro Bianchi (*The Virgin and Saints*), P. Costanzi (*The Resurrection of Tabitha*), Subleyras (*Saint Basil Celebrating Mass before the Emperor Valens*), and Pompeo Batoni (*The Fall of Simon Magus*). A canvas by Carlo Maratta adorns the altar. In the chancel are the *Martyrdom of Saint Sebastian* by Domenichino (from Saint Peter's), the dramatic *Death of Ananias and Saphira* by Pomarancio, and a canvas of the *Baptism of Christ* by Maratta.

Baths of Diocletian - The Baths of Diocletian were in all probability the largest *thermae* ever built in Rome. They went up in a relatively brief period of time, between 298 and 306 AD, under the two Augustan tetrarchs Diocletian and Maximinian, as the dedicatory inscription reminds us. The establishment was built in one of the most densely populated districts of Rome, between the Esquiline, Quirinale and Viminale hills. A special branch of the old Aqua Marcia aqueduct supplied water for the enormous cistern (91 meters in length), which was demolished once and for all in 1876. Reference to these baths is still to be found in the name "Termini" by which the nearby railroad station is now known. The structures of the original complex of buildings were greatly modified by later superstructures and variations in the fabric of the surrounding streets, but the original layout is in part still legible. The total area occupied measured 380 by 370 meters. The main bath building was at the center of a rectangular enclosure with a large semicircular exedra on one of the long sides (corresponding to what is now Piazza della Repubblica), two rotundas at the corners and numerous hemicycles along the perimeter. The plan of the main building is along the lines of the great imperial baths: a large central basilica, the *calidarium-tepidarium-frigidarium* complex on the median axis of the short side, and *palaestrae* and accessory services balancing each other on either side.
The entire structure is built in *opus latericium*, or brickwork. It has been calculated that about 3000 people could use the establishment at any one time. The *calidarium* (hot bath) was rectangular, with four semicircular alcoves; one of these is now the entrance to the Church of S. Maria degli Angeli, built by Michelangelo in 1566 in what was once the central basilica of the baths. Another part of the original building is now incorporated in the Museo Nazionale Romano, installed in the former Carthusian monastery that was built in the midst of the ruins of the baths.

San Lorenzo fuori le Mura - Although severely damaged by the World War II bombings, San Lorenzo still preserves much evidence of its remote and illustrious past. In truth, it arose from the fusion of the Pelagian Basilica, dedicated to Saint Lawrence, and Honorius' church dedicated to the Virgin, commissioned by the popes Pelagius II (6th century) and Honorius III (13th century), respectively. The Pelagian Basilica stood alongside the primitive Constantinian basilica that was destined for purely cemeterial functions and contained the relics of the titular saint, which were later moved to the adjacent Pelagian building. The lovely **portico** created by the Vassalletto family Cosmati workers, incorporating ancient columns with Ionic capitals, dates to the 13th century; under the portico are a number of *ancient tombs* and remains of medieval *frescoes*. Alongside are the monastery, with its beautiful **cloister**, and the late 12th-century Romanesque **bell tower**.
The **interior** shows evident signs of the origin of the building as the fusion of two churches that while contiguous were laid out on different axes: the front portion has a nave and two aisles divided by twenty-two ancient columns; the rear church, which forms the presbytery and the apse of the present-day basilica, has three aisles, divided by columns that probably came from the earlier Constantinian building, and upper **women's** galleries, marked out by small columns with a Byzantine cast. Examples of the alacritous activity of the Cosmati can also be found in the interior of the basilica: the beautiful mosaic *floor*, unfortunately damaged by the WWII bombings, the two *pulpits*, the *ciborium*, the *paschal candelabrum* and the *bishop's throne* at the back of the choir. The mosaic that decorates the triumphal arch with *Jesus with Saints Paul, Stephen, Hippolytus, Peter, Laurence and Pope Pelagius* instead dates to the 6th century.

MUSEO NAZIONALE ROMANO

The Museo Nazionale Romano, a prestigious archaeological institution founded in the late nineteenth century, brings together a great quantity and variety of precious finds and evidence of the history and the civilization of ancient Rome. Since 1997 the museum has enjoyed a new arrangement, being now split up among three main exhibition nuclei (enriched by temporary shows and exhibits) in the same number of buildings in different parts of the city. Thus the traditional seat of the museum at the Baths of Diocletian (the *Museo Nazionale Romano delle Terme*, and today dedicated exclusively to the epigraphical collections) has been flanked by two new centers born of the fission of the original collection and now housed in the rooms of *Palazzo Altemps* and of the *Collegio Massimo*. Palazzo Altemps is now home to the three celebrated Boncompagni-Ludovisi, Altemps and Mattei collections, never before visible to the public in their entirety. The second new center, instead, is arranged according to more strictly thematic criteria and is subdivided into sections that illustrate the phases of the historical and artistic evolution of Roman civilization from the republican through the imperial ages. The exhibit itinerary begins with a copious selection of works, above all busts and portraits from excavations both in the capital and in outlying areas (Palestrina, Mentana, Tivoli, etc.) that provide evidence of the variegated social composition of republican Rome and of the emergence of the patrician class that was to come to power later, at the beginning of the Empire. The creator and staunchest supporter of imperial ideas and politics was Augustus, who is here presented in his many different roles as founder, tutelar god and defender of the homeland in a wide-ranging iconographic repertoire rooted in the personality cult typical of Greek Hellenistic art (*Portrait of a Hellenistic Prince*, *Portrait of Philip of Macedon*). Augustus was fascinated by this art; he collected original works and also had many copies made. The museum proposes a number of the most interesting examples (the *Pugilist*, the *Caelian Athena*, the *Muse*, etc.) The evolution of the subject-matter and of the iconography itself under the Flavians and in late imperial times finds its highest expression in the decoration of the great imperial villas and the sumptuous homes of the aristocracy, whence come examples of celebratory statuary from the official portrait repertoire of the emperor, his family and the members of his court (the portraits of *Hadrian* and his wife *Sabina*, portrait of *Antinous*, the statue of *Antoninus Pius*) but also works inspired by Greek art, symbols of the taste and of the power of the dominant class (the *Maiden of Anzio*, the *Ephebe from Subiaco*, the *Boats of Nemi*, the *Chigi Apollo*). The cult of the body and of beauty, typical of this era, is amply represented in the

The remains of the Baths of Diocletian.

164

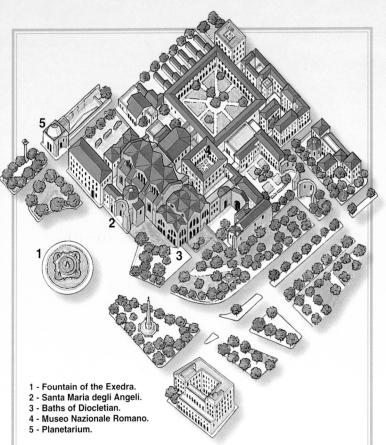

1 - Fountain of the Exedra.
2 - Santa Maria degli Angeli.
3 - Baths of Diocletian.
4 - Museo Nazionale Romano.
5 - Planetarium.

statues that once decorated the places consecrated to physical exercise, such as the bath establishments and the gymnasia (the Lancellotti *Discobolo*, the Castel Porziano *Discobolo*), while celebration of military might finds concrete expression in the narrative cycles and the representations of the heroic gestures of the warring armies (the *Portonaccio sarcophagus*).

The magnificence of the patrician homes and the interest in representation of nature, more often than not idealized, is instead documented by an extensive series of frescoes presenting many scenes from mythology, among other subjects. As part of the reorganization of the Museo Nazionale Romano, its historical premises at the Baths of Diocletian have been transformed into the Epigraphical Department of the museum, home to a rich collection of almost ten thousand inscriptions of different types, with ample explanatory material and adequate figurative supports for deciphering and placing the inscriptions in their correct historical/cultural context. The itinerary through the museum takes the visitor to different sections, ordered according to chronological criteria, and their subject-related subsections dedicated to different aspects of life in ancient Rome (politics, administration, religion and social relations). The collection goes from the first examples of epigraphs to development of the genre through the republican period (documents concerning the creation of the first public institutions and the first urban sanctuaries, documents relative to relations with other cities during the phase of expansion of Rome's power and of the transformation of the society in the late republican era) and to the wealth of epigraphic material dating to the imperial age, which is examined with an eye to highlighting the variations with respect to the earlier ages in the various historical and cultural subject-areas. Another portion of the museum, again arranged according to chronological criteria, is instead dedicated to the urban development of Rome and the cities of Latium and to their different natures and structures, all analyzed starting from different types of inscriptions.

QUIRINAL AND VIA VENETO

Piazza and Palazzo del Quirinale -
San Carlo alle Quattro Fontane - **Palazzo Barberini** - Galleria
Nazionale d'Arte Antica -
Fontana del Tritone - **Via Veneto**

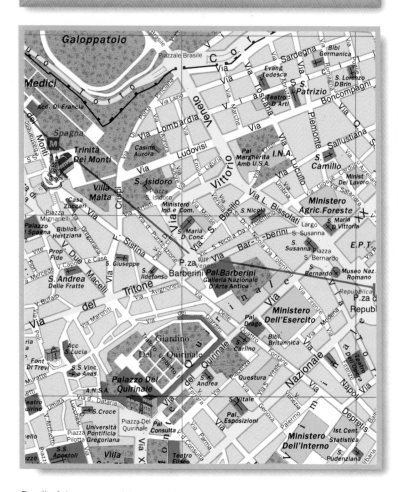

Detail of the statues of Castor and Pollux decorating the fountain and the obelisk in Piazza del Quirinale.

Piazza del Quirinale - This large square, which in a sense represents the "noble" center of Rome, is overlooked by some of the most interesting buildings of Renaissance, Baroque and rococo Rome (such as the Palazzo del Quirinale, the Palazzo della Consulta, the Church of Sant' Andrea al Quirinale); the fourth, open side is delimited by a theatrical balustrade graced by Roman statues.

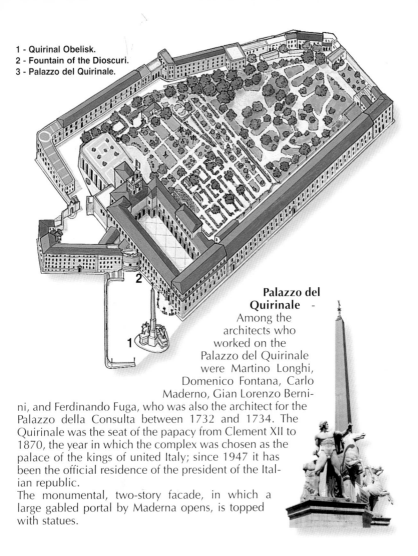

1 - Quirinal Obelisk.
2 - Fountain of the Dioscuri.
3 - Palazzo del Quirinale.

Palazzo del Quirinale -

Among the architects who worked on the Palazzo del Quirinale were Martino Longhi, Domenico Fontana, Carlo Maderno, Gian Lorenzo Berni-ni, and Ferdinando Fuga, who was also the architect for the Palazzo della Consulta between 1732 and 1734. The Quirinale was the seat of the papacy from Clement XII to 1870, the year in which the complex was chosen as the palace of the kings of united Italy; since 1947 it has been the official residence of the president of the Italian republic.

The monumental, two-story facade, in which a large gabled portal by Maderna opens, is topped with statues.

The Quirinal obelisk with the two statues.

A view of the facade of Palazzo del Quirinale.

Church of San Carlo alle Quattro Fontane - Purely Baroque in its layout, this stunning work by Borromini dates to the middle of the 17th century. The almost "undulating" *facade*, extremely innovative for the period, catches the light in an inspired play of chiaroscuro. It develops through two orders of four columns each and is decorated with sculptures. The oval plan of the *interior* is likewise extremely gracious. Of particular note here are the *Holy Trinity* by Mugnard, on the high altar, the *Rest on the Flight into Egypt* by Romanelli on its left, and above all, the splendid *San Carlo Borromeo Adoring the Holy Trinity* by Orazio Borgianni (1611), in the sacristy.

Above, a detail of the exterior of San Carlo alle Quattro Fontane, a marvelous work by Borromini; below, a view of the ceiling of the church.

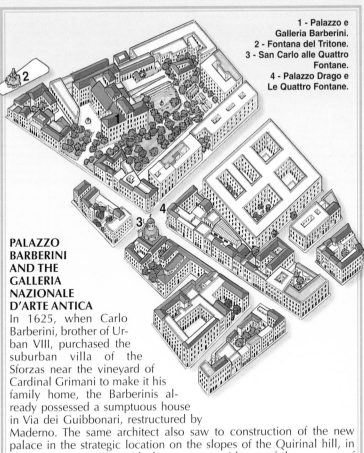

1 - Palazzo e
Galleria Barberini.
2 - Fontana del Tritone.
3 - San Carlo alle Quattro
Fontane.
4 - Palazzo Drago e
Le Quattro Fontane.

PALAZZO BARBERINI AND THE GALLERIA NAZIONALE D'ARTE ANTICA

In 1625, when Carlo Barberini, brother of Urban VIII, purchased the suburban villa of the Sforzas near the vineyard of Cardinal Grimani to make it his family home, the Barberinis already possessed a sumptuous house in Via dei Guibbonari, restructured by Maderno. The same architect also saw to construction of the new palace in the strategic location on the slopes of the Quirinal hill, in close communication with the summer residence of the popes - of which in a certain sense it could have been considered the direct extension. Maderno, whose designs called for a building on a square plan around a courtyard, died in 1629 before he could complete his work. He was succeeded as director of construction by Borromini, who was in turn succeeded by Bernini.

The latter architect revolutionized the original plan by inserting a rather compact building, with a facade lightened by a series of loggia-type windows with deep splays, between the two previously-built wings. In the interior, two staircases, one by Bernini, the other by Borromini, led from the atrium to the Gran Salone. From 1633 onward, Pietro da Cortona participated in the decoration of the latter with the grandiose ceiling painting of the *Triumph of Divine Providence*, exalting the glories of the Barberini family. But the decoration of the halls and the sumptuous rooms of the palace was also entrusted to the precious statues and Roman antiquities that the Barberinis had collected over the years, and to a conspicuous number of paintings, the nucleus of today's Galleria Nazionale d'Arte Antica founded in 1895. The absolute masterpiece of this collection, which includes, among many others, works by Filippo Lippi, Perugino, Bronzino, Tintoretto, Guido Reni, Guercino and many foreign masters, is Raphael's *La Fornarina*, in which criticism traditionally sees the portrait of the woman the artist "loved until his death." Particular interest also invests the *Judith and Holophernes* by Caravaggio and the *Narcissus* for many years attributed to the Baroque painter but now believed by criticism to have been painted by one of his pupils.

Besides the picture gallery, the palace also sported a library and, above all, many architectural features conceived to support its role as a reception facility. Among these were the famous theater designed by

The Heitz Madonna, *by Giulio Romano, in Palazzo Barberini. Below,* Festa a Palazzo Barberini, *a 17th-century work on exhibit in the* Museo di Roma.

Pietro da Cortona, a spheristerion (no longer existing), and the immense space in front of the building in which fêtes and carrousels were held, including a celebration organized in honor of Queen Christina of Sweden. In 1864, modification of the urban layout of the district and the construction of the monumental gate supported by colossal telamons radically changed the exterior aspect of the palace, which at the time stood out imposingly against the slope of the hill but today seems to be somewhat suffocated by the structures that surround it.

The Annunciation *by Filippo Lippi, in the Galleria Nazionale d'Arte Antica.*

Fontana del Tritone - Still another fascinating fountain by Gian Lorenzo Bernini is that which has stood at the center of Piazza Barberini since 1643, famous for the apparent lack of any kind of architectural support for the statue of the *Triton* from which it takes its name. He is in fact supported by a scallop shell that in turn rests on the arched tails of four dolphins; the spray of water that animates the whole ensemble is naturalistically blown upwards by the Triton through a conch.

Via Veneto - Via Vittorio Veneto, a salient element in the urban planning projects implemented in Rome in the early 20th century, and of particular importance for the development of the Ludovisi district, runs from Piazza Barberini to Porta Pinciana and is lined with world-famous hotels, shops and meeting places, but also with major works of architecture from different historical periods. The *Fontana delle Api* by Bernini, the *Church of Santa Maria della Concezione* by Antonio Casoni, and the *Church of Sant'Isidoro* all date to the 17th century; the *Ministry of Industry and Trade* building by Marcello Piacentini and Giuseppe Vaccaro and the headquarters of the *Banca Nazionale del Lavoro*, also by Piacentini, date to the 20th century, while *Palazzo Boncompagni-Ludovisi*, or Palazzo Margherita, is a late 19th-century work signed by Gaetano Koch.

Detail of the Fontana del Tritone, a masterpiece by Bernini, at the center of Piazza Barberini.

VILLA BORGHESE

Villa Borghese - Museo and Galleria Borghese - Galleria Nazionale d'Arte Moderna - Villa Giulia - Etruscan Museum - Pincio - Villa Medici

Villa Borghese - The villa and its park were designed for Cardinal Scipione Caffarelli Borghese in the early 1600s; although the villa was completely remodeled at the end of the following century to plans by the architects Antonio and Mario Asprucci and the painter Unterberger, it owes its present aspect to work conducted by Luigi Canina in the early 19th century.

When it was presented to the city of Rome in 1902 by King Umberto I, the villa was to have taken the name of the munificent sovereign, but its old denomination, linked to its founder Cardinal Borghese, has always continued to be used despite and notwithstanding any official names.

The **park** is the largest in the city, all of six kilometers around its perimeter, and it is also the loveliest and the most fascinating, with an incredible variety of plants and innumerable charming paths. At present, the main way into the park is from the overpass of Viale dell'Obelisco, but there are also convenient gates at Porta Pinciana and Piazzale Flaminio and other minor entrances.

In the midst of luxuriant plant life and a wealth of decorative elements (busts, statues, ruins, fountains, and small temples) lies a small artificial lake surrounded by an elegant garden known as the **Giardino del Lago**. An Ionic **temple** dedicated to Aesculapius, built in the late 18th century in imitation of the much more famous temples of ancient Greece, rises on the island at the center.

A little further on are evocative avenues leading to **Piazza di Siena**, designed as an amphitheater. Every year horse-lovers gather here to watch one the most famous equestrian events in the world. Not far off, in the southern corner of the park, is the **Galoppatoio** (riding track) of the Centro Ippico, a vast area under which an underground parking lot was created several years ago.

Above, a detail of a statue in the Museo Nazionale d'Arte Moderna in Villa Borghese. Left, the Temple of Diana and, below, the Temple of Aesculapius in the park of Villa Borghese.

MUSEO AND GALLERIA DI VILLA BORGHESE

The green slope of the Pincio overlooking Via Flaminia, delimited on the side toward the city center by the Aurelian Walls, was chosen in 1608 by Cardinal Scipione Borghese, nephew of Pope Paul V, as the site for a suburban villa immersed in an enormous park. The project was signed by Flaminio Ponzio, who however was unable to bring it to completion; this task instead fell to Vasanzio and Rainaldi. Work on both the villa, which housed the opulent art collections of the Borghese family, and the immense surrounding park continued in the following centuries in two major reprisals, one in 1766-1793 by Mario and Antonio Asprucci and another begun in 1822 by Luigi Canina. The latter gave a new look to the park, which had before his time been transformed from its original formal Italian style to English, by raising statues and constructions of neo-Classical inspiration (the Greek and Egyptian *propylaea*, the Fountain of Aesculapius, the Roman Arch) complementing those installed in the late 18th century by the Aspruccis (the Lion Portico, the Temple of Aesculapius on the island at the center of the lake, and Piazza di Siena, built on the model of the Roman stadium and today home to one of the world's most important equestrian meetings).

The recently-restored *palazzina*, also called the **Casino Borghese**, hosts the **Museo** and the **Galleria Borghese**, two of the most celebrated art collections in the world. Both got their start with Cardinal Scipione, who brought together not only many paintings but also antiquities of different origin and entrusted their restoration to the greatest artists of the time. First and foremost among these masters was Gian Lorenzo Bernini, who also created for his rich benefactor certain among the absolute masterpieces of Baroque statuary: the *David*, sculpted in 1623-1624, whose countenance is the self-portrait of the artist, and *Apollo and Daphne*, a marble group sculpted during the same period but of mythological inspiration, as was the *Rape of Proserpine*, an early but brilliant work. The younger Bernini also created works in collaboration with his father Pietro, among which *Aeneas Carrying Anchises* and *Truth*, an allegory dear to the heart of the Baroque era. These sculptures were placed in the rooms of the villa alongside ancient works such as the famous *Hermaphrodite*, the *Dancing Silenus*, and the many *portraits* of Roman emperors that alternate with the16th-century polychrome marble busts of Classical inspiration created by Della Porta. The collection was further enlarged in the 18th century and arranged in the rooms of the Casino, which were specially decorated by artists like Pacetti and Unterberger with ornamental motifs inspired by the works on exhibit.

In 1807, Prince Camillo Borghese sold the collection to his cousin, Napoleon Bonaparte, who carried off many pieces to the Louvre where they still form the main nucleus of the classical antiquities section. Two years earlier, Camillo's wife Pauline had been portrayed by Canova in the pose of *Venus*, a work that still today is one of the major attractions of the museum. Like the collection of statues and antiquities, the collection of paintings

The splendid David by Bernini, with the face of the sculptor, on exhibit at the Galleria Borghese.

that today graces the **Galleria Borghese** was also begun by Cardinal Scipione, who assembled a great number of masterpieces by the most illustrious exponents of 16th- and 17th-century painting. Caravaggio is represented here with some of his most interesting and most evocative works: the *Boy with a Fruit Basket*, one of the master's first Roman works, the *Little Bacchus*, the *Madonna dei Palafrenieri*, *Saint Jerome*, and the *David* with the head of Goliath, one of his last works, in which the slain giant wears his countenance. Alongside the works by the great Baroque artist from Lombardy, Cardinal Scipione collected paintings of enormous value by Raphael (the *Entombment of Christ*, perhaps better known as the *Borghese Deposition*), Titian (*Sacred and Profane Love*), and painters of the Ferrarese school (*Apollo* by Dosso Dossi). Later acquisitions (including the addition of the collection of Olimpia Aldobrandini, wife of Paolo Borghese) brought to the gallery such masterpieces as the *Virgin and Child with Young Saint John and Angels* by Botticelli, Correggio's *Danaë*, the *Portrait of a Man* by Antonello da Messina and works by many other Italian and foreign masters (Domenichino, Lorenzo Lotto, Parmigianino, Veronese, Rubens, and Cranach).

GALLERIA NAZIONALE D'ARTE MODERNA

In 1914, the gallery, with its vast series of collections representing the most important and prolific artistic movements of the 19th and 20th centuries, was transferred to the Palazzo delle Belle Arti, which had been built on occasion of the Exposition of 1911.

The arrangement of the works follows the chronological development of Italian art, beginning with Neoclassicism (Appiani, Canova, Bartolini) and Romanticism (Hayez, Induno). A space apart is reserved for the landscape painters, especially those of the so-called Sorrento School, whose painters used warm luminous tones to represent the landscapes of southern Italy. The Neapolitan School, which also arose in the mid-1800s, is instead represented by works with a clear Realist cast: historical and genre paintings (Camarano, Toma) and sculptures of historical and cultural figures of the Italy of the times (Gemito). The northern schools of the second half of the 19th century are also given ample breathing space with important series of the works of the Naturalists (Delelani, Ciardi) and above all of the currents more directly influenced by the contemporary French artistic movements such as Impressionism and Divisionism (Corcos, De Nittis, Segantini, Morbelli). That peculiarly Italian - and in particular Tuscan - phenomenon of the Macchiaioli, is represented by works of the most important exponents of this pictorial current, such as Fattori, Signorini, Cecioni, and Lega.

There are also many paintings by those foreign masters to whom 19th- and 20th-century Italian art is in more than

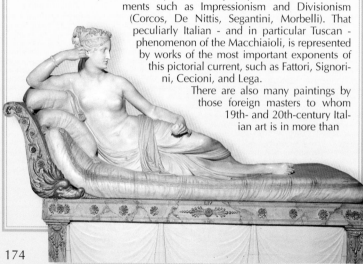

The Sacra Conversazione *by Lorenzo Lotto in the Galleria Borghese.
On the preceding page, two works on exhibit in the Museo di Villa
Borghese: above, the* Rape of Proserpine *by Bernini and below, the statue
of* Paolina Borghese *by Canova.*

one way indebted (Rodin, Van Gogh, Monet, Degas, etc.); besides its great intrinsic value, this section also provides the visitor with a yardstick for obtaining a better understanding of the tightly-woven mesh of artistic interchange among the various European countries.

Much space is also dedicated to the so-called "historical avant-garde" movements, from Symbolism to Futurism (Balla, Boccioni, Severini) and from Cubism to metaphysical painting (Morandi, Carrà, De Chirico) and the principal artistic movements of the postwar period, from Surrealism to abstract art to informal art (with Burri and Fontana), the experimental installations of kinetic art (Mari, Alviani, Munari), and the more contemporary trends with a large number of works by both Italian and foreign artists (Calder, Tinguely, Pollock).

VILLA GIULIA AND THE ETRUSCAN MUSEUM

One of the most fanciful realizations of architectural Mannerism is Villa Giulia, built for Pope Julius III in the area called the Vigna Vecchia against the walls of the city. Such famous names in mid-16th century art as Vasari, Ammannati, and Vignola collaborated on its construction. Villa Giulia is an admirable example of integration of plays of architectural spaces and volumes into the spectacular cornice of environmental green that from the Monti Parioli slopes down to the Tiber, in which the garden acts as a coordinating element for the complex of the villa and its outbuildings.

The villa as such is attributed to Vignola and characterized by a sober two-story facade, with two projecting portions, animated by pilaster strips, Doric columns and lateral niches. At the rear, Ammannati's loggia overlooks the first courtyard, also by Vignola, which gives access to the garden and the central courtyard. From here, two flights of stairs lead to the ideal center of the entire complex, the nymphaeum. This is a three-level structure with two series of overlaid loggias and, below, the Acqua Vergine Fountain, a work by Vasari and Ammannati decorated with river gods and caryatids. A third courtyard, remodeled in the 18th century, concludes the charming arrangement of the open spaces of this interesting suburban villa, one of the few left untouched by the expansion of Umbertine and contemporary Rome. Villa Giulia was chosen in 1889 to house the rich collection of Etruscan antiquities and relics of the Italic civilizations that flourished between the Iron Age and the beginning of

Roman hegemony in the territory between the lower Tiber valley and Tuscany. The finds on display are arranged according to topographical criteria based on place of discovery: Vulci, Veii, Cerveteri, the territory of Falerii Novi, Palestrina, and Umbria. The rich tomb furnishings on display testify to the high artistic level attained by Etruscan civilization: the *Husband and Wife Sarcophagus*, from the 6th century BC, is certainly one of the most evocative pieces of evidence regarding the cult of the dead of this civilization, and, together with the *Ficoroni Cist* and the elegant household goods found in the *Tomb of the Warrior* and in the *Barberini* and *Bernardini Tombs*, one of the major attractions in the museum. Much space is dedicated to

The precious decoration in the interior of Villa Giulia.

Greek and Etruscan-Italic ceramics; the outstanding *Castellani Collection* contains examples of this art form arranged in chronological order from the 8th century BC through the Roman era.

Pincio - The sloping public garden of the Pincio stretches out beyond the right exedra of the Piazza del Popolo. It was laid out, like the square, by Giuseppe Valadier between 1810 and 1818. The site was already famous in antiquity as the gardens (*horti*) of Lucullus, of the Acilians, of the Domitians and, lastly, of the Pincians, whose name continued to be used for the site and in particular for the future park. In typically Italian style, the Pincio is strewn with busts of famous figures from the world of history and art along tree-shaded avenues laid out in the form of a star.

The park also contains the lovely **Casina Valadier**, various picturesque fountains and above all, crowning a rocky reef at the beginning of a small artificial pond, the **water clock** built at the end of the 19th century by Fra' G. B. Embriaco. The **Viale del Muro Torto** runs along at the foot of the Pincio. This stretch of the city walls slopes sharply over the road, probably because of a landslip. Known also as the "Muro Malo," it was used in the past as the burial ground for prostitutes; the executed patriots Montanari and Targhini were later also buried here. A legend that arose at the end of the 16th century identifies this as the burial site of the emperor Nero.

Villa Medici - Construction of this villa began in 1564 on the remains of an earlier building. It belonged first to the Medici family but passed to the house of Lorraine when the latter replaced the former as Grand Dukes of Tuscany. Napoleon installed the French Academy here in 1803, so making it possible for many transalpine artists to come to Italy for their specializations. The external *facade* is perhaps excessively severe and contrasts sharply with the inner facade with its two avant-corps at the sides and animated architectural and sculptural decoration. The vast park, with its wealth of ancient Roman statues, is enchanting.

BATHS OF CARACALLA

Santo Stefano Rotondo - **Santa Maria in Domnica** -
Baths of Caracalla

Church of Santo Stefano Rotondo - The church, which may date as far back as the 5th century, was built over the *Macellum Magnum* of Nero's time; it derives its name from the circular ground plan. The **interior**, with 58 columns, each one different from the other and all taken from earlier buildings, is decorated with 16th-century frescoes, by Pomarancio and Tempesta, of 34 extremely realistic scenes describing the tortures of the first Christian martyrs. In addition to the so-called *Cathedra of Gregory the Great*, in marble, the church contains a fine 7th-century mosaic, highly unusual in its iconography, depicting Christ not crucified but in a mandorla above the Holy Cross (**Chapel of the Santi Primo e Feliciano**).

Church of Santa Maria in Domnica - This is the only church to have retained the denomination of *dominica*, as it was known prior to Constantine's time, of which Domnica is obviously a popular corruption. But the populace also called the church Santa Maria della Navicella, after a small marble boat that once stood in the neighboring piazza and that was replaced by the one there now by Leo X: some say in remembrance of a vow; others, as the *signum* of the chapter of Saint Peter in Vatican which owned this portion of the Caelian hill as well as the church of San Tommaso in Formis. The second denomination (both of the church and of the entire *contrada*) does not, however, appear until the 16th century, and prior to that time the area was known as *Mons Maior*. The first express mention of the church dates to the pontificate of Leo II and sanctions the more formal name of *Ecclesia sanctae Dei genitricis quae vocatur dominica*; not much later, the *Liber Pontificalis* mentions the building as "almost falling into ruin" and attributes its "renewal" and the decoration of the apse with mosaics to Pope Paschal I. These works, dating to the 9th century (Paschal I was pope from 817 to 824), gave Santa Maria the aspect it has conserved to the present day. This fact makes this cornerstone of the religious architecture of the time practically unique, since the coeval churches of Santa Prassede and Santa Cecilia were subjected to practically continual restructuring and renovation through the centuries. In fact, nothing worthy of note took place in Santa Maria in Domnica during the Middle Ages, with the extraordinary exception of the restoration commissioned by Giovanni de' Medici (later Pope Leo X) apparently, according to a reliable tradition, from Raphael. Other restoration work was directed by Sansovino (Andrea Contucci da Monte San Savino) in 1513 and 1514. Another Medici, Cardinal Ferdinando, had the old wooden ceiling of S. Maria in Domnica replaced, and this was then further restored under Pius VII by Cardinal Raffaele Riario Sforza. The **exterior** of S. Maria in Domnica is marked by the portico dating to the restoration under Leo X; it incorporates antique travertine elements taken from a house but originally from the forums of Caesar and of Augustus. The canonic entablature of this portico includes an equally canonic frieze with the dedicatory inscription "*Divae Virgini templum in Domnica dicatum / Io. Medices Diac. Card. Instauravit,*" the focus, as it were, of the original facade, which like the portico bears signs of the Medici restoration in the oculus in the center.

Villa Celimontana - The villa, particularly noteworthy for its magnificent late 16th-century portal, was acquired in 1553 by the wealthy Mattei family; its construction obviously predates that event. It is famous for its splendid gardens, now a public **park** with luxuriant vegetation, almost a grove of delights. A labyrinth drawn in green and studded with statues, small columns, architectural structures that almost seem to be fragmentary settings for a play.

The remains of the Baths of Caracalla (interior).

Park of Porta Capena - This park originated in 1911, when Guido Baccelli, then Minister of Public Instruction, decided to create a center for relaxation and for inspiration that would also be of cultural interest. The result was the park with its imaginative archaeological walk (***Passeggiata archeologica***) which includes the ancient Porta Capena at the beginning of the Via Appia, and other lesser elements which create a peaceful, "abstract" surround.

Baths of Caracalla - The Baths of Caracalla are a magnificent, and excellently-preserved, example of *thermae* from the Imperial period. Construction was begun by the emperor Caracalla in 212 AD. The site chosen was a small valley between the slopes of the knoll called the "Piccolo Aventino" and the Via Nova, where there may have already existed an artificial basin called the *Piscina Publica*. A special branch of the old Aqua Marcia aqueduct was created to bring water to the new baths. Work continued until 216, the year in which the complex was dedicated. The baths continued to function until 537 when, during the siege of Rome by Vitiges and his Goths, the aqueducts of the city were cut off.

In the 16th century, excavations carried out in the enormous building brought to light various works of art including the *Farnese Bull* and the *Hercules*, now in the National Museum of Naples. The mosaics of athletes that decorated the hemicycles of the large side courtyards of the *thermae* were discovered in 1824 (now in the Vatican Museums). The layout of the Baths of Caracalla made a clear distinction between the bath sector as such and the enclosure, in which all the accessory non-bathing services were located. The enclosure measured 337 x 328 meters and consisted of a portico; on the northeast side, where the monumental entrance was set, it was preceded by a series of concamerations on two levels, the extensive substructures of which supported one side of the immense artificial earthworks on which the baths were built. Two grandiose symmetrical exedrae still stand at the sides of the enclosure. Each one has three rooms: a central room with an apse, preceded by a colonnade and flanked by a rectangular chamber on one side and an interesting octagonal *nymphaeum*, covered with a dome on pendentives, on the other. At the back of the enclosure was a flattened exedra, like a stadium with one side missing, with tiers from which spectators watched gymnastic competitions. The enormous cisterns, with a total capacity of 80,000 liters of water, lay below on two levels. The two apsed rooms to the sides of the exedra were libraries. A colonnaded walkway, of which almost nothing remains, ran along the inner side of the enclosure. It was probably raised.

The building in the center, shifted toward the main entrance and separated from the enclosure by a vast garden, was the actual bathing establishment. Access was through four doors on the northeast facade. Two of these led to vestibules adjacent to the *natatio* (swimming pool), while the other two opened onto rooms leading to the *palaestrae*. At present, entrance is through the second door from the right and the itinerary is quite like that followed in antiquity by the bathers. The vestibule gives access, on the right, to a square chamber flanked by two small rooms on either side, covered with barrel vaults. This was the *apodyterium* (dressing-room). Next came one of the two large *palaestrae*, which were set symmetrically along the short sides of the building. They consisted of large peristyles (50 x 20 meters) with columns in yellow Numidian stone on three sides; a vast hemicycle opened off one side of the portico through six columns, while the other side, without a portico, had five rooms, the one in the center with an apse. This is where the bathing itinerary generally started after the bather's various exercises in the *palaestra*. This apsed room in fact led to a series of variously shaped, smaller and larger rooms with tubs for special baths and oiling (*unctuaria*). An elliptical chamber covered with a cross vault and with small oblique entrances (the whole designed to preserve the heat as much as possible) was a *laconicum* (Turkish bath); after this came the grand *calidarium* (hot bath), an enormous circular room (35 meters in diameter) covered by a dome supported on eight piers and illuminated by two rows of large windows in the drum. After the *calidarium* came the *tepidarium* (temperate bath), a more modest rectangular chamber flanked by two pools. Next came the large central hall, the *frigidarium*: it was a large basilica, 58 x 24 meters, with a triple cross-vaulted roof supported on eight piers against which stood eight granite columns. One of these remained in place until 1563, when it was transported to Florence and re-erected in Piazza Santa Trinita. On either side the *frigidarium* hall was a rectangular room, in the centers of which were the two granite basins now in the Piazza Farnese. The *natatio*, which could also be reached from the *frigidarium*, was unroofed. There has come down to us one of its facades with columns and groups of niches once meant to contain statues.

House of Cardinal Bessarion - This 15th-century building, with its aristocratic lines, cross-mullioned windows and spacious loggia, is known for having been the home of Cardinal Bessarion and the salon of the artists and scholars of early Renaissance Rome, who gathered here to hear dissertations on the many subjects that were an imperative part of intellectual life at the time: art, philosophy, theology, etc. A place, then, famous not for its architecture or its artistic merits but for its position as a center of the cultural ferment of the Renaissance.

Porta San Sebastiano and the Arch of Drusus - Once Porta Appia, this city gate was entirely rebuilt in the 5th century by Honorius. It is simple in form but provides an interesting perspective view of the lovely so-called Arch of Drusus, which from a distance seems to fuse with the gates. The solid, compact structure of the arch dates to the 2nd century.

VIA APPIA ANTICA

"Domine Quo Vadis?" - Catacombs of San Callisto -
Fosse Ardeatine - Basilica and Catacombs of San Sebastiano -
Catacombs of Domitilla - Circus of Maxentius -
Tomb of Cecilia Metella

Appia Antica - The most important of the Roman consular roads, known as the *Regina Viarum* (the queen of roads), begins at Porta San Sebastiano and winds towards the interior bordered with ancient and not-so-ancient monuments. Miraculous events such as the famous episode of "Domine quo vadis?" are thought to have taken place along this thoroughfare.

Church of Domine Quo Vadis? - The church known by this famous phrase actually seems to have been dedicated to Santa Maria in Palmis. The charming small building originally dates to the 9th century, although it was frequently remodeled, above all in the 17th century when the simple sober facade was also renovated.
But the worldwide fame of the building rests less on its artistic merits than on Christian tradition, which relates that the site on which the church stands was the spot where Jesus appeared to Peter as he was fleeing Rome for fear of being crucified. The apostle, taken aback, uttered the famous phrase "Domine quo vadis?" (Lord, where are you going?); Jesus is said to have answered "Venio iterum crucifigi" (I am returning to be crucified). Peter grasped the implicit invitation in Christ's words and returned to Rome and martyrdom.

Catacombs - These deep galleries were once quarries for travertine and pozzolana stone. Situated on the outskirts of Rome, they became meeting places for the early Christians and shortly thereafter were also used as cemeteries (1st - 4th centuries). Following many centuries of abandon, the catacombs were rediscovered and reappraised in the 16th century. The most suggestive portions of the vast maze of tunnels that spreads out to the sides of the Via Appia go by the names of Domitilla, San Callisto, San Sebastiano, Sant'Agnese and Santa Priscilla.

Catacombs of San Callisto - These catacombs are among Rome's best known, having been developed by Pope Calixtus III and become the official burial ground for the bishops of Rome. The catacombs extend for about 20 kilometers on four different levels and have been only partly explored. The part open to the public includes the *Crypt of the Popes*, where several of the early popes were buried; it contains interesting epigraphs relating to popes Pontianus, Lucius, Eutychianus, and Sixtus II. The *Crypt of Santa Cecilia*, where the remains of this Christian martyr were found, is decorated with painting from the 7th and 8th centuries. After this comes the *Gallery of the Sepulchers*, again with interesting paintings, the *Crypt of Pope Eusebius* and the *Crypt of Lucina*. The more remote part of the necropolis (2nd century AD) is decorated with paintings of the miraculous *Fish* and the *Symbols of the Eucharist*.

Fosse Ardeatine - The Fosse Ardeatine are remembered in history as the scene of a horrifying mass execution conducted by the Nazi troops in

1944, when the SS, by way of reprisal for the previous killing of thirty-two German soldiers, slaughtered 325 Italians (73 Jews, Italian officers, common people, a priest and a boy of fourteen) who had been detained in the prison of Regina Coeli. None of these persons had anything to do with the killing of the Germans. Today, after over half a century, the site is still visited by innumerable pilgrims who pay quiet homage to the dead.

Basilica of San Sebastiano - Built in the first half of the 4th century and originally dedicated to the apostles Peter and Paul, the church was subsequently sanctified to the soldier-saint Sebastian; it was entirely rebuilt in the early 17th century for Cardinal Scipione Borghese. The *facade* has a portico with three graceful arches resting on twin columns. The aisleless *interior* has a magnificent wooden ceiling with the representation of *Saint Sebastian*. The first chapel on the right contains a stone, with what are said to be the imprints of Christ's feet, and one of the arrows that pierced the body of Saint Sebastian. The beautiful second chapel on the right (Capella Albani), designed by Maratta on commission from Clement XI, is home to the painting of *Saint Fabian giving Communion to Philip the Arab* by P. L. Ghezzi.

Catacombs of San Sebastiano - The catacombs lie on four levels: the first, partially destroyed, still has a somber *chapel* where Saint Philip Neri prayed. Not far off is the compact *Crypt of San Sebastiano*, with a noble and the *bust of the saint*, probably by Bernini. From here, the underground itinerary leads to three decorated *hypogeum tombs* that have inscriptions dating to the 1st century of the Empire; the catacombs became a place of Christian burial around the middle of the 2nd century AD. On the way up toward the exit is the *Triclia*, a room where funerary banquets were held, with graffiti on the walls. After this comes the *ambulacrum*, which houses a rare collection of inscriptions, and then the *Chapel of Honorius III* adorned with mural paintings dating to the 8th century.

1 - Tomb of Cecilia Metella. 2 - Circus of Maxentius. 3 - Mausoleum of Romulus. 4 - San Sebastiano. 5 - Catacombs of San Callisto. 6 - "Domine Quo Vadis?". 7 - Porta San Sebastiano. 8 - Porta Latina. 9 - San Giovanni in Oleo. 10 - San Giovanni a Porta Latina.

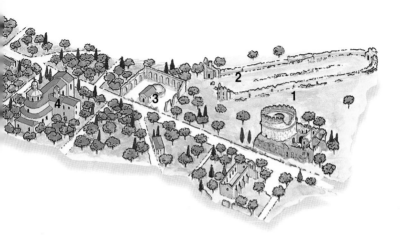

The Tomb of Cecilia Metella on Via Appia Antica.

Catacombs of Domitilla - Also known as the Catacombs of Santi Nereo e Achilleo, this network of tunnels is the largest in Rome and traditionally developed from a simple family burial ground that belonged to Domitilla, the wife or niece of the consul Flavius Clemens put to death by Domitian. The catacombs contain the ruins of the Basilica of Santi Nereo e Achilleo, with a cubicle behind the apse with the fresco of the *Deceased in Worship Invoking Saint Petronilla*. The ancient burial grounds of the Aurelian Flavians lie near the basilica. In the vault of another part of the catacombs, named after the *Good Shepherd* because the earliest representation of this subject was found here, are paintings from the 2nd century. Lastly, in the area of later date there are interesting depictions of the grain market and scenes of daily life and work (3rd-4th centuries).

Mausoleum of Romulus - Further along the Appian Way is the Mausoleum of Romulus, which has suffered badly with time. When it was built in about 309 AD as the final resting place of the mortal remains of the young son of Maxentius, the monumental mausoleum inspired by the forms of the Pantheon featured a large and elegant porticoed enclosure.

Circus of Maxentius - Dedicated, like the mausoleum nearby, to Maxentius' son Romulus after his premature death, the circus was erected in about 309 AD for chariot contests. The race consisted of seven laps around the dividing wall, and the stadium could contain an impressive number of spectators. An interesting clue to the structure of the complex is provided by the semi-cylindrical tower (its companion has disappeared) that marked the monumental entrance to the stadium.

Tomb of Cecilia Metella - This sumptuous and typically Roman mausoleum was originally built in the late republican period for Cecilia, the wife of Crassus and daughter of Quintus Metellus, the conqueror of Crete. It was modified in 1302 by the Caetani family, who adapted it to perform defensive functions for their neighboring castle. Even so, the cella of the ancient tomb, with its conical covering, can still identified.

SAN PAOLO FUORI LE MURA

Porta San Paolo - Pyramid of Caius Cestius -
Basilica of San Paolo fuori le Mura

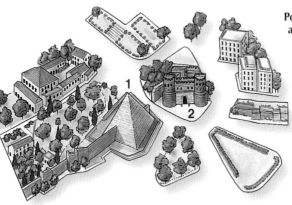

1 - Pyramid of Caio Cestio. 2 - Porta San Paolo.

Porta San Paolo and the Pyramid of Caius Cestius - What is now known as Porta San Paolo is one of the best preserved of Rome's city gates (the other is Porta San Sebastiano) in the formidable circuit of the Aurelian Walls. Its original name of Porta Ostiensis was as usual this was derived from the name of the road which started at the gate. Despite this, the oldest route followed by the Via Ostiense, the road that led to the great seaport of Rome, ran through a postern south of the Pyramid of Cestius, which was already closed in the time of Maxentius. The current name of the gate derives from the large early-Christian Basilica of San Paolo fuori le Mura, about two kilometers away. Originally, the gate had two entrances framed by semicircular towers; under Maxentius (306-312 AD), two pincer walls with an inner gate also consisting of two arches, in travertine, were

Aerial view of the Pyramid of Caius Cestius with Porta San Paolo in the background.

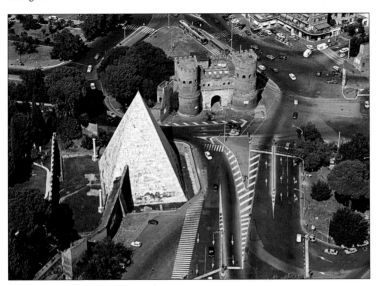

183

added. Under Honorius (395-423), the two passageways of the main entrance became one and the towers were raised. It was through this gate that Totila's Goths entered Rome in 544 during the Gothic-Byzantine war. The rooms inside the building now house the Museo della Via Ostiense.

A curious funeral monument of the early Imperial period, the Pyramid of Caius Cestius, was raised next to Porta Ostiensis during the construction of the Aurelian walls. The building was obviously inspired by Egyptian models, of the Ptolemaic period rather than that of the pharaohs, as was fashionable in Rome after the conquest of Egypt in 30 BC. The base measures 29.50 meters per side and the pyramid is 36.40 meters high. The foundations are in *opus caementicium* covered with blocks of travertine, while the walls are faced with marble slabs. On the west side is a small door that leads into the funeral chamber, a hollow in the concrete core on a rectangular ground plan (5,84 x 4 meters). It is roofed with a barrel vault and faced with *opus latericium* (brick); the wall thus made was then plastered and richly painted in what is called the "third Pompeiian" style. Interest has centered on the building ever since the Middle Ages, when it went by the name of "*Meta Remi*." An inscription placed on the monument records the fact that in 1600 Pope Alexander VII authorized its excavation. Four antique inscriptions, one on the east side, one on the west, and two engraved on the pedestals which supported the bronze statues of the deceased (in the Capitoline Museums), document the public offices held by the man for whom the tomb was made and list his heirs.

Basilica of San Paolo Fuori le Mura - Built by Constantine over the tomb of the apostle Paul, the church remained standing until 15 July 1823, when it was gutted by fire. It was not reconsecrated until 1854. The **exterior** of Saint Paul's now has a grandiose *quadriporticus* in front of the main facade (on the side toward the Tiber), with 146 granite columns that define a space dominated by the statue of the *Apostle Paul* by Pietro Canonica. The facade rising above the *quadriporticus* is richly decorated with mosaics both in the gable (the *Blessing Christ with Saints Peter and Paul)* and in the frieze (an *Agnus Dei* on a hill that rises up symbolically between the two holy cities of Jerusalem and Bethlehem), and with the four large *Symbols of the*

The facade and the colonnade of San Paolo fuori le Mura.

The Blessing Christ with Saints Peter and Paul *in the tympanum of San Paolo fuori le Mura.*
On the facing page, *the interior of the basilica; below, a view of the beautiful cloister.*

Prophets alternating with the three windows. The **interior** is divided into a nave and two aisles on either side with eighty columns, in Baveno granite, separating the five spaces, and is just as richly decorated as the exterior. An uninterrupted frieze with the *Portraits of 263 Popes* who succeeded Saint Peter runs along the transept and the aisles. On the walls, Corinthian pilasters rhythmically alternate with large windows with alabaster panes (which replace those destroyed in the explosion of 1893). The coffered ceiling has large gilded panels which stand out against the white ground.

Two stately statues of *Saint Peter* and *Saint Paul* overlook the raised transept with the sumptuous triumphal arch dating to the time of Leo the Great, called the *Arch of Galla Placidia*, which frames the apse and which was already decorated with mosaics in the 5th century. In the 13th century the mosaics were replaced by Honorius III, who employed Venetian craftsmen sent for the purpose to the pope by the doge of Venice. The mosaics depict a *Blessing Christ with Saints Peter, Paul, Andrew, and Luke*; Honorius himself, significantly in much smaller proportions, kisses the foot of the Savior. The *Redeemer* also dominates the gold-ground mosaic in the triumphal arch, this time flanked by two *Adoring Angels* and the *Symbols of the Evangelists* over the twenty-four *Elders of the Apocalypse* in two rows, with the slightly off-center figures of *Saint Peter* and *Saint Paul* on either side on a blue ground. Objects housed in the basilica include the Gothic **Ciborium** made by Arnolfo di Cambio in 1285 in collaboration with a certain "Petro" who some believe to have been Pietro Cavallini, the equally presumed author of the *mosaics* (of which only fragments remain) now decorating the reverse side of the arch of triumph and once part of the decoration of the exterior of the Basilica. Under the exquisite canopy of Arnolfo's tabernacle is the altar over the *tomb of Saint Paul* with the inevitable *fenestrella confessionis* (confessional window) through which can be seen the fourth-century epigraph reading *"Paulo Apostolo Mart."*

EUR

Palazzo della Civiltà del Lavoro - Museo Nazionale delle Arti e Tradizioni Popolari - Museo della Civiltà Romana - Museo dell'Alto Medioevo - Museo Preistorico-Etnografico Pigorini - Palazzo dello Sport

E.U.R. - This famous district, at one and the same time among the most recent and the most historical, was originally conceived as the site of the Esposizione Universale di Roma that was scheduled to have been held in 1942. Designed by a group of famous architects (Pagano, Piccinato, Vietti and Rossi) coordinated and directed by Marcello Piacentini, it covers an area of 420 hectares in the shape of a pentagon.

The formative concept was that of monumentality, and the district was developed with a view to the future expansion of Rome toward the Tyrrhenian Sea. Among the significant paradigms of Italian architecture of

the first half of the 20th century are the Palazzo della Civiltà del Lavoro and the buildings housing the Museo Preistorico-Etnografico Pigorini, the Museo dell'Alto Medioevo, the Museo delle Arti e Tradizioni Popolari, and the Museo della Civiltà Romana.

The 20th-century Palazzo della Civiltà del Lavoro.

Palazzo dei Congressi - Like the Palazzo della Civiltà del Lavoro, this building is one of the most interesting and "freest" examples of the architecture of the prewar period (1938). Designed and built by the architect Adalberto Libera, it has a sober facade with an eye-catching portico of columns and architraves in front. The building itself is quite innovative for the time in its cubic form and is roofed by cross-vaulting: a complex that while modern in concept was built with a clear awareness of the lessons of the past.

Palazzo della Civiltà del Lavoro - This relatively recent structure is an excellent example of 20th-century architecture, the result of a collaborative effort of the architects Guerrini, Romano and La Padula. It is vaguely inspired by the Colosseum even if it has a square ground plan; six tiers of 9 arches each create a forceful dynamic movement. It is "adorned" by four groups of statues that flank the front and back rooms.

Palazzo dello Sport - What may be the most interesting modern building in Rome is the result of the collaboration between the great architect Marcello Piacentini and the equally illustrious engineer Pier Luigi Nervi. The futuristic hemispherical silhouette is entirely glassed in to house a hall with a seating capacity of 15,000. Directly across from the entrance is Emilio Greco's interesting statue of a woman symbolizing the Olympic torch.

Church of the Santi Pietro e Paolo - This successful example of a modern church on a central plan with a strange hemispherical dome was designed by the architect Arnaldo Foschini. There are two interesting high reliefs inside: *Saint Paul Preaching in Trastevere* by G. Prini and the *Martyrdom of Saint Peter* by A. Monteleone.

MUSEO NAZIONALE DELLE ARTI E TRADIZIONI POPOLARI
The vast collection of objects from all parts of Italy is of inestimable interest from the point of view of art, anthropology, social studies, and history. The exhibits testify to the immense wealth of Italian folk traditions in Italy up to the period between the two world wars, which marked the end of the great Italian peasant culture.

MUSEO PREISTORICO-ETNOGRAFICO LUIGI PIGORINI
This is among the most important museums of ethnographical material in the world, containing the Kirchner Museum collections, the Albertis, Beccari, Loris, and Boggiani ethnographic collections, and many others, in addition to innumerable finds from excavation campaigns and surveys carried out in all parts of Italy. The *Ethnographical Section* and the *Prehistoric Section* are installed respectively on the first and second floors of the **Palazzo delle Scienze**. The former contains a wealth of man-made

The exterior of the Museo della Civiltà Romana.

articles of all kinds (arts and crafts objects, implements and tools, etc.) from various non-European cultures. The African room houses examples of figurative art as well as utensils, fetishes, etc. The room of the Americas houses material from sites ranging from Alaska to Latin America; the archaeological repertory of the South American cultures is splendid. The portion of the museum dedicated to Oceania contains material from Melanesia, Polynesia and Micronesia. Everything in the Prehistoric and Protohistoric Sections merits careful attention, but the extraordinarily rich collection of material from the Lazio area, with finds dating back to the early and late Paleolithic, is a true gem of its kind.

MUSEO DELLA CIVILTÀ ROMANA
The museum building was financed by the FIAT organization and donated to the city of Rome. Its 59 rooms contain exhibits and reconstructions illustrating the history of Rome, its civilization and its development up to the period of the Empire and Christianity. The first seven rooms narrate the origins of Rome and the expansion of Roman civilization in the Mediterranean.

MUSEO DELL'ALTO MEDIOEVO
On the first floor of the Palazzo delle Scienze, the Medieval Museum contains material ranging from the 4th through the 10th centuries. In its seven rooms are found craft objects (iron objects, weapons, ceramics, crockery, the remains of pavements, textiles, clothing), a few 5th-century marble portraits, and the interesting finds from the Lombard cemeteries of Nocera Umbra and Castel Trosino (near Ascoli Piceno).

INDEX

Project: CASA EDITRICE BONECHI
Editorial Director: Monica Bonechi
Graphic Design: Serena de Leonardis
Picture Research: Serena de Leonardis *and* Giovannella Masini
Editing: Giovannella Masini
Video Page Making and Cover: Laura Settesoldi
Drawings and Area Map: Stefano Benini
Texts compiled by the Casa Editrice Bonechi Editorial Department.

© CASA EDITRICE BONECHI
Via Cairoli 18b - 50131 Florence, Italy
Tel. 055/576841 - Fax 055/57000766
E-mail: bonechi@bonechi.it - Internet: www.bonechi.it

The photographs contained in this volume, taken by
Marco Banti, Gaetano Barone, Emanuela Crimini, Gianni degli Orti, Paolo Giambone,
Nicola Grifoni, Serena de Leonardis, Foto M.S.A., Stefano Masi, Andrea Pistolesi,
Gustavo Tomsich, Cesare Tonini *and* Michele Tonini
are property of the Casa Bonechi Editrice Archives.
The photographs of the restored Sistine Chapel are the property of the Vatican Museums
*and those on pages 114 and 115 (top left and right) are the property
of the* Archivio Fabbrica San Pietro in Vaticano.

Printed in Italy by
CENTRO STAMPA EDITORIALE BONECHI

ISBN 88-476-0136-3

* * *